Democracy after Covid

Kostas Chrysogonos • Anna Tsiftsoglou
Editors

Democracy after Covid

Challenges in Europe and Beyond

Springer

Editors
Kostas Chrysogonos
Faculty of Law
Aristotle University of Thessaloniki
Thessaloniki, Greece

Anna Tsiftsoglou
Faculty of Law
Aristotle University of Thessaloniki
Thessaloniki, Greece

ISBN 978-3-031-13900-0 ISBN 978-3-031-13901-7 (eBook)
https://doi.org/10.1007/978-3-031-13901-7

This Springer imprint is published by the registered company Springer Nature Switzerland AG
The registered company address is: Gewerbestrasse 11, 6330 Cham, Switzerland

To all the working people of the health sector who have fought against the pandemic.
K. Chrysogonos

To Yannis, for being always there for me & to all the scientists for their sacrifices to help make this world a better place
A. Tsiftsoglou

Acknowledgments

The idea behind creating a volume on *democracy after the pandemic* was born in late 2020, as Greece was facing an enormous consecutive wave of cases and fatalities caused by COVID-19. Since this was becoming a global issue, we decided to reach out to an international audience and selected colleagues from major liberal democracies in Europe and USA to contribute.

Some of the contributions in this collective volume have been presented, in earlier forms, at the International Society of Public Law (ICON) Annual Conference, under the theme 'The Future of Public Law', held online in July 2021, as accepted papers of a 'Democracy after COVID-19' panel that we formed to discuss our preliminary ideas behind this book. That includes Chapters 2 (Violante, *The COVID-19 Pandemic and the State of Emergency: Lessons from Portugal*), 3 (Delledonne, *Executives During the COVID-19 Pandemic: Contradictory Trends*), 7 (Tsiftsoglou, *American Lessons: The COVID-19 Pandemic and the US Supreme Court)* and 10 (Solanes Mullor, *Protecting Political Rights during the COVID-19 Pandemic: The Emergence of Strict Judicial Scrutiny in Spain).* We would like to thank all the workshop panelists and participants for their presentations and valuable comments, as well as the organisers of this conference.

We also thank all the book contributors for their stellar chapters. We could not have made this book happen without their valuable participation, research commitment and cooperation.

Moreover, this book has benefitted from a Postdoctoral Excellence Scholarship awarded to editor Anna Tsiftsoglou by the Aristotle University of Thessaloniki Research Committee for the academic year 2021–2022. This research funding is gratefully acknowledged.

Lastly, we thank our editor Laura Hofmann and the Springer Law editorial team in Heidelberg, Germany for accepting this volume for publication in their international legal series and for their professional coordination.

May this book give more food for thought for the future, even when the COVID-19 pandemic has hopefully subsided worldwide.

Thessaloniki, Greece
June 2022

Kostas Chrysogonos
Anna Tsiftsoglou

Contents

Part I The COVID-19 Pandemic as a State of Exception?

The Pandemic as an Idiosyncratic Case of a State of Exception 3
Kostas Chrysogonos and Panagiotis Viopoulos

The COVID-19 Pandemic and the State of Emergency: Lessons from Portugal 23
Teresa Violante

Part II Executives and Parliaments in a Pandemic

Executives During the COVID-19 Pandemic: Contradictory Trends . . . 47
Giacomo Delledonne

Parliamentarism in the Pandemic: Contemporary Challenges 61
Heike Merten

COVID-19 and the Federal State 77
Ekkehard Hofmann

The COVID-19 Pandemic in Cyprus: A Problematic Legal Regime, and the Potential of Rule of Law in Emergencies 91
Costas Stratilatis

Part III Balancing and Judicial Scrutiny in a Pandemic

American Lessons: The COVID-19 Pandemic and the US Supreme Court 113
Anna Tsiftsoglou

The Rule of Law and Fundamental Rights in the Coronavirus Pandemic in Germany 125
Wolfgang Kahl and Konstantina-Antigoni Poulou

The Impact of the Pandemic on the Greek Constitution 147
Ioannis A. Tassopoulos

Protecting Political Rights During the COVID-19 Pandemic: The Emergence of Strict Scrutiny in Spain 161
Joan Solanes Mullor

Part IV Conclusions: Liberal Democracy After COVID-19

Conclusions: Liberal Democracy After COVID-19: Challenges in Europe and Beyond 177
Kostas Chrysogonos and Anna Tsiftsoglou

Contributors

Kostas Chrysogonos Faculty of Law, Aristotle University of Thessaloniki, Thessaloniki, Greece

Giacomo Delledonne Institute for Law, Politics and Development (Dirpolis), Scuola Superiore Sant'Anna, Pisa, Italy

Ekkehard Hofmann Faculty of Law, University of Trier, Trier, Germany

Wolfgang Kahl Faculty of Law, Ruprecht-Karls-Universität, Heidelberg, Germany
Institute for German and European Administrative Law, Heidelberg, Germany

Heike Merten Party Research Institute, Heinrich Heine University Düsseldorf, Düsseldorf, Germany

Konstantina-Antigoni Poulou Faculty of Law, Ruprecht-Karls-Universität, Heidelberg, Germany

Joan Solanes Mullor Department of Law, Pompeu Fabra University, Barcelona, Spain

Costas Stratilatis School of Law, University of Nicosia, Nicosia, Cyprus

Ioannis A. Tassopoulos Department of Political Science and Public Administration, National and Kapodistrian University of Athens, Athens, Greece

Anna Tsiftsoglou Faculty of Law, Aristotle University of Thessaloniki, Thessaloniki, Greece

Teresa Violante Friedrich Alexander Universität Erlangen-Nürnberg, Erlangen, Germany
Max Planck Institute for Comparative Public Law and International Law, Heidelberg, Germany

Panagiotis Viopoulos Faculty of Law, Aristotle University of Thessaloniki, Thessaloniki, Greece

Part I
The COVID-19 Pandemic as a State of Exception?

The Pandemic as an Idiosyncratic Case of a State of Exception

Kostas Chrysogonos and Panagiotis Viopoulos

Abstract One of the characteristics of constitutionalism is that it usually flourishes in societies experiencing a state of normality. It is telling that its worldwide ascendance during the last two and a half centuries went hand-in-hand with a long-term mitigation of the use of mass organized violence in international as well as in national politics. COVID-19, however, is an asymmetric threat for humankind which could prove itself to have consequences comparable to those of a war. Whether this or eventual future pandemics might be enough to jeopardize the constitutional acquis is still an open question. Our aim shall be to show that the answer to such questions is not so much a matter of constitutional theory as of historical reality.

1 Introduction

Historical experience seems to indicate that the preservation of a relatively high level of political institutionalization in human societies goes hand-in-hand with circumstances of "normality," meaning that there is no clear and present danger threatening the very existence of a given society.[1] In most cases, such an imminent threat takes the shape of mass and organized use of violence by humans against humans, either coming from the outside (e.g., foreign invasion) or from the inside (e.g., civil strife).[2] From ancient times onward, this was frequently seen as justifying deviations from established rules and patterns of political behavior to avert that danger, as exemplified by the Roman maxim *salus populis suprema lex esto*.[3]

In as much as an exceptional situation demands exceptional answers, focused on efficacy through swift decision-making, it seems feasible to have an alternative

[1] Cf Rossiter (1948/2002), p. 5.

[2] Ferejohn and Pasquino (2004), p. 231.

[3] Cicero (edited by Keyes) (1928) De legibus, book III, sub. VIII.

K. Chrysogonos (✉) · P. Viopoulos
Faculty of Law, Aristotle University of Thessaloniki, Thessaloniki, Greece

K. Chrysogonos, A. Tsiftsoglou (eds.), *Democracy after Covid*,
https://doi.org/10.1007/978-3-031-13901-7_1

modus operandi to cope with such situations. A well-known example was the ancient Roman institution of "dictatorship," which originally meant the concentration of far-reaching, yet legally prescribed and delineated, emergency powers in an individual magistrate, called "dictator" for a certain (months-long) period to deal with extraordinary circumstances threatening the city-state. It has been calculated that within three centuries from 501 B.C. to 202 B.C. such a "dictatorship" was enacted no less than 76 times and it was connected, in most cases, with wars against foreign enemies or attempts of reconciliation at home.[4] Later, however, in the 1st century B.C., military leaders such as Sulla or Julius Caesar appropriated the title of the "dictator" for themselves to dress the violent and limitless imposition of their rule with a thin institutional veil.[5] In the case of Julius Caesar, even time limits were abolished, since he was proclaimed "dictator for life" in 44 B.C., shortly before being assassinated. This implied that the political institutions of the *res publica* were essentially put out of use, although they continued to formally exist.[6]

Likewise abuses of institutions foreseen to cope with exceptional situations occur frequently also in modern times. It is telling that the possibility to temporarily suspend the force of the Constitution to face extraordinary circumstances was first provided for in the French façade Constitution of 1799 (Art. 92), which essentially gave legal shape to the Napoleonic dictatorship.[7] Therefore, it seems that rules foreseeing a state of exception to overcome perilous circumstances, even when they are well-meant (which is not always the case), are susceptible to abuses, reminding a double-edged sword. Sometimes the (supposed) cure may be worse than the disease. Similarly, historical experience indicates that the exercise of political authority could acquire "dictatorial" features not only by applying derogation mechanisms, but also by openly violating constitutional provisions. For instance, in the context of the US Civil War, President Lincoln authorized the suspension of the writ of habeas corpus, enshrined in Article 1 of the US Constitution, and justified this deviation by invoking the "popular demand and public necessity."[8] These historical examples highlight the omnipresent risk of agents (political leaders, royals, military officers) who can utilize extraordinary circumstances to effectively set aside the juridical order and place themselves as *legibus soluti*.[9]

The question of governments functioning in a state of exception logic to deal with extraordinary circumstances and the threat of abuses and, consequently, of setbacks against the constitutional and democratic acquis recurred after the outbreak of the

---

[4] Gandhi (2008), p. 4.

[5] Lazar (2009), pp. 119–120.

[6] See Schmitt (1928), p. 3 (Fn. 3), König (2007), p. 79 ff.

[7] See Godechot (1979/1994), pp. 143 ff. and 161.

[8] See Rossiter (1948/2002), pp. 227–228 who refers to "Lincoln's dictatorship" and Agamben (2004), pp. 20–21 who refers to Lincoln's stance during this period as an example of the Schmittean "commissarial dictatorship."

[9] See Agamben (2004), p. 69, Raimondi (2021), p. 186.

COVID-19 pandemic. To address this problematic, we first provide an insight on how warfare, as a permanent threatening situation, determined states' institutional profile (Sect. 2). Then, we examine how the emergence of asymmetric threats, such as terrorism, formed a new type of "permanent" threatening situations and resulted to the so-called "normalization of the exception" (Sect. 3). The core idea behind Sect. 4 is that in, the era of the Anthropocene, "normal certainties are inverted or even dissolved," meaning that even our bare understanding of "normality" is questioned.[10] Indeed, the continuous feedback between humans and the natural environment leaves the door for future pandemics or other anthropogenic risks, for example natural disasters, wide open.[11] By recognizing that the threat of COVID-19 or of other future pandemics is more or less permanent, we conclude that institutional experience gained from the current pandemic showcases the demand for efficiency and the subsequent need for well-informed institutional preparedness and political consistency as the key factors for maintaining constitutional acquis.

2 From "War as Normality" to "War as Exception": The Impact of Warfare on States' Institutional Profile

The frequent participation of states in wars, some of which were extremely lengthy (e.g., the Hundred Years' War between England and France during 14th and 15th centuries), unavoidably had serious and enduring repercussions for the institutional profile of most states over thousands of years. It would not be an exaggeration to argue that the two main theses formulated by Carl von Clausewitz on the eve of the Napoleonic wars contained a concealed demand to overturn the relationship between state and war, as it was shaped throughout the preceding five millennia. His famous aphorism that war was the continuation of politics by other means, as well as his contention that the rational thing to do is to subjugate the military to the political point of view and that the vice versa position is irrational[12] (and therefore, we conclude, political control over the military is rational and military control over politics irrational) make sense and correspond to reality only insofar peace equals normality and war remains an exceptional situation.

On the contrary, if states usually conduct wars with only temporary peace intervals, then their foreign and even domestic politics look more like an effort to cope with the consequences of the one or the other outcome of the military operations, and with their collateral effects. In other words, in this case, politics rather resemble a continuation of war with other means. Even worse, during a war, decisions taken by the military leadership sometimes tend to dress themselves with the mantle of "necessity" and to be de facto imposed to the political leadership, even

[10] Vermeylen (2015), p. 138.

[11] See Vierck et al. (2017), p. 13, Deakin and Meng (2020), p. 562.

[12] von Clausewitz (1832/2004), book VIII, pp. 364 and 366.

when the latter is theoretically in charge (e.g., in imperial Germany in WWI, the Schlieffen Plan helped to provoke the entrance of Great Britain to the war, and again in 1916–1917, the unrestricted submarine warfare achieved the same regarding the United States of America).[13] A relatively innocuous result may be the election of retired officers, having won military glory, to top offices (e.g., generals Grant and Eisenhower served as President of the United States of America for two consecutive terms each). When, however, war tends to become an almost permanent situation, then the domestic organization of the state tends to become combative as well. When the people perceive that they fight for all they have, as ancient Greeks fighting in the battle of Salamis were singing,[14] then the fight naturally tends to be placed above all other things and consequently the leader in this fight is likely to be placed above all other persons. Similarly, the French slogan *Levée en masse*, developed during the Montagnard rule (1793–1794), reflects a situation in which the whole society must be involved in the war struggle.[15] Therefore, it is not only the function of the warlord that tends to absorb the function of the head of state (this is, in a degree, the historical origin of monarchy), but also, and more than that, the hierarchical logic of the army is likely to infiltrate the polity as a whole.

The ascent of constitutionalism during the last two centuries or so roughly coincides with a gradual receding of violence used in international relations. Up to the end of Napoleonic Wars, conflict between European Great Powers was, as far as time is concerned, rather the rule and peace was the exception. For instance, it has been estimated that, out of a total 950 years between 976 and 1925, France was belligerent in 657 years (80% of time) and, out of a total 875 years between 1051 and 1925, England was belligerent for 630 years (72% of time).[16] Besides, some of those wars (mainly Napoleonic and Seven Years') were essentially forerunners for what was later named a "World War," given that Europeans fought against each other not only within the boundaries of the Old Continent itself but also in their overseas colonial possessions (e.g., the Seven Years' War, 1756–1763, has been a catalytic event for the cultural identity of North America).[17] On the contrary, between 1815 and 1914, despite the major map changes in Europe as a continent (German and Italian national unifications, creation of new national states in the Balkan Peninsula etc.), wars usually lasted for a few months or, in the worst cases, for a few years. Out of the next 30 years, approximately one third was consumed by both world wars and, after that, wars between national states occur only sporadically and remain limited in time as well as in space.

Within the second decade after the end of the Napoleonic wars, a world-scale phenomenon that has been identified as the "first, long wave of democratization" by Samuel Huntington has emerged, which continued, with more or less impetus, for

[13] See Roberts (1976/2004), pp. 892 and 895–896.

[14] Aeschylus Persians, verse 405: "Fight for all we have!".

[15] Skocpol (1976/2008), p. 189.

[16] See Sorokin (1937/1941), pp. 309, 312, and 316.

[17] See also Colley (2021), pp. 5–7.

about a century (1828–1926). Two further waves followed, one at about the end of World War II (1943–1962), and the other roughly coinciding with a lessening of the international tension between the two major camps of the Cold War and then with the collapse of communist regimes in Eastern Europe, from 1974 onward.[18] The outcome of those "waves" was that, in the first decade of the new millennium, almost half of the existing national states could be evaluated as "free," with only slightly more than one fifth being rated as "not free."[19] Political power has been highly institutionalized with a written, formal Constitution, namely the "fundamental and paramount law of the nation,"[20] standing at the top of the legal pyramid in each and every country, with very few exceptions (e.g., the United Kingdom). However, state-building of the second and third waves sometimes suffered from the institutional pathogeny of a statehood limited in terms of capacities and capabilities, which rendered the respective societies vulnerable to any kind of turbulent circumstances, ranging from international or domestic warfare to outbreaks of epidemic diseases.[21]

3 The Gradual "Normalization" of the "Exception": "Emergencies" Beyond Warfare

War constitutes the main component of "emergency" constitutional provisions, as a situation clearly "threatening the life of the nation."[22] Nonetheless, historical experience indicates that "state of emergency" mechanisms were activated under the guise of "national danger" in circumstances beyond warfare (e.g., the *Preußenschlag* of July 1932, when President von Hindenburg applied Article 48 of the Weimar Constitution and issued an emergency decree enabling Chancellor von Papen to take control of the Land of Prussia).[23] This tendency was not limited to fragile constitutional frameworks like the Weimar Republic. Within 50 years (from 1920 to mid-1970s), consecutive British governments employed in 12 cases the Emergency Powers Act of 1920 to deal with incidents of lower tense, namely massive strikes and manifestations.[24] After 9/11, terrorism emerged through state practice as the most

[18] Huntington (1991), p. 13 ff.

[19] In its yearly "Freedom of the World" survey, released in 2008, the NGO "Freedom House" assessed that in the previous year—2007—out of a total of 193 countries, no less than 90 were free, 60 partially free and 43 not free. However, in its next survey (published in 2009), the respective numbers were 89, 62 and 42. Data retrieved from: Freedom House (2008), available at: https://freedomhouse.org/sites/default/files/2020-02/Freedom_in_the_World_2008_complete_book.pdf (last access: May 27, 2022).

[20] Marbury v Madison, 5 U.S. 137, 177-8 (1803).

[21] See Thauer (2017), pp. 375 and 378 and for further case studies see Guruparan (2020), pp. 69 and 76.

[22] See Table 1 in Bjornskov and Voigt (2018).

[23] Vinx (2015), pp. 1–14, Dyzenhaus (2012), p. 448.

[24] Agamben (2004), p. 19, Neocleous (2006), pp. 195–196.

notable case of "emergency," despite not literally putting the nation and the constitutional order into existential threat.[25]

Although the immediate aftermath of WWII revealed a tendency to weaken the attribution of emergency powers to the executive,[26] the trajectory of post-WWII constitutionalism, ascending in situations of relatively permanent peace, altered how the concept of "exception" is being perceived. First, most states have replaced recourse to derogation mechanisms with an infiltration of security concerns into normal governance.[27] Second, contrary to warfare situations, where they act as belligerent parties, state authorities are not necessarily involved in the context of novel threatening circumstances, such as terrorism or cyberattacks. These threats are asymmetric both in terms of location and duration. To this extent, the distinction between "friend" and "enemy" as an element shaping "emergency situations" (e.g., combatants against civilians in warfare) has been transcended and state responses rely on the idea that every person can be perceived as a potential "threat."[28] Warfare is not anymore the only potential "imminent" threat, meaning that the new perception of "normality" is not limited to peacetime as a relatively permanent situation, but it is also shaped by the perception of the asymmetric threats mentioned above as omnipresent.

However, when such asymmetric threats emerge and get materialized, the distinction between "friend" and "enemy" is still relevant as a basis to legitimize state responses. Political leaders often use "war rhetoric" to address and unite their citizens against the "unknown" or the "invisible" enemy (terrorists, viruses). In a political and social environment where security has acquired a primordial value, "fear" is a sentiment experienced by both those governing and those governed.[29] As the reaction against terrorist attacks indicates (e.g., France's response in the aftermath of 2015 terrorist attacks in Paris), "public mourning" and fear legitimize the resort to "states of emergency."[30] To this extent, "states of emergency" also function as a means to "reassure" the public and less as a means to achieve the goals anticipated, such as eliminating the likelihood of future terrorist attacks in the short- or long-term. The attempt to "reassure" serves two distinct purposes: first, the political leadership promises in a self-enforcing manner that it will not hesitate to do whatever it should be done to deal with the crisis and, second, the "assumption of separation between normality and emergency" gives the (vague) promise that once the threat disappears, then the enjoyment of fundamental rights and freedoms will be restored.[31]

---

[25] Fusco (2021), pp. 16 and 24, Poole (2015), p. 5, Tribe and Gudridge (2004), p. 1809.

[26] Bjornskov and Voigt (2018), p. 114.

[27] Agamben (2004), p. 14.

[28] Cf Greene (2011), p. 1769.

[29] Frankenberg (2010/2014), p. 153, Degerman et al. (2020), p. 4.

[30] Cf Yıldız (2021) p. 174, see also Agamben (2004), p. 64.

[31] For a critique on this "assumption," see Gross (2003), p. 1022.

The vagueness of this promise is illustrated on the blurry distinction between "normality" and "emergency" in cases of threats which are omnipresent, even if dormant for a certain period. This observation exceeds the classic dichotomy between the "fictitious" and the "real" state of exception[32] and it is the basis for the so-called "normalization" of the "exception."[33] On the one hand, the prominence of the executive on subjectively evaluating and declaring a "state of emergency" (even if parliaments typically confirm the relevant political choice and the judiciary legitimizes it by exercising a deferring review on the relevant acts)[34] leans towards the "fictitious" character. On the other hand, political authorities very often refrain from exercising the relevant constitutional powers, although the emergency can be classified as a "real" exceptional situation, in a sense similar to Agamben's observation that "the only circumstances that are necessary and objective are those that are declared to be so."[35] In cases where exceptional measures are not adopted under a formal suspension of constitutional or international human rights law obligations, the necessary accommodation between limiting fundamental rights and the legal requirements of fundamental rights protection is grounded on a sophisticated approach of the concept of proportionality.[36] However, especially when the measures taken are legitimized under the mantle of "security" (let alone "necessity" in extraordinary circumstances), then an innocuous externality might be the transformation of governmental "hyperboles" or unnecessary ideological radicalizations into political practice.[37]

In the context of post-WWII constitutionalism, developed under circumstances of political and institutional normality (which has lasted no more than 75 years so far), efficient risk management has emerged as a qualitative metric for the performance of political institutions.[38] This relatively short-term period of normality was enough to reflect that, apart from war, there can be other circumstances threatening all members of a human society, even if the latter behave with the utmost diligence.[39] To this extent, the re-emergence of the pandemic risk creates new dimensions on how human societies experience threat and this automatically creates new implications regarding the role of political institutions.

---

[32] See Humphreys (2006), p. 678.

[33] Kuo (2020), p. 37.

[34] Feinberg (2020), p. 120.

[35] Agamben (2004), p. 30.

[36] Dyzenhaus (2012), p. 460.

[37] See Kumm (2010), pp. 160–162 and 174.

[38] Poole (2015), p. 246.

[39] Parmet (2007), p. 22.

4 Evaluating the Potential Impact of COVID-19 on the Constitutional Acquis: The Pandemic as a Lesson for an Informed "Institutionalization"

4.1 Reassessing the "Novelty" of the Pandemic Threat: An "Ignored" Emergency

The pandemic of COVID-19 creates a "novel" kind of exceptional circumstances worldwide. In a way, it could be seen as a special kind of war, namely not a war between humans but a war of all of humankind against an asymmetric common enemy. Indeed, its consequences are undoubtedly comparable to those of a real war. It has been estimated by the World Health Organization that, from January 2020 onward, when the first confirmed death due to COVID-19 was reported in Wuhan (China), more than 528 million people have been infected and at least 6.2 million died.[40] Compared to the death toll rates of WWI (according to official UK statistics), the COVID-19 death toll rate per month is higher than that of WWI, when more than 8.2 million people died within a period less than 52 months.[41] The economic impact of COVID-19 is also severe. For instance, ILO assessed that income generated from labor worldwide in 2020 fell by 4.4% (equivalent to 3.7 trillion US dollars) compared to 2019.[42]

These statistics justify why COVID-19 pandemic has been experienced as a "novel" kind of exceptional situation. Nonetheless, its "novelty" should be properly contextualized. Human societies had been for long suffering from deadly epidemic diseases (e.g., plague, smallpox, etc.). To this extent, measures limiting the transmission of infectious diseases, such as quarantines and cordons sanitaires, have been very specific and invariable throughout history.[43] It is only from the 18th century onward that (mainly Western) societies have been experiencing an "epidemiological transition." In 1800, the global life expectancy was around 39 years and in 2019, it reached 79 years.[44] The "epidemiological transition" also embedded the sense of normality within most human societies and it is not a coincidence that it chronologically accompanies the period of revolutions and the development of constitutionalism.[45] Nonetheless, it had turned Western societies complacent about the effects generated by the interaction between humans and the natural environment, notably the evolution of new pathogens and the intensified risk of disease spread due to the

[40] Metrics retrieved from WHO's COVID-19 Dashboard, available at: https://covid19.who.int/ (last access: May 27, 2022).

[41] See War Office (1922), pp. 237 and 352–357.

[42] Data retrieved from ILO Monitor: COVID-19 and the World of Work (Seventh Edition), available at: https://www.ilo.org/wcmsp5/groups/public/%2D%2D-dgreports/%2D%2D-dcomm/documents/briefingnote/wcms_767028.pdf (last access: May 27, 2022).

[43] See Deakin and Meng (2020), pp. 539 and 594, Villarreal (2020), p. 226.

[44] Shaw-Taylor (2020), p. 1.

[45] Jensen (2021), p. 6.

high degree of interconnectivity between modern globalized societies.[46] It is quite characteristic that only two and a half years before the outbreak of COVID-19, Hurlbut was straightforwardly referring to the threat of a zoonotic virus by pointing that "whereas infectious disease and public health experts can see clearly the future is brewing in the poultry farms of Southeast Asia, the public has long since forgotten the pandemics of their grandparents' world."[47] Even in twenty-first century, outbreaks of infectious diseases affecting wide geographical areas, such as the Ebola epidemic in Western Africa, have not been unusual.[48] Therefore, COVID-19 pandemic should be preferably mentioned as a crisis *experienced* as novel and not as a crisis *been* novel.

Experiencing a predictable crisis as "novel" reflects a divergence between epistemic knowledge and the anticipated institutional knowledge and preparedness.[49] Responses against the outbreak of COVID-19 showcased the role of two epistemic communities (epidemiologists and policy makers) on balancing competing perceptions on how to deal with the pandemic and how to weigh the (epidemiological and economic) stakes involved.[50] However, dealing with a pandemic is not just a matter of implementing epistemically informed political decisions into state coercion. Since every member of the society is potentially both a "victim" (infected) and a "carrier" (transmitter) of the threat (pathogen), the initial "entrustment" of political institutions towards the epidemiological epistemic community[51] would have no impact without a high degree of compliance on behalf of the citizens. As empirically observed, guidance-based approaches without specific coercive measures, such as lockdowns, were inefficient (e.g., the initial stance of the British Government against the pandemic), meaning that the required scale of compliance and, subsequently, the epidemiologically anticipated results can be achieved neither by solely relying on state coercion mechanisms nor by anticipating that merely nudging practices would be sufficient.[52] At least some coercive measures are necessary and, thus, limitations to the enjoyment of certain fundamental rights are inevitable.

In the context of "epistemic democracy," acceptance goes hand-in-hand with an output legitimation of political institutions, based on the quality of outcomes rather than on the bare—but perhaps inefficient—compliance with procedural safeguards, which are sometimes perceived as useless technicalities.[53] Contrary to large-scale warfare, which can be prevented by deterministic political means like diplomacy, anthropogenic risks emerge through nature and cannot abide by exogenous "rules"

[46] For the pre-COVID-19 literature see Fidler (2004), pp. 259–260 and 273–274, Hurlbut (2017), p. 1 and for post-COVID-19 literature see Deakin and Meng (2020), p. 584, Jensen (2021), p. 3.

[47] Hurlbut (2017), p. 4.

[48] See Villarreal (2020), p. 231.

[49] Hurlbut (2017), pp. 3–4, Abiri and Guidi (2021), p. 4.

[50] Scheinin and Molboek-Steensing (2021), p. 19.

[51] Walby (2020), p. 12.

[52] Deakin and Meng (2020), pp. 541 and 578.

[53] See Boschele (2020), p. 3, Villarreal (2020), p. 226.

and political decisions.[54] After all, "normality," as a determinant of constitutionalism, was a by-product of the absence of both warfare and pandemics. The experience of COVID-19 reminds us that when a pandemic breaks out, political institutions (as agents) and human societies (as principals) are immediately involved in "crisis management." Hence, the threat of pandemics resembles the threat of terrorism, as understood after 9/11. Even in a situation of normality, the omnipresence of such large-scale risks questions the existence of "normality" itself.

4.2 *COVID-19 As a Reminder of the Omnipresent Risk of Abusing "Emergency Situations"*

Pandemics can asymmetrically jeopardize the physical and economic survival of human societies and, thus, can be classified as "emergencies," either pragmatically or juridically.[55] The experience of COVID-19 pandemic reminded to state institutions and human societies in general the special nature of pandemics as a large-scale threat and as an "exceptional situation." For instance, France shaped a completely new "state of health emergency" regime (état d' urgence sanitaire) to deal with the exigencies of the pandemic.[56]

By May 2020, roughly two months after the outbreak of COVID-19 pandemic in most countries, more than one fifth of the ECHR state parties (10 out of 47) and more than half of the ACHR state parties (12 out of 23) had activated the derogation clauses of Articles 15 ECHR and 27 ACHR.[57] Nonetheless, this formal criterion cannot offer a comprehensive assessment on whether and how the rule of law has been undermined in the pandemic context.[58] For example, according to the Pandemic Violations of Democratic Standards (PanDem) index, certain states, such as Romania, recorded a "minor violations" score despite having activated a constitutional or international derogation mechanism,[59] whilst other states recorded violations of "moderate" or "major" score without recourse to such a mechanism.[60] Indeed, undermining democratic standards is not a matter of juridical technicality, but mainly a matter of political practice and institutional consistency. For instance, Hungarian authorities did not invoke COVID-19 to derogate from the standards of

[54] See Hamilton (2015), p. 39, Vermeylen (2015), p. 159.

[55] Cf Villarreal (2020), p. 225, Lebret (2020), p. 5, Greene (2011), p. 1767.

[56] See Platon (2020), available at: https://verfassungsblog.de/from-one-state-of-emergency-to-another-emergency-powers-in-france/ (last access: May 27, 2022).

[57] See Coghlan (2020), available at: https://verfassungsblog.de/dissecting-covid-19-derogations/ (last access: May 27, 2022).

[58] Helfer (2021), pp. 21 and 25.

[59] See Coghlan (2020).

[60] Data retrieved from: https://www.v-dem.net/pandem.html (last access: May 27, 2022).

the European Convention on Human Rights, but they severely undermined rule of law by enacting the "Enabling Act" of March 2020.

The Hungarian Enabling act (30th March 2020) is a quite indicative example of setbacks against constitutional acquis and the rule of law. It did not only attribute to the Executive the super-power to suspend or alter, without former special delegation, legislation enacted by the Parliament, but it also refrained from including any sunset clause or other provision safeguarding its temporary character.[61] From the period of Roman "dictatorship" to liberal constitutionalism, "emergencies" have been historically understood as temporary circumstances and, thus, any relevant legislation should envisage the re-establishment of constitutional and institutional normality when the pragmatic background will be also normalized,[62] especially in cases where this normalization can be foreseen, at least situation-wise if not time-wise (e.g., the "flattening" of the epidemiological curve or the progress of vaccinations and the achievement of "herd immunity" against COVID-19).[63] Furthermore, "state of exception" mechanisms are abusively employed by political authorities when the latter utilize them to serve irrelevant political purposes, mainly by establishing a multi-scale exceptionality. For example, by invoking the temporary prohibition of non-essential medical and surgical acts and by inscribing abortion as a "non-essential" act, certain US states practically issued anti-abortion legislation under the mantle of enacting "emergency" legislation against the spread of COVID-19.[64]

If "state of exception" is to be perceived as a "factual" extraordinary situation which cannot be confronted without disregarding rule of law safeguards,[65] then the "juridical" activation of "state of emergency" mechanisms cannot per se undermine the constitutional acquis. Nonetheless, governmental practice against the permanence of certain invisible threats, such as terrorism, has revealed that "state of exception" is mainly materialized as a fictitious concept which has juridically and politically infiltrated human societies. Within these antithetical positions, the experience of COVID-19 showcases the idiosyncratic characteristics of the pandemic threat as a potential "state of exception." Contrary to the "warfare state," where historical experience underlines the imposition of military will upon political leadership, the "pandemic state" indicates the pivotal role of the political leadership for establishing trust towards the epidemiological epistemic community and adopting relevant efficient measures. Regardless of previous formal recourse to emergency mechanisms, the necessary measures to deal with the pandemic risk are very specific and—if adopted and executed in a non-abusive and informed manner—they are constitutionally acceptable. Nonetheless, similarly to the historical experience gathered from the periods of mass organized violence, the exceptional situation of the

[61] See Greene (2011), pp. 1766 and 1782 and for the value and functioning of sunset clauses, see generally Kouroutakis (2017).

[62] Ferejohn and Pasquino (2004), p. 210, Bertolini (2020), p. 213.

[63] Scheinin and Molboek-Steensing (2021), p. 24.

[64] Hill (2020), pp. 99–100.

[65] Kuo (2020), p. 22, note 1.

COVID-19 pandemic reflected once again the propensity of political institutions to abuse emergency situations to establish political dominance, especially if the epistemic criteria are blurred by merely political purposes.

4.3 *"Efficiency" as a Factor of Trust Towards Democratic Political Institutions and as a Prerequisite for Maintaining Constitutional Acquis*

From a comparative standpoint, China has presented an example of a very efficient response against the spread of COVID-19, which has, however, been mainly attributed to the illiberal nature of Chinese governing political institutions.[66] This Schmittean-like equation between, on the one hand, "illiberal" and "efficient" policies and, on the other hand, "liberal" and "inefficient" ones is rather arbitrary. As Deakin and Meng develop, our assessment on China's (and every state's) efficiency should not be limited to generic observations based on the type of the political regime in place.[67] Such an approach undermines the ability of democratic political systems to prove themselves efficient and it jeopardizes constitutional acquis by creating public's perception that only draconian and illiberally oriented measures can provide the necessary response, legitimizing propensity towards authoritarianism whenever an "emergency" occurs.[68] Contrary to Western governments and societies, which initially undermined the severity reflected on available scientific evidence on COVID-19,[69] East-Asian countries (e.g., Japan, China, Republic of Korea, etc.) have recently experienced the threats posed by infectious diseases (e.g., the first SARS epidemic in early 2000s or MERS in mid-2010s). Hence, they have achieved a high degree of "institutional preparedness," analyzed into expediency in relevant decision-making and clear knowledge about the types of measures capable of dealing with an outbreaking pandemic.[70]

Moreover, the contention that "efficiency" is not a privilege of undemocratic political leaderships is also confirmed by the stance of certain authoritarian and populist political leaders against COVID-19. When it comes to such kind of political leadership, the main concern is no other than the potential propagandistic characterization of a crisis as an "exceptional situation" to provide space for an "executive overreach," as it has happened in the case of Hungary. However, the choice of

---

[66] See, among others, Degerman et al. (2020), pp. 14–15.

[67] Deakin and Meng (2020), pp. 541–542.

[68] Tribe and Gudridge (2004), p. 1829, Daly (2020), available at: https://verfassungsblog.de/democracy-and-the-global-emergency-shared-experiences-starkly-uneven-impacts (last access: May 27, 2022), Abiri and Guidi (2021), p. 37.

[69] Degerman et al. (2020), p. 4.

[70] See Deakin and Meng (2020), pp. 541 et seq.

Brazilian President Bolsonaro to act in a form of "executive underreach,"[71] reflected on his unwillingness to enforce lockdowns or follow the epistemic apparatus against the transmission of COVID-19 (e.g., his personal anti-vaccine stance) has been severely criticized. Although the laissez-faire approaches towards the pandemic risk are sought to be justified under a libertarian guise of protecting fundamental and mainly economic liberties, Bolsonaro's inefficient policy undermined any sympathy to his authoritarian profile and strengthened public's trust towards democratically consistent political behavior (e.g., many public officials have resisted central governmental choices and that reaction has politically strengthened checks and balances against Bolsonaro's *golpismo*).[72] Hence, when authoritarian politicians exercise inefficient policies and disregard fundamental values such as life and health, then trust to democratically consistent political institutions, who do not disregard these values, can be strengthened and halt already ongoing decays of the constitutional acquis.

Constitutional acquis is not a blank slate, but it is shaped by the political institutions of a given society and by the feedback generated between those governing and those governed. Hence, even in highly institutionalized constitutional polities, when institutions are proven inefficient in achieving the results anticipated, then they risk being undermined. From an evolutionary standpoint, efficiency entails survival, to the sense that "efficient" institutions survive, while "inefficient" institutions get extinct.[73] However, institutions are dynamic concepts which can be efficient (and thus survive) by adapting to changing circumstances, although their initial design might not have been fit to deal with them. For example, the economic institutions of the European Union showed a great degree of adaptivity to deal with Eurozone crisis from 2010 onward.[74] "Variations" with regard to dealing with emergency situations do not necessarily attach to the temporary nature of the emergency, but they may acquire relatively permanent characteristics due to overriding political interests or social demands.[75] However, if "adaptivity" is limited within the mantle of the "law of necessity," then "efficiency" acquires a monosemantic content and the relevant emergencies are in practice dealt with under the "There Is No Alternative" (TINA) doctrine.[76] Functioning under the TINA doctrine may have two important consequences: first, any institutional framework (including rules and practices) applied to deal with the crisis may remain intact in the post-emergency "normality" as an obstacle against a new emergence of the

---

[71] For the distinction between "executive overreach" and "executive underreach," see Scheppele and Pozen (2020), pp. 38–53.

[72] Smith (2020), p. 77.

[73] Roe (1996), p. 641.

[74] See Delledonne (2020), pp. 256 et seq.

[75] Kouroutakis and Ranchordas (2016), p. 51.

[76] Séville (2016), p. 3.

crisis[77] or it may generate predicted or unpredicted long-term effects.[78] Second, it may obscure a clear evaluation on whether political institutions had had the appropriate "institutional knowledge" and, thus, the future acquisition of such a knowledge remains uncertain.

Both aspects are relevant when it comes to epidemic diseases: "efficiency" is measured not only with reference to the rate of cases and the death toll suffered, but also with reference to the detriment of restrictive measures like lockdowns to the national economy. To this extent, a basic factor of "institutional preparedness" against pandemics is no other than "social" or "welfare" state institutions.[79] Public health systems constitute a pivotal welfare state institution, which significantly contributed to the "epidemiological transition," mainly because of the welfare state's ability to employ resources and deal with infectious diseases at their very beginning (e.g., vaccination programs against diseases related to infant mortality).[80] Therefore, welfare state institutions, as the reflection of practically implementing social rights, also belong to the post-war constitutional acquis[81] and the relevant institutional arsenal forms an integral part of the collective responses of societies against epidemics. It is quite characteristic that political authorities justified lockdowns and other restrictive measures and established confidence to their actions by invoking the need to protect public health systems from a massive influx of COVID-19 cases (e.g., the slogan of the British government: "Stay Home, Protect the NHS, Save Lives").[82]

Therefore, "efficiency" arises as a key factor for maintaining constitutional acquis in times of pandemic. The demand for efficiency incites political institutions to be really cognizant of the exigencies of the pandemic risks and, therefore, to be institutionally prepared to deal with the outbreaks of pandemic diseases in a timely and efficient manner. Maintaining the constitutional acquis requires from political institutions to guarantee circumstances of factual and juridical "normality." In case the threat excels beyond the limits of normality and amounts to "emergency," then political institutions shall apply their relevant competences in a non-abusive and above all politically consistent way.

[77] See Farrand and Rizzi (2019), pp. 23–24 and 44–45.

[78] See Tsiftsoglou (2015), p. 36.

[79] See Erikson (2017), pp. 362 and 365 referring to the underdeveloped public health systems of West Africa countries as factors deteriorating the spread of Ebola. Jensen (2021), p. 7.

[80] Deakin and Meng (2020), pp. 539, 541 and 544 use the term "mortality revolution."

[81] See King (2012), p. 23.

[82] See Tan et al. (2021), pp. 1–4.

5 Conclusion

In a constitutional system, political institutions function as agents and the subjects of their authority function as their principals. On the one hand, political institutions are "rule governed," meaning that they are bound by specific legal rules establishing procedural and substantial limits to their decision-making.[83] On the other hand, they are not "rule determined," meaning that the agent possesses discretion with regard to whether a specific decision should be made and what the content of this decision—if made—will be.[84] Therefore, the recourse to "state of exception" mechanisms and, if such recourse happens, the abuse of the relevant mechanisms constitute after all a matter of political morality and institutional coherence.[85]

The divergence between what the law prescribes and how the office holder of a political institution would be inclined to behave is also reflected on the way science and law interreact. According to Luhman's systems' theory, science follows a different code than law, the former understood within the binary "true/false," and the latter understood within the binary "legal/illegal."[86] Thus, "efficiency" is determined through scientific knowledge, but an "efficient" measure is not in all circumstances a "legal" measure and vice versa. Moreover, contrary to incidents of mass organized violence, where the distinction between "normality" and "exception" is quite clear, science and law (as the reflection of political decision-making) assess different criteria to determine when an "emergency" exists. For example, in the case of Liberia, WHO, reflecting the scientific input, declared the country as Ebola-free on 2016, whereas the juridical "state of emergency," activated under the relevant constitutional rule as a response against the Ebola epidemic had been lifted two years earlier in November 2014.[87] However, scientific input is useful to determine whether certain measures are "necessary or not," but the crucial part of *stricto sensu* proportionality—where the limits between law and politics are not clear—is mainly blurred and it favors judicial deference. Thus, in the modern post-national constitutional landscape, governance relies even more on the possession of the "right knowledge" and the demand for efficiency has rendered science an integral part of decision-making.

As historical experience and reality indicate, the restoration or the maintenance of constitutional acquis cannot be an automatic outcome of the transition from the "state of exception" to the "state of normality." It cannot also rely on the bare anticipation of judgments finding specific "emergency" measures to be unconstitutional. This observation should not be understood as an adherence to the Schmittean idea that the exercise of emergency powers is merely a political rather than a legal

[83] Lazar (2009), p. 9.

[84] Lazar (2009), pp. 9–10.

[85] See Lazar pp. 9 et seq.

[86] Luhman (2002), p. 20.

[87] Villarreal (2020), p. 230.

question.[88] Although "emergency powers" and the relevant logic have infiltrated the administrative state as legitimate policy choices,[89] exceptional circumstances make emergency mechanisms more vulnerable to abuses and this is the point where (constitutional) law is even more essential.[90] It is the exact point where the untenable idea of a limitless executive power shall meet juridical limits.[91]

To summarize, "efficiency" in case of emergencies shall not only be understood as an individual goal, alienated from the stakes involved with regard to the maintenance of the constitutional acquis.[92] COVID-19 will not be the last infectious disease affecting humankind.[93] The omnipresent threat of a new pandemic disease does not allow human societies and their political institutions to approach future pandemics as "novel" circumstances. Contrary, the fallacies and contradictions experienced in the context of the COVID-19 pandemic shall above all determine a new "institutional knowledge," which does not prejudice against constitutional and democratic acquis. The main components of this "knowledge" shall be no other than efficient proactive and responsive mechanisms, included in the "umbrella" of the welfare state institutions, as well as a profound understanding that "state of exception" rationale shall not be abusively implemented.

References

Abiri G, Guidi S (2021) The pandemic constitution. Columbia J Transnatl Law (forthcoming), Available at SSRN: https://doi.org/10.2139/ssrn.3797023 (last access: May 27, 2022)

Agamben G (2004) State of Exception (trans: Attel K). University of Chicago Press, Chicago

Barak A (2020) Human rights in times of terror – a judicial point of view. In: Albert R, Roznai Y (eds) Constitutionalism under extreme conditions: law, emergency, exception. Springer Nature, Cham, pp 109–120

Bertolini E (2020) Financial crisis as a new genus of constitutional emergency. In: Albert R, Roznai Y (eds) Constitutionalism under extreme conditions: law, emergency, exception. Springer Nature, Cham, pp 197–216

Bjornskov C, Voigt S (2018) The architecture of emergency constitutions. ICON 16(1):101–127

Boschele M (2020) COVID-19 science policy, experts, and publics: why epistemic democracy matters in ecological crises. OMICS A J Integr Biol 24(8):1–4

Cicero (printed 1928) De re publica. De legibus, by Clinton Walker Keyes (ed) Cicero, On the Republic. On the Laws. Harvard University Press, Cambridge

Coghlan N (2020) Dissecting Covid-19 Derogations, available at: https://verfassungsblog.de/dissecting-covid-19-derogations/ (last access: May 27, 2022)

Colley L (2021) The gun, the ship, and the pen: warfare, constitutions, and the making of the modern world. Profile Books, London

---

[88] See Schmitt (translated by Vinx) (1932/2015), p. 222, Dyzenhaus (2012), pp. 448–450.

[89] Kuo (2020), p. 37.

[90] Barak (2020), p. 111.

[91] See Tsiftsoglou (2015), p. 201.

[92] Gross (2003), p. 1031.

[93] Dobson et al. (2020), p. 381.

Deakin S, Meng G (2020) The governance of Covid-19: anthropogenic risk, evolutionary learning, and the future of the social state. Ind Law J 49(4):540–594

Degerman D, Flinders M, Johnson M T (2020) In Defence of Fear: COVID-19, Crises and Democracy. Crit Rev Int Soc Polit Philos, pp 1–22. https://doi.org/10.1080/13698230.2020.1834744

Delledonne G (2020) Crises, emergencies and constitutional change. In: Contiades X, Fotiadou A (eds) Routledge handbook of comparative constitutional change. Routledge, New York, pp 245–260

Dobson AP et al (2020) Ecology and economics for pandemic prevention. Science 369(6502): 379–381. https://doi.org/10.1126/science.abc3189

Dyzenhaus D (2012) States of Emergency. In: Rosenfeld M, Sajó A (eds) The Oxford handbook of comparative constitutional law. OUP, Oxford, pp 442–461

Erikson S (2017) The limits of the international health regulations: Ebola Governance, regulatory breach, and the non-negotiable necessity of national healthcare. In: Vierck L, Villarreal P, Weilert KA (eds) The Governance of Disease Outbreaks. Nomos, Baden, pp 351–372

Farrand B, Rizzi M (2019) There is no (legal) alternative: codifying economic ideology into law. In: Nanopoulos E, Vergis F (eds) The crisis behind the Euro-Crisis - the Euro-Crisis as a multi-dimensional systematic crisis of the EU. CUP, Cambridge, pp 23–48

Feinberg M (2020) Introduction: terrorism and warfare – extreme conditions or the new normal. In: Albert R, Roznai Y (eds) Constitutionalism under extreme conditions: law, emergency, exception. Springer Nature, Cham, pp 103–108

Ferejohn J, Pasquino P (2004) The law of the exception: a typology of emergency powers. ICON 2(2):210–239

Fidler D (2004) Constitutional Outlines of Public Health Constitutional Outlines of Public Health's "New World Order." Articles by Maurer Faculty. Available at: https://www.repository.law.indiana.edu/facpub/401: 247–290 (last access: May 27, 2022)

Frankenberg G (2010/2014) political technology and the erosion of the rule of law. Elgar, Cheltenham

Freedom House (2008) Freedom in the World 2008: The Annual Survey of Political Rights and Civil Liberties, Rowman and Littlefield Publishers, Lanham. Available at: https://freedomhouse.org/sites/default/files/2020-02/Freedom_in_the_World_2008_complete_book.pdf (last access: May 27, 2022)

Fusco GG (2021) Exception, fiction, performativity. In: Cercel C, Fusco GG, Lavis S (eds) States of exception: law, history, theory. Routledge, New York, pp 15–33

Gandhi J (2008) Political institutions under dictatorship. CUP, Cambridge

Godechot J (1979/1994) Les Constitutions de la France depuis 1789. Garnier Flammarion, Paris

Greene A (2011) Separating normalcy from emergency: the Jurisprudence of Article 15 of the European Convention on Human Rights. Ger Law J 12(10):1765–1785

Gross O (2003) Chaos and rules: should responses to violent crises always be constitutional. Yale Law J 112:1011–1134

Guruparan K (2020) Constitution and law as instruments for Normalising Abnormalcy: states of exception in the Plurinational context. In: Albert R, Roznai Y (eds) Constitutionalism under extreme conditions: law, emergency, exception. Springer Nature, Cham, pp 63–80

Hamilton C (2015) Human destiny in the Anthropocene. In: Hamilton C, Bonneuil C, Gemenne F (eds) The Anthropocene and the global environmental crisis: rethinking Modernity in a New Epoch. Routledge, New York, pp 32–43

Helfer L (2021) Editorial comment: rethinking derogations from human rights treaties. ASIL 115(1):20–40

Hill J (2020) Essentially elective: the law and ideology of restricting abortion during Covid-19 pandemic. Va Law Rev Online 106:99–123

Humphreys S (2006) Legalizing lawlessness: on Giorgio Agamben's state of exception. Eur J Int Law 17(3):677–687

Huntington S (1991) The third wave: democratization in the late twentieth century. Oklahoma University Press, Norman
Hurlbut BJ (2017) A science that knows no country: pandemic preparedness, global risk, sovereign science. BIG DATA SOC (July–December): 1–14. https://doi.org/10.1177/2053951717742417
International Labour Organization (2021) ILO Monitor: COVID-19 and the world of work. Seventh Edition, available at: https://www.ilo.org/wcmsp5/groups/public/%2D%2D-dgreports/%2D%2D-dcomm/documents/briefingnote/wcms_767028.pdf (last access: May 27, 2022)
Jensen S (2021) 'Human Rights against Human Arbitrariness': Pandemics in a human rights historical perspective. In: Kjaerum M, Davis M, Lyons A (eds) Covid-19 and human rights. Routledge, New York, pp 3–18
King J (2012) Judging social rights. CUP, Cambridge
König I (2007) Der römische Staat. Ein Handbuch. Reclam, Stuttgart
Kouroutakis A (2017) The constitutional value of sunset clauses. Routledge, New York
Kouroutakis A, Ranchordas S (2016) Snoozing democracy: sunset clauses, de-Juridification, and emergencies. Minn J Int Law 264:29–77
Kumm M (2010) The idea of socratic contestation and the right to justification: the point of rights-based proportionality review. Law Ethics Hum Rights 4(2):142–175
Kuo MS (2020) From institutional sovereignty to constitutional mindset: rethinking the domestication of the state of exception in the age of normalization. In: Albert R, Roznai Y (eds) Constitutionalism under extreme conditions: law, emergency, exception. Springer Nature, Cham, pp 21–40
Lazar NC (2009) States of emergency in liberal democracies. CUP, New York
Lebret A (2020) COVID-19 pandemic and derogation to human rights. J Law Biosci 7(1):1–15. https://doi.org/10.1093/jlb/lsaa015
Luhman N (2002/2013) Introduction to systems theory (trans: Gilgen P). Polity Press, Cambridge
Neocleous M (2006) The problem with normality: taking exception to "Permanent Emergency". Alternatives 31:191–213
Parmet W (2007) Public health and constitutional law: recognizing the relationship. J Health Care Law Policy 10(1):13–25
Platon S (2020) From One State of Emergency to Another – Emergency Powers in France, available at: https://verfassungsblog.de/from-one-state-of-emergency-to-another-emergency-powers-in-france/ (last access: May 27, 2022)
Poole T (2015) Reason for State: law, prerogative and empire. CUP, Cambridge
Raimondi S (2021) Beyond 'the most serious suspension of rights' of Genoa: violence, anomie and force (of law). In: Cercel C, Fusco GG, Lavis S (eds) States of exception: law, history, theory. Routledge, New York, pp 184–202
Roberts JM (1976/2004) The new penguin history of the world. Penguin (first published by Hutchinson), London
Roe M (1996) Chaos and evolution in law and economics. Harv Law Rev 109(3):641–668
Rossiter C (1948/2002) Constitutional Dictatorship (with a new introduction by William J. Quirk). Routledge, New York
Scheinin M, Molboek-Steensing H (2021) Human rights-based versus populist responses to the pandemic. In: Kjaerum M, Davis M, Lyons A (eds) Covid-19 and human rights. Routledge, New York, pp 19–34
Scheppele KL, Pozen D (2020) Executive overreach and underreach in the pandemic. In: Maduro MP, Kahn P (eds) Democracy in times of pandemic. CUP, Cambridge
Schmitt C (1928) Die Diktatur. Von den Anfangen des modernen Souveranitatsgedankens bis zum proletarischen Klassenkampf 2.ed. Duncker und Humblot, Munich-Leipzig
Schmitt C (1932) Schlußrede vor dem Staatsgerichtshof in Leipzig in dem Prozeß Preußen contra Reich' in Carl Schmitt Positionen und Begriffe im Kampf mitWeimar – Genf – Versailles 1923–1939, 3rd edn. Duncker and Humblot, Berlin, pp 205–210, translated by Vinx L (2015). In Vinx L (ed) The Guardian of the constitution: Hans Kelsen and Carl Schmitt on the limits of constitutional law. CUP, Cambridge, pp 222–227

Séville A (2016) From 'one right way' to 'one ruinous way'? Discursive shifts in 'there is no alternative'. Eur Polit Sci Rev 9(3):1–22

Shaw-Taylor M (2020) An introduction to the history of infectious diseases, epidemics and the early phases of the long-run decline in mortality. Econ Hist Rev 73(3):1–19

Skocpol T (1976, reprinted: 2008), States and social revolutions. CUP, New York

Smith AE (2020) Covid vs. Democracy: Brazil's populist playbook. J Democr 31(4):76–90

Sorokin P (1937/1941) Social and cultural dynamics, vol 3. American Book Co., New York

Tan MC, Owuamalan CK, Ng PN (2021) Stay at home, protect the NHS and save lives! Confidence in government moderates the negative effects of staying at home on mental health. Pers. Individ. Differ 179, https://doi.org/10.1016/j.paid.2021.110948

Thauer C (2017) The governance of infectious diseases. An international relations perspective. In: Vierck L, Villarreal P, Weilert KA (eds) The governance of disease outbreaks. Baden Baden, Nomos, pp 373–393

Tribe L, Gudridge OP (2004) The anti-emergency constitution. Yale Law J 113:1801–1870

Tsiftsoglou A (2015) Public Security and Privacy (in Greek: Δημόσια Ασφάλεια και Ιδιωτικότητα). Sakkoulas Publications, Athens - Thessaloniki

Vermeylen S (2015) Materiality and the ontological turn in the Anthropocene: establishing a dialogue between law, anthropology and eco-philosophy. In: Kotze L (ed) Environmental law and governance for the Anthropocene. Hart Publishing, Oxford, pp 137–162

Vierck L, Villarreal P, Weilert KA (2017) The concept of the book. In: Vierck L, Villarreal P, Weilert KA (eds) The governance of disease outbreaks. Nomos, Baden Baden, pp 13–42

Villarreal P (2020) Public health emergencies and constitutionalism before COVID-19: between the National and the International. In: Albert R, Roznai Y (eds) Constitutionalism under extreme conditions: law, emergency, exception. Springer Nature, Cham, pp 217–238

Vinx L (2015) Introduction: In Vinx L (transl, ed) The Guardian of the constitution: Hans Kelsen and Carl Schmitt on the limits of constitutional law. CUP, Cambridge, pp 1–21

von Clausewitz C (1832, reprinted 2004). Von Kriege. Erfhstadt, Area

Walby S (2020) The COVID pandemic and social theory: social democracy and public health in the crisis. Eur J Soc Theory 10(5):1–22. https://doi.org/10.1177/1368431020970127

War Office (1922) Statistics of the military effort of the British Empire during the Great War 1914–1920. Naval and Military Press Ltd (2015), London

Yıldız CB (2021) A state in anomie: an analysis of modern Turkey's states of exception. In: Cercel C, Fusco GG, Lavis S (eds) States of exception: law, history, theory. Routledge, New York, pp 167–183

The COVID-19 Pandemic and the State of Emergency: Lessons from Portugal

Teresa Violante

Abstract The present chapter analyses the normative response of Portugal to the coronavirus crisis. As in other European Member States, the reaction to the pandemic was developed through a combination of enactment of the constitutional state of emergency with the statutory administrative emergency regime. Under both frameworks, there has been a strengthening of the executive at the expense of a parliamentary retreat. This chapter covers both responses to the pandemic and their shortcomings, mainly regarding the lack of democratic legitimation of the fight against the pandemic in face of a parliamentary circumvention and abdication.

1 Introduction

"Who asks about the law when death is at the doorstep?".[1] This existential doubt has tormented lawyers and constitutional law since the coronavirus pandemic confronted humanity with unprecedented challenges at the level of public health, human life, and economic stress. Tackling the pandemic has forced governments to limit individual rights and freedoms to an extent rarely experienced in peacetime, often pushing liberal democracies to stretch the limits of the rule of law.

This chapter deals with the normative responses adopted in Portugal to handle the COVID-19 pandemic. Since the Constitution entails special provisions for dealing with emergency and specific crises' situations, and this exceptional framework was

The research leading to this chapter has been funded by the German Research Foundation/Deutsche Forschungsgemeinschaft (DFG) in the framework of the Emmy-Noether-Project on "Transnational Solidarity Conflicts".

[1] Frankenberg (2019), p. 15.

T. Violante (✉)
Friedrich-Alexander-Universität Erlangen-Nürnberg, Erlangen, Germany

Max Planck Institute for Comparative Public Law and International Law, Heidelberg, Germany
e-mail: teresa.nunes.violante@fau.de

K. Chrysogonos, A. Tsiftsoglou (eds.), *Democracy after Covid*,
https://doi.org/10.1007/978-3-031-13901-7_2

triggered, for the first time, to respond to the pandemic challenge, this analysis provides a valuable case study to test the adequacy of constitutional emergency powers in such a concrete factual context. Furthermore, the Portuguese authorities combined the constitutional emergency powers with the application of legislative emergency regimes entailed in ordinary statutes,[2] sometimes simultaneously. The twofold approach to pandemic containment allows testing the theoretical framework of the constitutional state of emergency, which presupposes a clear analytic distinction between constitutional and legislative exceptions. However, this theoretical distinction does not always provide a clear-cut contrast in practice, as some literature had already noted.

Moreover, it is also confronted by challenges posed by contemporary emergencies such as terrorism and, more recently, global pandemics. The illustration of the Portuguese practice in the context of COVID-19 feeds into these debates. It also substantiates the questionable position of Parliament in the management of the emergency and raises the difficulty of power-sharing between the legislature and the executive under times of dire stress. The analysis concludes that under constitutional and legislative exceptions, a parliamentarisation of the emergency is advisable as it can provide more democratic legitimacy to the executive action and lead to better decision-making.

2 The Emergency Framework in Portugal

Portugal is a representative democratic republic with a directly elected President and a unicameral Parliament. The regime is semi-presidential:[3] the President of the Republic, elected by direct popular vote, has significant constitutional and political powers, including the competence to dissolve Parliament. The Prime Minister has the competencies to direct the Government's general policy and coordinate and orient all the Ministers' actions. The Government is politically accountable to the Parliament and the President of the Republic. The Government and the Parliament enjoy legislative powers, although some matters are reserved for the Parliament.[4]

Portugal is a unitary state with two autonomous regions in the Madeira and Azores archipelagos with self-governing bodies and legislative, executive, and international powers. The independent Ombudsperson is tasked with safeguarding and promoting individuals' freedoms, rights, and guarantees and has the right to initiate abstract constitutional review[5] near the Constitutional Court.

[2] For a typology of emergency powers, see Ferejohn and Pasquino (2014).

[3] Novais (2021).

[4] Articles 164 and 165 of the Constitution. Unless otherwise specified, quotation of normative provisions refers to the constitutional text.

[5] The distinction between abstract and concrete review will be explained subsequently.

When the World Health Organization declared a global pandemic on 11 March 2020, there were two normative mechanisms at the disposal of the Portuguese authorities to react and adopt the necessary containment measures. On the one hand, the statutory instruments addressed to the administrative authorities are called administrative emergency or statutory administrative emergency. These instruments are provided by statute. On the other, the constitutional state of exception is addressed to the State's highest political authorities. The Constitution provides the state of exception which is divided into the "state of siege" and the "state of emergency".[6]

2.1 *The Administrative Emergency*

Administrative emergency encompasses statutory regimes provided in civil protection and health.[7] In Portugal, as in several other countries, administrative authorities are legally competent to adopt measures to tackle dangers and risk control situations. The current Framework Law on Civil Protection dated 2006 was last amended in 2015.[8] Under Article 8, the competent bodies may declare a situation of alert, a situation of contingency, and a situation of calamity, "depending on the nature of the events to be prevented or addressed and the gravity and extent of their current or expected effects". While in the less severe circumstances of alert or contingency, the competence to declare the situation may belong to a municipal or district authority, in the more severe calamity circumstances, the competent body for the declaration is the Government as the highest body of the Public Administration, gathered in the Council of Ministers. The declaration of calamity allows the establishment of more intense limits to individual rights.

The Framework Law on Civil Protection allows for nuanced centralisation of powers and substantial restrictions of fundamental rights, imposing limits to the circulation of persons and vehicles, fixation of cordons sanitaires, access to private property, and temporary requisition of products and services. This act was framed as a middle option between constitutional normalcy and the state of constitutional exception. It is tailored to address meteorological phenomena, floods, fires, technological hazards, earthquakes, and tsunamis, i.e. specific and localised events. On the other hand, epidemics are prolonged, and their effects spread among the population.[9]

---

[6]Different normative possibilities have been identified in other States such as measures adopted by the executive under urgent or exceptional circumstances and subject to parliamentary scrutiny. This hypothesis lacks constitutional basis in Portugal. On this, see Diaz Crego and Kotanidis (2020).

[7]On the administrative state of necessity, see Gomes (2020b).

[8]Law 27/2006, of 3 July 2006, last amended by Law 80/2015, of 3 August 2015.

[9]Gomes (2020a), p. 69.

Two other statutes, aimed at regulating public policies in the field of health, entail specific provisions on the powers that administrative authorities can take in health emergencies. First, the Framework Health Law[10] assigns powers to health authorities in case of serious risk to public health. Such powers include suspending or closing public and private facilities, the internment of individuals,[11] and requisition of health facilities and workers. Second, the Law on Public Vigilance of Health Risks[12] allows the adoption of exceptional and necessary measures in cases of public health emergencies, such as the suspension or closure of activities or the separation of sick and non-sick persons.

The Government and, more specifically, the Minister of Health lead the executive response to the pandemic, mainly centered in the Directorate General of Health and the Regional Health Administrations. In continental Portugal, the national health system is centralised. However, local authorities have some devolved powers on primary health care and significant powers on civil protection, such as closing parks and other public areas. The regional governments direct regional health systems in the autonomous regions. Resource allocation and priority setting rest mainly in the hands of the Government and, in the case of the autonomous regions, the regional governments. As regional legislative powers are limited, most of the sanitary measures aimed at responding to the pandemic were adopted through executive regulations approved by the regional governments. Legislative powers in health protection matters belong to the Parliament, although the Government may also legislate if it respects the Framework Health Law.

2.2 *The Constitutional Exception*

States of exception are self-protective mechanisms designed to deal with unexpected threats or dangers to the State or the community and restore constitutional normalcy. They impact the exercise of fundamental rights and the division of state powers. According to the Schmittian account of emergency powers, the sovereign is "he who has the power to decide on the state of emergency".[13] The concept of exception would be crucial to the idea of sovereignty and implies that the law does not constrain emergency power. Emergency governance would be governance by an unbound executive, as it has been argued in the context of the United States.[14]

---

[10] Law 95/2019, of 4 September 2019.

[11] It is controversial that there is legal basis for confinement and general and compulsory quarantines of non-sick persons, as well as compulsory hospitalisation of patients outside the framework of a constitutional state of emergency. See Novais (2020).

[12] Law 81/2009, of 21 August 2009.

[13] Schmitt (2005), p. 5.

[14] Vermeule and Posner (2011).

But the weight of history looms large in contemporary European constitutionalism,[15] and the Schmittian approach to exception has not prevailed. Several European constitutional texts entrench obstacles to the suspension of fundamental rights and do not provide for the possibility of constitutional exception.[16] On the other side of the spectrum, other constitutional texts adopt constitutional emergency frameworks tamed by the rule of law. That is also the case of Portugal: after 48 years of dictatorship, the democratic Portuguese Constitution of 1976 has defined within the constitutional order the procedural and material conditions that enable the suspension of fundamental rights and the declaration of constitutional exception. The Constitution expressly recognises that grave dangers and threats may pose risks to the democratic and constitutional order. However, it demands that such crises be dealt with inside the legal order in constitutionally-regulated spaces. In the words of Ferejohn and Pasquino, Portugal is one of "those advanced democracies whose constitutions contain provisions for emergency powers".[17]

The crisis that poses a constitutional threat is first domesticated by Constitutional Law, which recognises the necessity to develop a sufficiently flexible framework for the executive to act without jeopardising the rule of law and essential human rights protection. Under the Portuguese Constitution, the constitutional exception is divided into "state of siege" and "state of emergency". These concepts relate to the intensity and seriousness of the factual preconditions. The state of emergency applies when such contexts are less severe[18] and only allows for the suspension of some rights and freedoms (in the context of the Covid-19 crisis, we always refer to the state of emergency).[19]

The Portuguese Constitution limits the rights that can be suspended and imposes a time limit and the obligation to respect proportionality. The state of constitutional exception, either in the modality of state of siege or state of emergency, can only be declared for 15 days, subject to renewals following Government consultation and binding parliamentary authorisation.[20] During constitutional exception, the Parliament cannot be dissolved, and constitutional amendments and referenda are

[15] Influenced by the dramatic experience with the use of Article 48 of the Weimar Constitution. This provision warranted the President of the Reich vast emergency powers that availed the legal establishment of the national socialist regime. See Agamben (2005), pp. 14–15.

[16] Specifically, Austria, Belgium, and Denmark. See Diaz Crego and Kotanidis (2020).

[17] Ferejohn and Pasquino (2014), p. 215.

[18] Article 19(3) of the Portuguese Constitution.

[19] The Law on the State of Siege and State of Emergency – Law 44/86, of 30 September 1986 (last amended by Organic Law 1/2012, of 11 May) further details the circumstances in which the state of siege or the state of emergency applies. Cases of "military aggression" and "disruption of the constitutional order" fall under the state of siege whereas situations of "public calamity" are reserved for the state of emergency. That explains why, in the context of this chapter, we speak essentially of the constitutional state of emergency.

[20] Article 19(5).

prohibited.[21] The Constitution expressly states that the rights to life, personal integrity, personal identity, civil capacity and citizenship, the non-retroactivity of criminal law, the accused persons' right to a defense, and freedom of conscience and religion are off-limits, as they can never be suspended.[22] Furthermore, the declaration of the state of emergency can only determine the affection of some of the suspendable fundamental rights. In contrast, the state of siege allows for the suspension of all rights that are not off-limits.

To avoid a unilateral suspension of rights, the Constitution provides a mechanism of mutual control. Hence, the state of constitutional exception is agreed between the three central political institutions: the President, the Government, and Parliament. The following formula enforces checks and balances: the President of the Republic has the power to declare the state of constitutional exception, but only after consulting the Government and seeking parliamentary authorisation.[23] Once declared, it is for the Government to execute the state of siege or the state of emergency. However, it must keep the Parliament, and the President informed of its actions.[24] The President declares, the Parliament authorises, and the Government executes the state of constitutional exception. It is thus a case of "presidential prominence mitigated by the interdependence of the Parliament and the Government".[25] Whereas the President holds power to declare the state of exception, he must first hear the Government and seek binding parliamentary authorisation. Once declared, it is for the Government to execute the state of exception.

The Law on the State of Siege and the State of Emergency expressly guarantees full access to courts to individuals harmed or threatened by any illegal or unconstitutional measure.[26] Parliament oversight and judicial review of the state of exception are theoretically envisaged, and its institutional design promotes the use of all the branches of power. Moreover, the declaration of a state of siege or a state of emergency may only alter constitutional normalcy under the terms laid down in the Constitution itself, and it cannot affect the application of constitutional rules on the competence and functioning of the sovereign organs as well as the self-governing bodies of the autonomous regions.[27]

In sum, the model of constitutional exception enshrined in the Portuguese Constitution corresponds to the constitutionalised emergency paradigm that entails the following requirements: "formal declaration, temporary application, reference to a system of powers under the rule of law and its aim of re-establishing normal constitutional conditions".[28]

---

[21] Articles 172(1) and 289 and Article 9(1) of the Referendum Organic Law – Law 15-A/98, of 3 April 1998 (last amended by Organic Law 4/2020, of 11 November 2020.

[22] Article 19(6).

[23] Article 138.

[24] Article 17 of the Law on the State of Siege and the State of Emergency.

[25] Botelho (2020), p. 68.

[26] Article 6 of the Law on the State of Siege and the State of Emergency.

[27] Article 19(7).

[28] Frankenberg (2014), p. 100.

3 Coping with COVID-19 in Portugal: Between the Constitutional and the Administrative State of Emergency

3.1 The Constitutional State of Emergency

When the first cases of COVID-19 were known in Portugal, in the beginning of March 2020, the Government reacted quickly based on administrative emergency legislation to adopt measures aimed at reducing social contact. During this stage, the Government acted through legislation without proper delegation and administrative orders. It approved the closure of all schools and restricted access to restaurants and bars.[29] It also framed teleworking as mandatory and established an exceptional and speedy public procurement regime for hospitals and public health services. Other fundamental rights were also affected, such as the right to strike of port workers and the freedom of enterprise as some economic activities were suspended. The use of administrative orders to restrict fundamental rights and the approval of governmental legislation without proper delegation raised issues of constitutionality and legality.[30]

Despite the political divide about the need to declare a constitutional state of emergency,[31] the President of the Republic initiated the relevant proceedings to declare it on 18 March 2020. For the first time since the coming into force of the democratic Portuguese Constitution, in 1976, the constitutional state of exception was declared, in the modality of the state of emergency, to address the COVID-19 pandemic. The paradox already noted by Anna-Betina Kaiser, that the increasing talk on the state of emergency prompted by the war on terror and other contemporary emergencies was not matched with an effective application of its constitutional provisions, came to an end.[32] The initial declaration and subsequent renewals lasted in the first phase between 19 March 2020–2 May 2020. On the second phase, it lasted between 9 November 2020–30 April 2021. Stricter suspensions of fundamental rights were enforced. A generalised ban on movement and cordons sanitaires was applied to the most affected municipalities, and an extensive list of economic activities was shut down.

[29] Decree-Law 10-A/2020, of 13 March 2020.

[30] Violante and Lanceiro (2020). Lanceiro (2020), pp. 734–735.

[31] Botelho (2020), p. 71 ff.

[32] Kaiser (2020), p. 13. When the Eurocrisis first struck Portugal there was a discussion on the legal literature whether the situation of financial distress should be articulated under a state of financial exception. See Urbano (2013). The Portuguese Constitutional Court dismissed any controversies in this regard in Decision 353/2012, as it affirmed the following: "The Constitution certainly cannot remain unaware of the economic and financial reality, and in particular of a situation that can be considered to be of serious difficulty. But it has a specific normative autonomy that prevents economic or financial objectives from prevailing, without any limits, over parameters such as equality, which the Constitution defends and must enforce."

The number and type of fundamental rights suspended evolved. In the original declaration of the state of emergency, the following rights were partially suspended: the freedom to travel and settle within the Portuguese territory, allowing public authorities to impose the compulsory confinement at home or in a medical facility;[33] the freedom to cross the national borders; the right to private property and the freedom of enterprise, giving the Government the power to requisition property, material, and facilities, to issue orders to the private sector; some workers' rights, including the right to strike under some circumstances; the right to assembly and to demonstrate, as well as the freedom of worship in its collective dimension,[34] allowing for the restriction of public gatherings; and the right of resistance against unlawful orders.[35]

The renewals of the declaration of the state of emergency built upon the previous suspension of rights, adding powers to the executive to restrict dismissals, control prices, and hoarding, and interfere in the operation of companies and production units. The right to education and freedom to learn was suspended for the first time, although schools had been closed earlier, on 16 March 2020, giving a stronger legal basis to the prohibition of face-to-face classes and the changing of the school year limits.

The second phase of the state of emergency lasted between 9 November 2020 and 30 April 2021. Initially, the fundamental rights suspended were fewer than the first period, but the list grew longer over time. They included: the right to freedom and the freedom to travel within the Portuguese territory; the freedom of enterprise, allowing the mobilisation of resources from the private sector; workers' rights, allowing the mobilisation of medical and non-medical personnel from the public and private sector; and the right to the free development of personality and the negative side of the right to health, allowing the imposition of non-invasive body temperature checks and diagnostic tests for SARS-CoV-2. In the first renewal, some other dimensions were added, with the power given to authorities to impose masks in public spaces and the suspension of the right to data protection of workers, namely, to allow the recording of body temperature. The suspension of these rights was

[33] There was a strong controversy among scholars on whether the suspension of the right or freedom to travel would provide sufficient legal basis for the compulsory confinement. The difficulty lies in the apparent fact that the Portuguese constitutional text, on the regulation of the right to freedom (Article 27), does not allow for the compulsory internment of carriers of a contagious disease or the confinement of non-sick people. See Novais (2020), de Brito (2020), Alexandrino (2020), Ramião (2020).

[34] The suspension of the freedom of worship was criticised due to its connection to the freedom of religion, a right that cannot be suspended according to Article 19(6). See Gouveia (2020b), p. 100.

[35] The suspension of the right of resistance was subject to criticism since it is considered an implicit limit to the constitutional exception as a last resort means of defense against unconstitutional suspensions of rights. See Canotilho and Moreira (2007), p. 422, Gouveia (2020a), p. 293, Gouveia (2020b), pp. 100–101, Ramião (2020), pp. 14–15, Sánchez (2021b), p. 772. Perhaps acknowledging the criticism, in the subsequent renewals of the original declaration, the right of resistance was no longer formally suspended but regulated to prevent any act exclusively directed against lawful orders issued by public authorities in the execution of the state of emergency.

maintained until the fifth renewal of the state of emergency in January 2021, which broadened the suspension of the right to work, establishing the power to impose telework, and of the freedom of enterprise, allowing the imposition of price controls. In the sixth renewal of the state of emergency, invoking the worsening of the pandemic situation, the right to education was also suspended, allowing the prohibition of face-to-face classes, and the suspension of the right to data protection was broadened to include online classes.

In both periods of the state of emergency, under the principle of proportionality, the presidential decrees have only suspended the aforementioned fundamental rights to the extent considered necessary by the competent public authorities to make decisions deemed essential to reduce the risk of contagion and to implement measures to prevent and combat the epidemic. The presidential decrees enumerated the fundamental rights that were suspended, detailed the conditions under which the suspensions should be executed, and narrowed down the measures that the executive could adopt.[36]

3.2 The Administrative State of Emergency

From a constitutional state of emergency, the country moved, on 3 May 2020, and later 1 May 2021, to the less severe statutory administrative state of emergency, in the modality of state of calamity, declared by the Council of Ministers (Government) and governed by the Framework Laws on Civil Protection and Health and the Law on Public Vigilance of Health Risks. Neither the Parliament nor the President of the Republic plays any role in these declarations.

The transition from the constitutional state of emergency to the statutory administrative state of emergency did not entail substantial changes because the Government made a broad interpretation of its statutory and administrative powers. Still, it allowed the Government to regain ownership of the situation, as in the first days of the pandemic, not being bound by the initiative and the framework defined by the President of the Republic and the need to present periodic reports to the Parliament. Moreover, during the constitutional state of emergency, both the legislature and the President of the Republic are competent to supervise the executive action.[37]

In May 2020, a "civic duty" of confinement replaced the ban on movement. Nevertheless, fundamental rights' remaining affections were mainly maintained through regulatory instruments that were not subject to parliamentary oversight or presidential promulgation.[38] In Portugal, whereas the constitutional state of emergency allows for the *suspension* of fundamental rights, the remaining mechanisms related to the administrative exception only provide for the possibility of their

[36] For a strong critique, see Terrinha (2019), p. 195 ff.

[37] Article 162(b).

[38] For a critique, see Castro (2020), p. 669 ff. For more details, see below Sect. 3.1.

restriction.[39] On the other hand, restrictions of rights, freedoms, and guarantees, such as freedom of movement, are the exclusive province of the parliamentary legislature, and the Government can only legislate under express delegation. The suspension model resembles the derogation paradigm enshrined in Article 15 of the European Convention of Human Rights.[40] However, Portugal did not file any notification under the said provision, unlike Albania, Armenia, Estonia, Georgia, North Macedonia, Republic of Moldova, Romania, San Marino, and Serbia.

The transitions between the state of emergency and administrative emergency raised complex constitutional issues due to the lack of a clear differentiation of the restrictive normative framework. Theoretically, there should not be a continuum between constitutional and administrative exception but rather a sharp distinction: it is precisely such sharp distinction that provides the material preconditions that will ground the political and legal decision to declare the constitutional exception or, rather, to abolish it or not have it renewed. Only in the most extreme cases can the constitutional exception be declared. That is why there should be a structural distinction between the "measures" of the state of emergency and the "law of the normal state of affairs", as Böckenförde has argued, to prevent emergency measures from penetrating the normal state of affairs through their "statutorification".[41] It should be noted, however, that one important element prevented the "normalization of the state of emergency"[42] as these restrictions have been mainly introduced through sunset clauses whose prorogation demands express re-approval. As the first and second renewals of calamity were declared (each declaration is subject to a two-week duration), in May 2020, it became clearer that deconfinement was gradually in motion and that the Government was slowly but steadily lifting the restrictions.

During the summer of 2020, the territory was divided between areas under the state of alert, state of contingency, and state of calamity. In October 2020, as the second wave began to hit the country, a state of calamity was again declared for the whole mainland territory. This was eventually replaced by the second state of constitutional emergency period, which came into force on 6 November 2020.

4 Oversight and Judicial Review

4.1 Parliamentary Scrutiny

We must distinguish between the period encompassed by the declarations of state of emergency under the Constitution and the periods covered by the administrative

[39] On the distinction between restriction and suspension of fundamental rights, see Gil (2021), Botelho (2020), p. 57 ff., and Moniz (2020).

[40] Kaiser (2020), pp. 247–248.

[41] See Böckenförde (2017), pp. 120–121.

[42] Frankenberg (2014), p. 189 ff.

state of emergency, declared by the Government. As mentioned above, the state of emergency is agreed upon between the three leading political institutions: it is declared by the President after hearing the Government. The Parliament must authorise it—and the Government executes it. The declaration of the state of emergency can be amended or revoked at the sole initiative of the President. This power is free from the input of the other powers if the amendment aims at narrowing the extension of the emergency. Should the President wish to broaden the scope of the measures, the Government and the Parliament must also be involved.

During the constitutional state of emergency, both the legislature and the President of the Republic are competent to supervise the executive action. According to the Law on the State of Siege and State of Emergency, the Government must keep the legislature, and the President informed of the execution of the state of constitutional emergency. Moreover, and under the same act, at the end of each state of emergency, the Government must provide the Parliament a documented report of the arrangements and measures adopted in the execution of the emergency. Based on said report, the Parliament evaluates the execution of the declaration of the state of emergency by the Government. This means that during the period covered by the regime of quarterly declarations of a state of emergency (between 18 March–2 May 2020 and 6 November 2020–30 April 2021), the Government was subject to the supervision of the legislature by giving notice of the emergency measures and presenting interim reports to Parliament at the end of each period, enabling the Parliament to exercise also an ex post control.[43] These reports were subject to discussion in parliamentary plenary debates. Moreover, an ad hoc parliamentary committee was created to monitor the measures adopted to respond to the pandemic.

The execution of the state of emergency has been translated into detailed regulations enacted by the Government in the framework of the presidential decrees that the Parliament previously authorised. Hence, both the Parliament and the President have the theoretical power to define the scope for the executive action during a state of emergency. In practice, however, the presidential decrees worked as deferrals of power to the Government instead of binding frameworks limiting the executive action.[44]

The oversight mission of Parliament was also affected during the first phase of the constitutional state of emergency (18 March–2 May 2020) by a reduction in parliamentary works. At the beginning of the pandemic, the Parliament adopted a deliberation maintaining face-to-face plenary meetings but only once per week and decided to operate with just one-fifth of the members, reflecting the proportion of the parliamentary groups.[45] Plenary deliberations were taken in the presence of more than half of the members (the constitutional quorum limit), so at least 116 members should be present to vote. Remote voting in plenary sessions is not possible. Together with reducing the number of representatives present, the Parliament also

---

[43] Following Article 28 of the Law on the State of Siege and State of Emergency.

[44] See the poignant analysis by Sánchez (2021b).

[45] This deliberation is not public.

deliberated to maintain parliamentary committee meetings only if necessary and limited to the coordinators. Parliamentary committees have also switched some sessions to videoconferences using Skype. These conditions have affected the individual rights of parliamentarians. Moreover, the reduced role of Parliament endangered political deliberation, and the symbolism of keeping the Parliament's doors open came at a democratic cost. By reducing plenary meetings and the committee's works, the Parliament's oversight role was effectively curtailed during this period.[46] However, these rules have not caused significant political turmoil or criticism and were accepted by parliamentarian groups. Moreover, during the later stages of the pandemic, plenary meetings were resumed under their normal conditions, sticking to social distancing requirements. These require that MPs are spread between the plenary hall and their offices, but the reduction of works was later dropped.

On the other hand, under the state of administrative emergency, the Government is not bound by the initiative, and the framework defined by the President and does not need to present periodic reports to the Parliament. Still, it is politically accountable to the Parliament in general terms.[47] Under this accountability model, the Parliament can raise questions[48] and interpellations[49] to the Government and be informed on the topics of high public relevance.[50] During the administrative state of emergency, the Government enjoys a broader margin of action as it is not constrained to the checks and balances entrenched in the constitutional state of emergency. Parliament's abdication has also enabled this freedom of action in matters concerning the restriction of fundamental rights in the realm of sanitary policy. In fact, the Parliament has allowed the Government to remain the chief normative conductor of administrative emergency action, abdicating from its constitutional function as the primary legislator on matters related to fundamental rights in the framework of sanitary measures.[51] It has silently acquiesced to executive power-grabs in these areas covering mandatory confinements of infected persons, public gatherings and intercity traveling, mandatory use of indoor masks, and other fundamental rights and freedoms restrictions. A problem of separation of powers arises when the executive encroaches on the constitutionally reserved sphere of the Parliament since restrictions of freedom require a parliamentary legislative basis.

---

[46] Violante and Lanceiro (2020).

[47] Article 191(1).

[48] Articles 156(d) and 177(2).

[49] Article 180(2)(d).

[50] Article 180(2)(j).

[51] The most significant exception concerns the mandatory use of masks in public spaces which was required by parliamentary law. See Law 62-A/2020, of 27 October 2020, subsequently renewed by Law 75-D/2020, of 31 December 2020, Law 13-A/2021, of 5 April 2021, and Law 36-A/2021, of 14 June 2021. More recently, see Law 88/2021, 15 December 2021. Mandatory use of mask indoor is required by undelegated governmental legislation. See Article 13-B of Decree Law 10-A/2020, of 13 March 2020, last amended by Decree Law 6-A/2022, of 7 January 2022.

Nevertheless, despite enjoying significant legislative competence in the face of the Constitution, the Government has introduced these limitations primarily through resolutions (orders) of the Council of Ministers and not through legislative acts. On legislative powers, the Portuguese Constitution assigns normal legislative competence to the Government, alongside the legislative competence of Parliament.[52] This legislative competence is not limited to the right of legislative initiative common in other jurisdictions but also includes a significant range of concurrent legislative competencies shared between the Government and the Parliament. The sharing between these two organs of sovereignty of a broad sphere of legislative competence is a Portuguese singularity.[53] However, by choosing to implement many restrictions through administrative orders approved through resolutions of the Council of Ministers and not ordinary legislation, or even regulatory decrees, the Government has further reduced legal checks on its action. First, if the Government had acted primarily through legislation, it would have safeguarded the Parliament's right to hold the *last word*[54] through the mechanism of parliamentary scrutiny of legislative acts enshrined in Article 169. Even if the hurdle of restriction of freedom through undelegated legislation still existed in that hypothesis, the Parliament would still have the possibility to act through the mechanism entailed in Article 169. According to this mechanism, the Parliament can scrutinise the legislative acts of the Government and eventually terminate their validity under the constitutional principle of the primacy of Parliament in the legislative process. By choosing to tackle the pandemic mainly through executive orders, the Government evaded this important mechanism of parliamentary control. Moreover, it also avoided the political control of the President of the Republic and the possibility of *a priori* review by the Constitutional Court.[55] Parliamentary control was limited to essentially providing a forum to prepare and inform decision-making through the exercise of the right, mostly of the opposition, to question the Government.

Second, the Government also did not resort to regulatory decrees that could still trigger the political control of the President of the Republic. It primarily acted through resolutions of the Council of Ministers which are not subject to the political

[52] In Portugal, the Government enjoys three types of legislative competence: (i) reserved or exclusive (includes matters relating to its own organisation and functioning—Article 198(2)); (ii) concurrent (includes matters not reserved to the Assembly of the Republic—Article 198(1)(a)); (iii) authorised or derived (includes matters in the relative reserve of the Assembly of the Republic, subject to its authorization or delegation—Article 198(1)(b) of the Constitution); (iv) complementary or developmental (decree-laws developing the principles or general bases of the regimes of the Republic—Article 198(1)(c) of the Constitution). (iv) complementary or developmental (decree-laws developing the principles or general bases of the legal systems contained in laws that are limited to them—Article 198(1)(c) of the Portuguese Constitution).

[53] Although the Parliament remains the primary legislator considering the constitutional division of powers, empirically the Government authors most of the legislation. Furthermore, the most significant legislative reforms have been introduced by governmental decrees (decree-laws). See Otero (2010), p. 232. For a critical account, see Alexandrino (2018), pp. 210–215.

[54] Alexandrino (2018), p. 215.

[55] Article 278(1).

control of the President of the Republic[56] and enjoy weaker protection at the level of constitutional review,[57] attesting for the "erosion of legal checks" typical of the new paradigm of the state of exception as conceptualised by Günter Frankenberg.[58] On the other hand, by circumventing the principle of requirement of law for fundamental rights restrictions, individuals' legal protection is also undermined.

4.2 Access to Courts and Judicial Review

As mentioned earlier, under the Law on the State of Siege and the State of Emergency, ordinary courts remain fully operational during the constitutional state of emergency. Moreover, a transitory and exceptional procedural regime was introduced in the first phase.[59] This regime allowed online proceedings when face-to-face proceedings were not possible for sanitary reasons. It also determined the suspension of specific deadlines, such as the deadline of a debtor to require the insolvency and eviction orders. The regime was terminated in June 2020 and reinstated at the end of January 2021, when the number of COVID-19 cases peaked. An amendment was then introduced to suspend all the judicial proceedings in every court, except for the Court of Auditors. The suspension did not include the proceedings related to fundamental rights or involving any unconstitutional or illegal measure. A security protocol was adopted on 3 June 2020, including a combination of measures such as the requirement of maintaining two meters' physical distance, the use of facemasks (unless giving testimony), a special cleaning protocol, and the recommended use of only those courtrooms with windows, not those with air conditioning unless necessary and air circulation is feasible.[60]

On emergency litigation near the administrative courts, there have been challenges on the constitutionality of resolutions of the Council of Ministers, limiting the inter-municipal circulation[61] and restricting freedom of assembly[62] without success. The administrative courts found the requests inadmissible on procedural grounds in several cases. That was the case with the writ for the protection of rights, freedoms, and guarantees proposed by extreme right-wing political party Chega against the travel ban across municipalities,[63] which was not admitted because the party's

[56] Article 136(4) *a contrario*.

[57] If a court disapplies a provision entailed in a resolution of the Council of Minister such decision is not subject to mandatory appeal to the Constitutional Court by the Public Prosecutor. See Article 72(3) of the Act on the Constitutional Court (Law 28/82, of 15 November 1982). It is also not reviewable by the Constitutional Court under *ex ante* or *a priori* proceedings. See Article 278(1).

[58] Frankenberg (2014), pp. 203–204.

[59] See Article 6-A of Law 1-A/2020, of 19 March 2020.

[60] See OSCE (2020), p. 32.

[61] Judgment Case No 0122/20.1BALSB (10 September 2020) (Supreme Administrative Court).

[62] Judgment Case No 088/20.8BALSB (31 October 2020) (Supreme Administrative Court).

[63] Ordered by Resolution of the Council of Ministers 89-A/2020 on 26 October 2020.

legitimacy to submit such actions was not recognised.[64] Interim injunctions concerning the protection of civil liberties, including the demand for the lifting of the suspension of teaching and non-teaching activities[65] or the restriction on private property and freedom of enterprise invoked by night club owners who were forced to keep their establishments closed, were also found inadmissible by the Court, mainly on procedural grounds.[66]

In several contentious rulings on the merits of challenges on governmental orders on restrictive measures concerning the prohibition of gatherings,[67] intercity traffic restrictions,[68] and prophylactic home isolations,[69] the Supreme Administrative Court adopted a generous approach towards the executive encroachment of parliamentary powers.

In fact judicial review of emergency executive action by the administrative courts has been a "façade"[70] and the administrative judiciary has given the Government a blank check to operate free of constraints.[71] On the other hand, civil and criminal courts have reacted against confinements imposed by regional authorities and the Government in the context of administrative emergency. In the first case, the challenges were successful, whereas the results have been mixed in the latter. The Constitutional Court will settle the issue as several appeals are currently pending.

The Constitutional Court can assess the constitutional state of emergency declaration in abstract or concrete review.[72] Abstract review is initiated by certain institutional petitioners (the President of the Republic, the President of Parliament, the Prime Minister, the Ombudsperson, the Prosecutor General, or one-tenth of MPs). In comparative terms, the Portuguese institutional design of abstract review is very generous since it recognises legitimacy to initiate the proceedings to a high number of institutions.[73] On the other hand, concrete review arises during judicial disputes. All lower courts that apply the measures taken in the scope of the state of emergency declaration are competent to check their legality or constitutionality. Since all courts have direct access to the Constitution, should a court find any measure unconstitutional, it would be bound to refuse its application, this decision being subject to mandatory appeal to the Constitutional Court. Courts can also

[64] Judgment Case No 01958/20.9BELSB (31 October 2020) (Supreme Administrative Court).

[65] Determined by Decree No 3-C/2021, of 22 January, 2021.

[66] Judgment Case No 012/21.0BALSB (5 February 2021) (Supreme Administrative Court); Judgment Case No 0136/20.1BALSB (18 February 2021) (Supreme Administrative Court).

[67] Judgment Case No 088/20.8BALSB (31 October 2020) (Supreme Administrative Court).

[68] Judgment Case No 086/21.4BALSB (27 June 2021) (Supreme Administrative Court). Judgment Case No 085/21.6BALSB (27 June 2021).

[69] Judgment Case No 0105/21.4BALSB (24 August 2021) (Supreme Administrative Court).

[70] Dyzenhaus (2006), p. 47.

[71] In Germany, a similar criticism is made in relation to the review of sanitary measures by administrative courts at least as to what concerns restrictions of gatherings. See Arzt (2022).

[72] On this, see Bargado (2020), p. 293 ff.

[73] Garoupa et al. (2019), p. 248.

review the declaration of administrative emergency and the measures adopted in said context. Under this context, it is expected that judicial restraint in this area is less intensive as the framework of the administrative emergency is not triggered by the combined action of three sovereign organs (the President, the Parliament, and the Government) and is not subject to interinstitutional oversight.

The Portuguese Constitutional Court has not dealt with any request on constitutional or administrative emergency declarations. Moreover, despite the generous framework of abstract review, there has been only one request, filed by the Ombudsperson, challenging a statute that exempted tenants in shopping malls from paying minimum rents.[74] According to the request, this measure breached the right to property and private enterprise. In a controversial and polarized ruling,[75] the Constitutional Court found that there was a breach of the right to property of owners and managers of shopping malls. The grounds of the decision raised criticism because the judges failed to pay due account to the sanitary crisis that justified the measure aimed at redistributing the economic costs caused by the pandemic, on the one hand, and, on the other, extended the constitutional protection of the right to property to contractual rights without assigning them any social function. Other COVID-19 related cases have recently been addressed by the Constitutional Court but they all concern concrete review issues. Thus far, the Court has censored regional regulations imposing mandatory confinements and criminal prosecution in cases of disobedience for breach of emergency requirements for lack of parliamentary delegation.[76]

The Constitutional Court was initially more deferent towards the powers of the Government in the constitutional emergency context. In a first ruling, it recognised that the Government has the power to enact rules on crimes that fall within the legislative competence of the Parliament, namely by increasing the minimum and maximum criminal limits of the crime of disobedience. The Court controversially acknowledged that under the constitutional framework of emergency, the executive operates as an extraordinary legislator *ex ratione necessitates*.[77] Although this ruling was delivered in chambers and by a narrow majority vote,[78] it is doubtful that the Court will continue to accept executive grabs of power and claims of necessity even against express constitutionally protected interests such as separation of powers during the constitutional (and administrative) state of emergency. The Portuguese Constitutional Court has proved an active watchdog in times of financial and

[74] The case is still pending. The referral was submitted on 20 November 2020 and can be accessed at https://www.provedor-jus.pt/documentos/2020_11_20_Tribunal_Constitucional.pdf. (access 1 May 2022).

[75] Judgment 468/2022.

[76] Judgments 424/2020 and 687/2020.

[77] Judgment 352/2021. For a critique of this ruling, see Sánchez (2021a) and Caldeira (2021), pp. 11–15.

[78] Meaning that it does not produce erga omnes effect and is only binding in the dispute at stake. For an overview of the Portuguese system of constitutional review, see Cortês and Violante (2011).

economic crises,[79] and lately it has shown the stamina to substantially uphold the rule of law in the context of a pandemic even when there is a broad social and political consensus on the necessity of solid containment measures. In fact, more recently, a different chamber of the Court delivered an unconstitutionality ruling in a similar question.[80] Moreover, in the context of the administrative state of emergency, several recent rulings have censored the executive strategy to restrict fundamental rights through administrative regulations. Such rulings have mainly stated that the governmental strategy is procedurally flawed since the restrictions should have been enacted by parliamentary legislation or delegated legislation.[81] Some of them have further stated that the administrative regulations at stake are substantially unconstitutional for breach of the right to freedom.[82] The Constitutional Court has therefore invalidated several measures imposing mandatory confinements either in case of travellers or high-risk contacts.

The lack of an instrument of constitutional complaint on fundamental rights and the broad political consensus underlying the crisis management account for the late constitutional litigation. Whereas in other jurisdictions, the constitutional court has been, since the early days of the pandemic, an active watchdog of the democratic integrity of executive and legislative action to handle the pandemic, in Portugal, emergency litigation has been chiefly circumscribed to the administrative courts, with the Constitutional Court remaining on the sidelines until recently. That has helped the executive a peaceful management of the political impact caused by the judicial vetoes, further reduced by their inter partes effects resulting from the lack of abstract review requests. In Spain, for instance, the Spanish Constitutional Court has been challenged to review some of the most restrictive measures adopted by the Government to contain the pandemic. Through the *Sentencia* delivered on appeal 2054-2020, initiated by the far-right political party Vox, by a slim majority of six to five, the Constitutional Court declared the unconstitutionality of the lockdown imposed by the Government in 2020. According to the Court, the lockdown would have required the stricter state of emergency, an institutional mechanism that involves parliamentary authorisation, instead of the simple state of alarm triggered solely by the Government. Similarly, albeit in the framework of concrete review proceedings, which nevertheless bear the potential for erga omnes effects, the German Federal Constitutional Court has been called to rule on mobility restrictions,[83] freedom of assembly concerning the prohibition of demonstrations,[84] and

---

[79] Violante (2019, 2021).

[80] Judgment 477/2022.

[81] Judgments 88/2022, 89/2022, 510/2022.

[82] Judgments 465/2022, 466/2022, 489/2022, 490/2022.

[83] See Order of the Third Chamber of the First Senate of 7 April 2020 – 1 BvR 755/20; see also Order of the First Chamber of the First Senate of 1 May 2020 – 1 BvR 996/20; Order of the Second Chamber of the First Senate of 3 June 2020 – 1 BvR 990/20.

[84] See Order of the First Chamber of the First Senate of 17 April 2020 – 1 BvQ 37/20; see also Order of the First Chamber of the First Senate of 15 April 2020 – 1 BvR 828/20.

gatherings also applied to worship services.[85,86] More recently, in the context of constitutional complaints, the German Federal Constitutional Court also ruled on exit and contact restrictions,[87] school closures,[88] and the protection of persons with disabilities in triage situations caused by the pandemic.[89]

5 Conclusion: The "Hour of the Executive"?

The declaration of the state of constitutional exception has the effect of disempowering the Parliament from its natural role of leading legislator in situations concerning restrictions of fundamental rights. Although the Parliament is competent to authorise the declaration of the state of exception, the emergency framework shifts the normative competence to affect fundamental rights from the Parliament to the President and the Government. The Parliament's role is weakened when there is a strengthening of the executive dimension of the emergency.[90] With the declaration of the state of emergency, we noticed a "parliamentary abdication" since the legislature refrained from producing the norms that should frame the executive action.[91]

On the other hand, under the state of statutory administrative emergency, the Government regained ownership of the situation as it was no longer bound by the initiative and the framework defined by the President of the Republic and enjoyed a broader margin to operate freely from supervision from the legislature and the President. This freedom of action was also attributed to the fact that Parliament allowed the Government to remain the chief normative conductor of emergency action, abdicating its constitutional function as the primary legislator on matters related to fundamental rights.[92] Even during the state of statutory administrative emergency, with few exceptions, the Parliament relinquished and surrendered the Government the right to legislate and regulate on the topics related to restrictions of freedom. There was a parliamentary surrender to the executive as the chief conductor of emergency even when tackling the pandemic required harsh abridgments of individual rights and freedoms, which is the typical province of Parliament. One can raise the question of how Parliament could legislate in the face of scientific and factual uncertainty and the lack of readily available information. Although this is not the forum to explore in detail such a topic, it bears noting that between a vague and

[85] See Order of the Second Chamber of the First Senate of 29 April 2020 – 1 BvQ 44/20.

[86] Kaiser and Hensel (2020).

[87] Decision of the First Senate of 19 November 2021 – 1 BvR 781/21 et. al.

[88] Decision of the First Senate of 19 November 2021 – 1 BvR971/21, 1 BvR 1069/21.

[89] Order of the First Senate of 16 December 2021 – 1 BvR 1541/20.

[90] Lomba (2020a, b).

[91] Gonçalves (2020).

[92] Gonçalves (2020).

an "open-ended"[93] delegation, there is a spectrum of available possibilities to be explored, and comparative law exemplifies that parliaments can still play a meaningful role in pandemic emergencies without jeopardising the executive margin of action.[94]

The fight against the pandemic was mainly conducted through decrees and resolutions: presidential decrees declaring or renewing the declaration of a state of emergency; parliamentary resolutions authorising the presidential declarations; governmental decrees or resolutions regulating them. "Between the moment of administrative regulation issued by the Government and the moment of the most serious political decision taken by presidential decrees, there is a missing link: that of the legislative moment, which is the proper role of the Parliament".[95] The normative framework of emergency—constitutional and legislative exception dimensions—lacked proper parliamentary delegation to the executive power. Legislative delegation allows the Parliament "to take advantages of the capabilities of the executive organization"[96] without running the risks of contradicting the "necessary openness of the political process".[97]

Furthermore, due to a broad political consensus on the measures adopted to tackle the pandemic and the absence of procedural mechanisms that allow for individual complaints about breaches of fundamental rights, the Constitutional Court has maintained a passive role concerning the emergency measures. Judicial review of emergency action by the administrative courts has been a façade. It is doubtful that the judiciary can substantially uphold the rule of law when "it is difficult to find an area of intervention of the sovereign bodies in which some unconstitutionality has not been incurred",[98] especially as what concerns the division of powers and the primacy of Parliament.

There has been a growing critique on using the combined constitutional and statutory administrative emergency tools to handle the pandemic situation. Recently, the Prime Minister appointed a Technical Commission[99] in charge of preparing the draft reform to adapt the legal framework to a future sanitary emergency law that can address several of the shortcomings pointed. In a future pandemic, the Portuguese authorities will therefore be equipped with a statutory framework specifically designed to handle pandemic emergencies similar to those developed in France and Germany at the outset of the coronavirus outbreak. The draft[100] produced has

---

[93] Möllers (2013), p. 118.

[94] On Germany, still with critiques for the disempowerment of the Bundestag, see Möllers (2020) and Mangold (2021).

[95] Provedor de Justiça (2021), p. 42.

[96] Möllers (2013), p. 118.

[97] Möllers (2013), p. 117.

[98] Sánchez (2021b), p. 782.

[99] Diário da República, I Série, Parte C, n.° 131, 8 July 2021, pp. 24–25.

[100] The draft is available at https://www.portugal.gov.pt/download-ficheiros/ficheiro.aspx?v=%3d%3dBQAAAB%2bLCAAAAAAABAAzNLKwNAQAqW9jdQUAAAA%3d (accessed 16 August 2022).

been criticized for not taking into account the constitutional case law and reinforcing the powers of the executive. The President of the Republic has publicly announced that he will request an a priori review of the future bill.

However, it is doubtful that the constitutional state of emergency can be discarded entirely if drastic measures are needed to handle a pandemic such as a complete lockdown. Since the Constitution entails a specific legal regime for the suspension of fundamental rights, the difficult issue will be where to draw the line between an ordinary restriction, under the constitutional normalcy, where containment measures are adopted under a statutory administrative framework, or an actual suspension, that should convey the extraordinary constitutional exception.

References

Agamben G (2005) State of exception. The University of Chicago Press, Chicago

Alexandrino JdM (2020) Devia o direito à liberdade ser suspenso? - Resposta a Jorge Reis Novais. Observatório Almedina, 7 de abril de 2020. https://observatorio.almedina.net/index.php/2020/04/07/devia-o-direito-a-liberdade-ser-suspenso-resposta-a-jorge-reis-novais/. Accessed 31 May 2022

Alexandrino J d M (2018) Lições de Direito Constitucional, vol II. AAFDL Editora, Lisboa

Arzt C (2022) Versammlungsfreiheit unter Druck. Eine Auswertung des verwaltungsgerichtlichen Schutzes von Art. 8 GG in der Pandemie. Verfassungsblog, 12 Januar 2022. https://verfassungsblog.de/versammlungsfreiheit-unter-druck/. Accessed 31 May 2022

Bargado G (2020) O estado de exceção constitucional – Teoria e prática. O Direito 152:253–306

Böckenförde E-W (2017) The repressed state of emergency. In: Künkler M, Stein T (eds) Constitutional and political theory. Selected writings. Oxford University Press, Oxford, pp 108–132

Botelho CS (2020) Os estados de exceção constitucional: estado de sítio e estado de emergência. In: Gomes CA, Pedro R (eds) Direito Administrativo de Necessidade e de Exceção. AAFDL, Lisboa, pp 47–95

Caldeira M (2021) A pandemia e a jurisprudência: primeiros desenvolvimentos. Revista Jurídica – AAFDL 32–33:7–24

Canotilho JJG, Moreira V (2007) Constituição da República Portuguesa Anotada, vol I. Coimbra Editora, Coimbra

Castro RB (2020) Direito Constitucional em tempos de pandemia: Pode a Constituição sobreviver a crises sanitárias? Revista da Faculdade de Direito da Universidade de Lisboa – Lisbon Law Review LXI 1:645–679

Cortês A, Violante T (2011) Concrete control of constitutionality in Portugal: a means towards effective protection of fundamental rights. Penn State Int Law Rev 29:759–776

de Brito MN (2020) Pensar no estado de exceção na sua exigência. Observatório Almedina, 2 de abril de 2020. https://observatorio.almedina.net/index.php/2020/04/02/pensar-no-estado-da-excecao-na-sua-exigencia/. Accessed 31 May 2022

Diaz Crego M, Kotanidis S (2020) States of Emergency in Response to the Coronavirus Crisis. Normative Response and Parliamentary Oversight in EU Member States During the First Wave of the Pandemic. European Parliamentary Research Service. Available at https://www.europarl.europa.eu/thinktank/en/document.html?reference=EPRS_STU(2020)659385 Accessed 31 May 2022

Dyzenhaus D (2006) The constitution of law. Legality in a time of emergency. Cambridge University Press, Cambridge

Ferejohn J, Pasquino P (2014) The law of the exception: a typology of emergency powers. I.CON 2(2):210–239

Frankenberg G (2014) Political technology and the erosion of the rule of law: normalizing the state of exception. Edward Elgar, Cheltenham

Frankenberg G (2019) The pandemic of authoritarianism. Comp Law Rev 10(1):9–19

Garoupa N, Solanes Mullor J, Violante T (2019) Constitutional Courts and National Parliaments in Spain and Portugal. In: Fernandes JM, Leston-Bandeira C (eds) The Iberian legislatures in comparative perspective. Routledge, London, pp 241–256

Gil AR (2021) Em busca de uma perspetiva substancial do conceito de "suspensão de direitos fundamentais". In: Gomes ACN, Albergaria B, Canotilho MR (eds) Direito Constitucional: Diálogos em Homenagem ao 80.° aniversário de J. J. Gomes Canotilho. Fórum, Belo Horizonte, pp 631–646

Gomes CA (2020a) Legalidade em tempos atípicos: notas sobre as medidas de polícia sanitária no âmbito da pandemia. Revista do Ministério Público, Número Especial Covid-19, 43–77

Gomes CA (2020b) O estado de necessidade administrativo. In: Gomes CA, Pedro R (eds) Direito Administrativo de necessidade e de exceção. AAFDL Editora, Lisboa, pp 23–46

Gonçalves P (2020) Abdicação parlamentar na emergência e continuação da abdicação na calamidade. Observatório Almedina. Available https://observatorio.almedina.net/index.php/2020/05/21/abdicacao-parlamentar-na-emergencia-e-continuacao-da-abdicacao-na-calamidade/ Accessed 31 May 2022

Gouveia JB (2020a) Estado de exceção no Direito Constitucional. Almedina, Coimbra

Gouveia JB (2020b) Portugal e a COVID-19: balanço e perspetivas de uma Ordem Jurídica de Crise. Revista do Ministério Público, Número Especial Covid-19: 93–106

Kaiser A-B, Hensel R (2020) Federal Republic of Germany: Legal Response to Covid-19. Oxford Constitutional Law. Available https://oxcon.ouplaw.com/view/10.1093/law-occ19/law-occ19-e2. Accessed 3 May 2022

Kaiser A-B (2020) Ausnahmeverfassungsrecht. Mohr Siebeck, Tübingen

Lanceiro R (2020) Breves notas sobre a resposta normativa portuguesa à crise da Covid-19. Revista da Faculdade de Direito da Universidade de Lisboa – Lisbon Law Review LXI 1:729–746

Lomba P (2020a) The Constitutionalized State of Emergency. Verfassungsblog, 15 April 2020. Available https://verfassungsblog.de/the-constitutionalized-state-of-emergency/ Accessed 31 May 2022

Lomba P (2020b) Constituição, estado de emergência e administração sanitária: alguns problemas. E-pública 7(1):27–43

Mangold AK (2021) Germany and Covid-19: A Most Eventful Year. Verfassungsblog, 7 April 2021. https://verfassungsblog.de/germany-and-covid-19-a-most-eventful-year/. Accessed 31 May 2022

Möllers C (2013) The three branches. A comparative model of separation of powers. Oxford University Press, Oxford

Möllers C (2020) Parlamentarische Selbstentmächtigung im Zeichen des Virus. Verfassungsblog, 26 März 2020. https://verfassungsblog.de/parlamentarische-selbstentmaechtigung-im-zeichen-des-virus/. Accessed 31 May 2022

Moniz PL (2020) Significado e alcance da "suspensão" do exercício de direitos fundamentais na declaração do estado de emergência. E-pública – Revista Eletrónica de Direito Público 7:118–152

Novais JR (2020) Estado de emergência – Quatro notas jurídico-constitucionais sobre o Decreto Presidencial. https://observatorio.almedina.net/index.php/2020/03/19/estado-de-emergencia-quatro-notas-juridico-constitucionais-sobre-o-decreto-presidencial. Accessed 31 May 2022

Novais JR (2021) Semipresidencialismo. Teoria geral e sistema português. 3.ª edição. Almedina, Coimbra

OSCE (2020) The Functioning of Courts in the Covid-19 Pandemic – Primer. Available at https://www.osce.org/files/f/documents/5/5/469170.pdf. Accessed 31 May 2022

Otero P (2010) Direito Constitucional Português. Volume I – Identidade Constitucional. Almedina, Coimbra

Provedor de Justiça (2021). Estado de direito. Cadernos da Pandemia. Available https://www.provedor-jus.pt/documentos/cadernos-da-pandemia-estado-de-direito/. Accessed 31 May 2022

Ramião R (2020) Lendo a Constituição em estado de emergência (3.ª resposta a Jorge Reis Novais), Instituto de Ciências Jurídico-Políticas, Centro de Investigação em Direito Público, https://www.icjp.pt/sites/default/files/papers/lendo_a_constituicao_em_estado_de_emergencia_3a_resposta_a_jorge_reis_novais.pdf. Accessed 31 May 2022

Sánchez PF (2021a) A modificação das regras de competência dos órgãos de soberania em estado de exceção: o caso exemplar da aprovação de normas sem autorização parlamentar em matéria penal. Revista Portuguesa de Direito Constitucional – Portuguese Rev Const Law 1:103–139

Sánchez PF (2021b) Sobre os poderes normativos do Presidente da República e do Governo em Estado de exceção. Revista da Ordem dos Advogados, III/IV, pp 755–805

Schmitt C (2005) Political theology: four chapters on the concept of sovereignty (trans: Schwab G). The University of Chicago Press, Chicago (1922)

Terrinha LH (2019) A suspensão de direitos fundamentais em estado de exceção biopolítico. RDeS – Revista de Direito e Segurança 14:167–213

Urbano MB (2013) Estado de crise económico-financeira e o papel do Tribunal Constitucional. In: Gonçalves, Pedro, Gomes, Carla Amado et. al. A crise e o Direito Público. VI Encontro de Professores Portugueses de Direito Público. Available https://www.icjp.pt/sites/default/files/publicacoes/files/ebook_encontrosdp_31out2013a.pdf. Accessed 31 May 2022

Vermeule A, Posner E (2011) The executive unbound: after the madisonian republic. Oxford University Press, Oxford

Violante T (2019) The Portuguese constitutional court and its austerity case law. In: Costa Pinto A, Pequito C (eds) Political institutions and democracy in Portugal. Assessing the impact of the eurocrisis. Palgrave, Cham

Violante T (2021) Constitutional adjudication as a forum for contesting austerity: the case of Portugal. In: Farahat A, Arzoz X (eds) Contesting austerity. A socio-legal inquiry. Hart Publishing, Oxford, pp 173–190

Violante T, Lanceiro R (2020) Coping with Covid-19 in Portugal: from constitutional normality to the state of emergency. Verfassungsblog 12 April 2020. Available at https://verfassungsblog.de/coping-with-covid-19-in-portugal-from-constitutional-normality-to-the-state-of-emergency. Accessed 31 May 2022

Part II
Executives and Parliaments in a Pandemic

Executives During the COVID-19 Pandemic: Contradictory Trends

Giacomo Delledonne

Abstract This chapter focuses on how the executives have adapted to the pandemic challenge since March 2020. To do so, it develops a comparative analysis of the role of the executives in facing the COVID-19 pandemic in three selected European jurisdictions, namely, Belgium, Germany, and Italy. An underlying assumption in this chapter is that executives, more or less inevitably, are crucial actors in major crises; still, it remains to be seen how these very crises impact on their structure and functioning.

1 Preliminary Remarks

The COVID-19 pandemic crisis and its handling have severely affected nearly every aspect of public law. Great attention has been devoted to the limitations on fundamental rights, with an "unprecedented" number of derogations from related international law obligations.[1] However, the COVID-19 crisis has also impacted upon the institutional architecture in constitutional democracies as well as in hybrid regimes and non-democratic systems. In times of constitutional stress, the balance of power between the branches of government is frequently altered to allow for swifter decision-making. This generally happens to the advantage of the executive, which is better placed for responding to a serious crisis or an existential threat. In fact, although comparative analyses show that this assumption is mostly correct, the evolution of the constitutional law of emergency in several legal systems can be described as an attempt to mitigate the subversive potential of extraordinary

[1] Committee on Legal Affairs and Human Rights of the Parliamentary Assembly of the Council of Europe, *The impact of the Covid-19 pandemic on human rights and the rule of law*, Report by Vladimir Vardanyan (AS/JUR (2020) 13), available at www.assembly.coe.int (website last accessed 20 May 2022).

G. Delledonne (✉)
Institute for Law, Politics and Development (Dirpolis), Scuola Superiore Sant'Anna, Pisa, Italy
e-mail: giacomo.delledonne@santannapisa.it

K. Chrysogonos, A. Tsiftsoglou (eds.), *Democracy after Covid*,
https://doi.org/10.1007/978-3-031-13901-7_3

regimes.[2] Over the last few decades, the drafters of constitutional amendments or entirely new constitutions have taken care to avoid entrenching strong executive-centred emergency regimes; rather, they have focused on how to develop "a normative framework for understanding how, in the light of experience, the grip of constitutional principles can be maintained".[3]

Although the pandemic crisis does not fully fall under the standard model of constitutional emergency, the response to COVID-19 can be analysed against this background. Typically, scholars have focused on the relationship between the executive and the legislature, and factual developments have been tested against an initial hypothesis: "It is conventional wisdom that emergencies require massive delegation of power to the executive, which is the only branch of government with the information, decisiveness, and speed to respond to crises".[4] Moving from this preliminary assumption, scholars have also investigated the role of parliaments during the health crisis. Assuming that legislatures have been able to work, their involvement in decision-making processes and their ability to hold to account the executive have been carefully scrutinised.[5] As claimed by Ginsburg and Versteeg, "executives have not become 'unbound' during this current crisis".[6] The involvement of multiple branches of government, including legislatures and courts, in the handling of this existential threat may even have contributed to establishing the closest thing to an optimal response to the pandemic challenge.

The object and purpose of this chapter is slightly different. It considers not so much the interactions between the branches of government as the very structure of the executive. How have executives been affected by the significant responsibility that they have quite often taken over for facing the pandemic? How does this impact on the distribution of power between the branches of government? To answer these research questions, the chapter compares developments in selected European jurisdictions, namely Belgium, Germany, and Italy. All these constitutional systems have a parliamentary form of government and leave greater or lesser room for the autonomy of substate entities, ranging from regional to federal; moreover, they are all member states of the European Union and were severely hit by the crisis, albeit to different extents, as early as Spring 2020. Non-European cases in which the changing role of the executive(s) came to the forefront are no less interesting but may not fit in very well with the purpose of this comparative analysis.

The reasons for the choice of this topic can be traced back to the need for ad hoc reactions tools, which was most evident at different stages of the pandemic. One of the lessons of the health crisis is that the existing emergency regimes, be they regulated in constitutional or legislative provisions, proved to be of limited use. More often than not, national governments did not take advantage of these

[2]Delledonne (2017).

[3]Dyzenhaus (2012), p. 460.

[4]Ginsburg and Versteeg (2021), p. 1499.

[5]Bar-Siman-Tov (2020).

[6]Ginsburg and Versteeg (2021), p. 1533.

mechanisms or did so only partially. New ad hoc mechanisms were introduced, or the existing ones were modified to tackle the COVID-19 crisis. This has called into question the role of the executives, which were supposed to play a key role in the management of the crisis and, simultaneously, were affected and (re)shaped by the need for appropriate responses to this challenge.

2 The Limited Relevance of Emergency Clauses

Quantitative analyses of the constitutions that are currently in force throughout the world show that emergency clauses are, more often than not, an integral part of constitutional charters.[7] This may run counter to expectations based on distrust of such tools. Constitutions that were drafted in the 18th century, such as the Belgian charter of 1831, tend to explicitly prohibit the suspension of constitutional provisions under all circumstances (Art. 187 of the Belgian Constitution). Around the middle of the 20th century, the drafters of post-totalitarian constitutions in the aftermath of World War II, for instance, the Constitution of the Italian Republic and the Basic Law of the Federal Republic of Germany, were deeply suspicious of any kind of emergency clause or extraordinary powers, which they saw as the possible starting point of a slippery slope towards the demise of constitutional democracy. Massive resort to extraordinary presidential powers in the final years of the Weimar Republic served as a cautionary tale for the drafters of the constitutions that followed the downfall of totalitarian regimes in Western Europe. By now, things have clearly changed. The constitutional entrenchment of emergency clauses can be seen as part of a comprehensive effort to rationalise,[8] that is, juridicise political power. Extraordinary circumstances may require a response that cannot be implemented by ordinary means. Therefore, limited derogation from the ordinary constitutional framework is allowed for the sole purpose of coping with a major crisis, following which constitutional normalcy should be fully restored.

As mentioned above, the peculiar challenges raised by the pandemic may not be fully encompassed by an average emergency clause, where the focus is generally put, to quote from section 37 of the South African Constitution of 1996, on "war, invasion, general insurrection, disorder, [or] natural disaster".[9] Due to the distinctive features of COVID-19, the spread of this infectious disease may seriously undermine the normal functioning of constitutional organs, parliaments in the first place,[10] and put a terrible strain on the internal distribution of power in decentralised or federal polities. Depending on whether the contagion was uniformly distributed or was

[7] Bjørnskov and Voigt (2018).

[8] I am borrowing from Boris Mirkine-Guetzévitch's theory of *rationalisation du pouvoir* (Mirkine-Guetzévitch 1931).

[9] See also Pizzorusso (1993).

[10] Bar-Siman-Tov (2020), pp. 14–19.

concentrated in one or more parts of the country, requests for centralised or decentralised crisis management have almost inevitably emerged.

If attention shifts to empirical data, that is, to how selected jurisdictions have actually addressed the pandemic crisis, one point is striking. Quite often, governments refrained from resorting to constitutional emergency clauses or did not simply enforce pre-existing ordinary laws that regulate the response to extraordinary occurrences. The German example is quite telling. The Basic Law of 1949 contains some clauses that can be relied on to cope with a serious threat. However, Articles 35, 91, and 115a to 115l of the Basic Law make reference, respectively, to "a grave accident or a natural disaster", to "an imminent danger to the existence or free democratic basic order of the Federation or of a *Land*", and to an actual or imminent attack to the federal territory. The pandemic threat seems to lie outside the scope of these (quite detailed) constitutional clauses.[11] Therefore, the response to the COVID-19 threat was based on ordinary, albeit adapted, constitutional tools. The Constitution of the Italian Republic does not contain any clause that specifically aims to face an internal emergency; the conferral of war powers on the executive, regulated in Article 78 of the Constitution, does not seem to apply to a health crisis.[12] The Civil Protection Code, a piece of ordinary legislation that entered into force in 2018, regulates the handling, among other occurrences, of "emergencies of national significance". Article 24 of the Code regulates the declaration of a state of national emergency, which has to be agreed upon by the Council of Ministers. However, the Civil Protection Code has been criticised for not providing the governmental authorities with appropriate instruments to address a crisis such as the COVID-19 pandemic.[13]

For all their differences, all these constitutional systems based the response to COVID-19 on ad hoc legislative frameworks that were introduced in Spring 2020 and were modified in the following months. This demonstrates an inherent flaw of several emergency clauses; due to the multiform nature of the existential challenges that a constitutional system may face from time to time, the appropriate response instruments may not be fully encompassed by the relevant constitutional provisions. This seems to have been the case for the COVID-19 pandemic, not only because of the peculiar nature of the threat and its worldwide spread but also because of the far-reaching impact of the pandemic on the ordinary functioning of democratic institutions.

What is relevant for the purpose of this chapter is that the customised regimes that were devised to face the pandemic also had a significant impact on the executive, that is, the branch of government that is called upon to make the most significant decisions under such circumstances. Not only is the executive often seen as best placed for taking action under such circumstances, but its relative flexibility may turn to the advantage of the overall resilience of the system. Primarily due to historical reasons, the constitutional regulation of the executive tends to be more

[11] See Thielbörger and Behlert (2020); Woelk (2020), pp. 1715–1717.

[12] See analyses by Luciani (2020), pp. 137–138; Lupo (2020), pp. 139–140.

[13] See De Siervo (2020), pp. 310–311.

elusive than those of the legislature or of the head of state. It took some time for the government to stand out from the monarch, on the one hand,[14] and the civil service, on the other hand. On a different note, in parliamentary regimes such as Italy and Germany, the inner workings of the executive generally rely on the interplay and balance between three somewhat overlapping principles, namely, prime ministerial leadership, collegiality, and the autonomy of ministerial departments. In Italy, all these principles can be derived from Article 95 of the Constitution, whose open-texture wording seems to allow for a few different interpretations.[15] In Germany, in turn, Article 65 and several other provisions of the Basic Law of 1949 (*Grundgesetz*, hereinafter GG) define the respective tasks of the Federal Chancellor (*Bundeskanzler*), the individual ministers, and the Federal Government (*Bundesregierung*) as a collegial body; in so doing, the relatively detailed constitutional provisions strike a balance between the *Kanzlerprinzip*, the *Ressortprinzip*, and the *Kollegialprinzip*.[16] As German scholars have noticed, the tripartite division of the competences of the composing units of the federal government is not exempt from problematic aspects.[17] What really matters are not the three principles considered separately but, rather, their evolving interaction, whose final outcome cannot be determined in advance.[18]

3 A Stronger Position for Individual Members of the Executive

A first recognisable trend can be detected in Germany and Italy, with one member of the executive empowered to exert significant responsibilities in the fight against the pandemic. The centralisation of decision-making has its upsides, for instance, the possibility of rapid action; however, this may come at the expense of the internal collegiality of the cabinet.

---

[14] A persuasive example for this claim is the "constitutional fluidity" of the status and powers of the executive in the United Kingdom (McHarg (2018), p. 961).

[15] See Paladin (1970), p. 676; Capotosti (1989), pp. 9–12. Article 95 of the Italian Constitution reads: "The President of the Council shall conduct and be accountable for the general policy of the Government. The President of the Council shall ensure the consistency of political and administrative policies, by promoting and coordinating the activities of Ministers. The Ministers shall be collectively responsible for the decisions of the Council of Ministers; they shall be individually responsible for the decisions of their own ministries".

[16] Article 65 GG reads: "The Federal Chancellor shall determine and be responsible for the general guidelines of policy. Within these limits each Federal Minister shall conduct the affairs of his department independently and on his own responsibility. The Federal Government shall resolve differences of opinion between Federal Ministers. The Federal Chancellor shall conduct the proceedings of the Federal Government in accordance with rules of procedure adopted by the Government and approved by the Federal Parliament".

[17] See Maurer (2007), pp. 466–471.

[18] See Busse and Hofmann (2019), p. 67.

In Germany, "measures to combat human and animal diseases that pose a danger to the public or are transmissible" are listed among shared competences by Article 74(1) GG. This means that the *Länder* have the power to legislate in this area so long as and to the extent that the Federation has not exercised its legislative power. In 2000, the federal parliament legislated by adopting the Law on Prevention and control of Infectious Diseases (*Infektionsschutzgesetz*, IfSG). The IfSG has been repeatedly modified since March 2020 to adapt its content to the problems raised by the COVID-19 pandemic. In its previous wording, the law relied on the exchange of information between the Federation and the Länder to prevent the introduction of transmissible diseases and their spread within the Federal Republic of Germany. The new legislative framework is based on the declaration of an epidemic emergency of national significance (*epidemische Lage von nationaler Tragweite*). The existence of such an emergency leads to empower the Minister of Health to exercise special responsibilities. If an epidemic emergency of national significance is declared, the Minister of Health will adopt the necessary measures, which may take of form of regulations (*Rechtsverordnungen*) that can derogate from the laws currently in force. The existence of an epidemic emergency of national significance is declared by the federal parliament, that is, the *Bundestag*, which is also competent to declare its termination. When it was introduced, the draft amendment to the IfSG conferred upon the Minister of Health even this power. Scholars such as Möllers criticised this (ultimately unsuccessful) move as an act of self-empowerment (*Selbstermächtigung*) of the Minister.[19] In any case, the amendment of the IfSG considerably strengthened the role of the Minister of Health as a key decision-maker within the federal government. Möllers denounced this as "the renouncement of a final democratic coordination" within the federal government: "The fact that all these competencies, which are at the centre of political attention in an emergency like the current one, can be carried out by a single ministry ... takes the depoliticization of far-reaching decisions to the extreme".[20] The risk of depoliticisation is further highlighted by the role of expert bodies with consultative tasks within the Ministry of Health.

At first sight, the COVID-19 pandemic strongly boosted the *Ressortprinzip*, with the Minister of Health being granted key rule-making functions. It may not be trivial to mention that in the fourth (and last) Merkel cabinet the post of Minister of Health was held by Jens Spahn, a senior member of the Christian Democratic Union (CDU) and a would-be successor to Angela Merkel as leader of the CDU at the party congress in 2018. Still, this move, which was formalised in the amendment to the IfSG, was counterbalanced by other developments that emerged through institutional practice. This confirms that the balance between *Kanzlerprinzip*, *Ressortprinzip* and *Kollegialprinzip* is a dynamic one and may (have to) adapt to specific circumstances. To strengthen the collegial dimension of the executive activity, a core group of members of the cabinet, known as the Corona Cabinet (*Corona-Kabinett*), met every Monday from March 2020 to 23 August 2021.

[19] See Möllers (2020).

[20] Ibid.

The corona cabinet was chaired by the chancellor, and its meetings were attended by the Minister of Defence, the Minister of Finance, the Minister of the Interior, the Minister of Foreign Affairs, the Minister of Health, and the Head of the Federal Chancellery. The Merkel cabinet being supported by a grand coalition of Christian Democrats, Bavarian Social Christians and Social Democrats, the composition of the Corona Cabinet included representatives from all three political parties. Finally, these informal arrangements also contributed to preserving the primacy of the Chancellor within the cabinet and, consequently, the *Kanzlerprinzip*. Chancellor Merkel played a key role in ensuring informal coordination between the federal government and the *Länder* governments and conducted the meetings of the Corona Cabinet.

The relevance of the Corona Cabinet can be understood, at least to some extent, in the light of the need for pluralistic decision-making when it comes to introduce limitations on fundamental rights to tackle the pandemic. The amended provisions of the IfSG that confer a stronger role on the Minister of Health have raised criticism because, among other reasons, they have not been counterbalanced by the formal involvement of other members of the cabinet, for instance, the ministers who are in charge of public order and fundamental rights protection.[21]

After a new federal cabinet took office under Chancellor Olaf Scholz on 8 December 2021, some moderate innovation may surface in the German approach to the fight against COVID-19. One of the first decisions of Chancellor Scholz has been to set up a Council of Experts *within the Federal Chancellery*. The task of the Council, whose establishment was agreed upon by the federal and regional executives, is to provide advice and to formulate recommendations for coping with the pandemic; its institutional position testifies to the role of the Federal Chancellery as a nodal point of the relations between the federal and regional executives.[22]

Having in mind the possible flaws and intimate contradictions of the German legislative framework for the fight against the pandemic threat, the Italian case looks no less problematic. Here again, two significant trends can be found: the quest for ad hoc anti-crisis procedures, which are complementary to the already existing legislative framework, and the decision to grant one member of the executive extended powers to face the pandemic.

As early as 31 January 2020, the Italian government declared a national state of emergency based on Article 24 of the Civil Protection Code. When a national state of emergency is declared, the Head of the Department for Civil Protection may adopt bylaws (*ordinanze di protezione civile*) after seeking an agreement with the governments of the affected regions. The *ordinanze di protezione civile* can derogate from the laws in force but must respect the general principles of the legal system.[23] However, after the first major COVID-19 clusters were detected in Lombardy and

---

[21] See Lepsius (2020).

[22] More information available here: www.bundesregierung.de/breg-de/themen/coronavirus/expertenrat-covid-19-1991526 (website last accessed 20 May 2022).

[23] More detailed information available in Delledonne and Padula (2021).

Veneto, the executive put in place a different legal framework to face the pandemic. The executive adopted decree laws, that is, acts with the same legal value as ordinary laws passed by the legislature; the decree-laws can be adopted under extraordinary circumstances, "in case of necessity and urgency" (Article 77(2) of the Constitution). Provisions in the decree-laws adopted in February and March 2020 enabled the head of government (*Presidente del Consiglio dei ministri*, hereinafter the Italian Prime Minister) to adopt non-legislative decrees "in order to avoid the spread of Covid-19" (Article 1(1) of decree-law no. 6/2020). These prime ministerial decrees (*decreti del Presidente del Consiglio dei ministri*, dPCm) were to be adopted upon the proposal of the Minister of Health and after consultations with other ministers. A crucial and controversial point is that the Prime Minister is not required to seek an agreement with the presidents of the affected regions, as decree-law no. 6/2020 mentions a mere duty to consult them or the President of the Conference of regional presidents. Also, the legal regime of these prime ministerial decrees allows to get a sense of the centralisation of decision-making power in the person of the Italian Prime Minister. Unlike, decree-laws, prime ministerial decrees do not need to be converted into law by the Parliament and cannot be reviewed by the Constitutional Court on the grounds of their constitutionality. Another relevant point is that the prime ministerial decrees, unlike other sub-legislative acts, do not need to be submitted to the Council of State for advice and are not enacted by the President of the Republic after adoption by the Council of Ministers.

Resort to prime ministerial decrees to tackle the pandemic threat can be justified in pragmatic terms, since the very possibility to convene the Parliament was called into question during the first wave of the pandemic. Still, this course of action has given rise to criticism both in the scholarly debate and in public discussion.

With all probability, the early version of this anti-COVID-19 legal framework as regulated in decree-law no. 6/2020 was unconstitutional as it resulted in a blanket delegation of quasi-legislative power to the Prime Minister, who would adopt "all containment and management measures that are appropriate and proportionate to the evolution of the epidemiological situation".[24] Most of all, limitations on fundamental rights contained in Prime Minister's decrees were highly problematic because of the very generic wording of the enabling legislative norms. A few weeks later, this procedural framework was modified to put it in line with some basic constitutional requirements. In addition to specifying some substantive constraints, Article 2-(5) of decree-law no. 19/2020 provided that the Parliament would be notified of all the Prime Minister's decrees adopted over the course of the pandemic.

After the fall of the Conte government, Mario Draghi took office as the new Prime Minister. The advent of the Draghi government had been facilitated, among other reasons, by growing dissatisfaction with Conte's management of the crisis. The unclear balance of power within the bicameral legislature led the President of the Republic to appoint "a high-profile government that does not identify with any

[24] See Luciani (2020), p. 112; Tripodina (2020), pp. 83–84; Delledonne and Padula (2021), p. 305.

political formulas".[25] Meanwhile, the Committee for Legislation (*Comitato per la legislazione*), an internal body of the Chamber of Deputies, had pleaded in favour of a departure from massive resort to Prime Minister's decrees.[26]

However, it is difficult to describe the agenda of the Draghi government as a sharp break in continuity with its predecessor, also because some of its senior members, including Health Minister Roberto Speranza, were retained. The newly appointed government abode to the legal framework put in place by its predecessor, but it tried to favour the use of decree-laws over Prime Minister's decrees. The reasons for this choice are related, first, to the perceived need for greater involvement of the legislature and, second, to the promotion of collegiality within the cabinet. On the one side, decree-laws, as mentioned above, are converted into law by the Parliament, on the other side, and quite importantly for the purpose of this chapter, they are agreed upon by the Council of Ministers. In April 2021, a decree-law granted the Council of Ministers the power to derogate from some of the measures contained in a Prime Minister's decree enacted on 2 March. On the whole, the relative continuity with its predecessor did not prevent the Draghi government from promoting the internal collegiality of the government at the expense of (quasi-)unilateral decision-making by the Prime Minister. Aside from constitutional concerns, the broad and heterogeneous coalition that supported the Draghi government is a crucial political factor for explaining the evolution since February 2021.

The Prime Minister-centred approach was ultimately vindicated by the Constitutional Court in a judgment that upheld the constitutionality of decree-law no. 19/2020. "In a nutshell", the Constitutional Court said, "decree-law no. 19/2020 does not bestow upon the Prime Minister any legislative powers, which would run counter to Articles 76 and 77 of the Constitution; rather, it just entitles him to implement the measures that are listed [in the decree-law itself]".[27]

4 Response to the COVID-19 Threat in a Consensual Democracy

For the purpose of this chapter, the Belgian case stands apart from the others. In Belgium, the response to the pandemic did not lead to the empowerment of one or more members of the cabinet for the sake of swift and efficient executive action. Rather, executive response was structured so as to reflect the huge diversity of the country. These arrangements can be understood in the light of the serious political instability from which Belgium had been suffering since December 2018, when a minority coalition took office following the breakup of the so-called "Swedish"

[25] Declaration by President Sergio Mattarella, 2 February 2021, available at www.quirinale.it (website last accessed 20 May 2022).

[26] See Cavino (2021).

[27] Italian Constitutional Court (*Corte costituzionale*), judgment no. 198/2021.

right-of-centre coalition. The formation of a new government after the federal election of May 2019 soon proved to be cumbersome. This may give rise both to political and constitutional problems: in this respect, it should be kept in mind that the federal government of Belgium is supposed to act as an arbiter between the Dutch-speaking and French-speaking linguistic groups.[28] When the first wave of the pandemic hit continental Europe, it found Belgium with a caretaker minority government, supported by the Flemish Christian Democrats and the Flemish and francophone Liberals. Although there was consensus on granting the federal government special powers to fight the pandemic, the issue of the political legitimacy of such measures soon emerged.

The minority government led by Sophie Wilmès stayed in office, although almost all the political parties represented in the Chamber of Representatives agreed that this was only for a limited period of time. Meanwhile, the first measures adopted to counter the spread of the contagion through Belgium took the form of decrees of the Minister of Security and the Interior. However, much of the content of these decrees had been decided earlier within a select ministerial committee, the National Security Council (NSC). The NSC played a significant role at the time of the Islamist terrorist attacks, when its regulation was last amended; basically, its mission is "to coordinate government action in times of crisis or threat".[29] What should be kept in mind is that the ordinary composition of the NSC, that is, one of the main decision-making fora during the first wave of the pandemic, was adjusted to meet the concerns of the moment. By virtue of a royal decree of 28 January 2015, the Council for National Security is composed of the Prime Minister, the Deputy Prime Ministers, the Minister of Justice, the Minister of Defence, the Minister of the Interior, and the Minister of Foreign Affairs. In March 2020, the leaders of the governments of the three regions and the three communities were also invited to attend the meetings of the NSC. The informal adaptation of the composition of the Council deserves mention because some of the leaders of the subnational governments are members of political parties that were in the opposition at the federal level. Such was the case with Jan Jambon, Minister-President of Flanders and member of the New Flemish Alliance (N-VA), and with Elio Di Rupo and Rudi Vervoort, both members of the francophone Socialist Party (PS) and Ministers-President of, respectively, Wallonia and Brussels.[30] According to Clarenne and Romainville, the involvement of the NSC and the change in its composition can be described as a new consociational tool of the consensual democracy of Belgium.[31] Having in mind the political stalemate that could not be resolved until Autumn 2020, the risk of an escalation of the political crisis into a constitutional one and the practical difficulties faced by the federal parliament, this pragmatic solution allowed, at least for a while, to take into

[28] See Popelier and Lemmens (2015).

[29] Popelier (2020), p. 134.

[30] See Bouhon et al. (2020), pp. 12–13.

[31] See Clarenne and Romainville (2020).

consideration the multiple political and cultural cleavages of the country during the management of an all-embracing crisis.

5 Concluding Assessment

The trends and developments that have been presented in this chapter lend themselves to mixed reviews. The particular viewpoint that I have chosen, that is, how governments have been (re)shaped by the response to the pandemic, may have farther-reaching implications for the understanding of the legal dimension of this largely unprecedented crisis.

The first relevant point is *experimentalism*: national governments seldom relied only on already existing legal frameworks for the management of emergencies. Rather, they introduced ad hoc solutions that have often supplemented the existing legal tools.

In this respect, the relative flexibility of the constitutional and legislative arrangements related to the executives should be assessed positively. During the first acute stage of the pandemic in Spring 2020, the very ability of legislative assemblies to perform their functions was a reason for concern. In Italy, a pragmatic justification for the response strategy based on the Prime Minister's decrees was that the Parliament might not have been able to convene and, therefore, to legislate and to convert decree-laws into law. A recurring trend was the centralisation of decision-making power in one member of the executive, such as the Italian Prime Minister or the German Minister of Health. This was countervailed by the enhancement of safeguards of the collegiality of the executive, which, by the way, was more evident in Germany than in Italy. The internal collegiality and pluralism of the executive was a topical issue even in Belgium, as the informal enlargement of the National Security Council reveals. An open point, which lies outside the scope of this brief study, is how these innovations can be reconciled with parliamentary supervision and decision-making powers.

As I have tried to show throughout the chapter, political contingency played a role in defining the contours of the response to COVID-19 in each of these jurisdictions. Both Italy and Belgium were hit by the first wave of the pandemic in a time of serious political instability, which may reflect a wider crisis of representative democracy (from which even Germany may not be completely exempt). What remains to be seen, however, is whether and to what extent these formal and informal changes will subsist in a post-COVID constitutional universe and will be of benefit to European constitutional democracies.

References

Bar-Siman-Tov I (2020) Covid-19 meets politics: the novel coronavirus as a novel challenge for legislatures. Theory Pract Legis 8:11–48

Bjørnskov C, Voigt S (2018) The architecture of emergency constitutions. Int J Const Law 16:101–127

Bouhon F, Jousten A, Miny X, Slautsky E (2020) L'État belge face à la pandémie de Covid-19: esquisse d'un régime d'exception. Courrier hebdomadaire du CRISP 62(1):5–53

Busse V, Hofmann H (2019) Bundeskanzleramt und Bundesregierung. Handbuch für Wissenschaft und Praxis, 7th edn. Nomos, Baden-Baden

Capotosti PA (1989) Governo. In: Enciclopedia giuridica, vol 19. Istituto dell'Enciclopedia italiana, Roma

Cavino M (2021) Comitato per la legislazione e d.P.C.M.: il diavolo si cela nei dettagli. Quaderni costituzionali 41:401–404

Clarenne J, Romainville C (2020) Le droit constitutionnel belge à l'épreuve du COVID-19 (1/2). JP Blog, 23 April. https://blog.juspoliticum.com/2020/04/23/le-droit-constitutionnel-belge-a-lepreuve-du-covid-19-1-2-par-julian-clarenne-et-celine-romainville (website last accessed 20 May 2022)

De Siervo U (2020) Emergenza Covid e sistema delle fonti: prime impressioni. Osservatorio sulle fonti 13 (special issue): 299–312. https://www.osservatoriosullefonti.it (website last accessed 20 May 2022)

Delledonne G (2017) History and concepts of emergency. In: Grote R, Lachenmann F, Wolfrum R (eds) Max Planck Encyclopedia of comparative constitutional law. Oxford University Press, Oxford. http://oxcon.ouplaw.com (website last accessed 20 May 2022)

Delledonne G, Padula C (2021) Italy: the impact of the pandemic crisis on the relations between the state and the regions. In: Hondius E, Santos Silva M, Wendehorst C, Nicolussi A, Salvador Coderch P, Zoll F (eds) Coronavirus and the law in Europe. Intersentia, Antwerp, pp 301–318

Dyzenhaus D (2012) States of emergency. In: Rosenfeld M, Sajó A (eds) The Oxford handbook of comparative constitutional law. Oxford University Press, Oxford, pp 442–462

Ginsburg T, Versteeg M (2021) The bound executive: emergency powers during the pandemic. Int J Const Law 19:1498–1535

Lepsius O (2020). Vom Niedergang grundrechtlicher Denkkategorien in der Corona-Pandemie. Verfassungsblog, 6 April. https://verfassungsblog.de/vom-niedergang-grundrechtlicher-denkkategorien-in-der-corona-pandemie (website last accessed 20 May 2022)

Luciani M (2020) Il sistema delle fonti del diritto alla prova dell'emergenza. Rivista AIC 11(2): 109–141. https://www.rivistaaic.it (website last accessed 20 May 2022)

Lupo N (2020) L'attività parlamentare in tempi di coronavirus. Forum di Quaderni costituzionali Rassegna 9(2):122–142. http://www.forumcostituzionale.it (website last accessed 20 May 2022)

Maurer H (2007) Staatsrecht I: Grundlagen – Verfassungsorgane – Staatsfunktionen, 5th edn. C.H. Beck, München

McHarg A (2018) Navigating without maps: constitutional silence and the management of the Brexit crisis. Int J Const Law 16:952–968

Mirkine-Guetzévitch B (1931) Les nouvelles tendances du droit constitutionnel. Marcel Giard, Paris

Möllers C (2020) Parlamentarische Selbstentmächtigung im Zeichen des Virus. Verfassungsblog, 26 March. https://verfassungsblog.de/parlamentarische-selbstentmaechtigung-im-zeichen-des-virus (website last accessed 20 May 2022)

Paladin L (1970) Governo italiano. In: Enciclopedia del diritto, vol 19. Giuffrè, Milano, pp 675–711

Pizzorusso A (1993) Emergenza (stato di). In: Enciclopedia delle scienze sociali, vol 3. Istituto dell'Enciclopedia italiana, Roma, pp 551–559

Popelier P (2020) COVID-19 legislation in Belgium at the crossroad of a political and a health crisis. Theory Pract Legis 8:131–153

Popelier P, Lemmens K (2015) The constitution of Belgium: a contextual analysis. Hart Publishing, Oxford

Thielbörger P, Behlert B (2020) COVID-19 und das Grundgesetz: Zur (Un)tauglichkeit des verfassungsrechtlichen 'Immunsystems'. Verfassungsblog, 19 March. https://verfassungsblog.de/covid-19-und-das-grundgesetz (website last accessed 20 May 2022)

Tripodina C (2020) La Costituzione al tempo del Coronavirus. Costituzionalismo.it 18(1):78–88. https://www.costituzionalismo.it (website last accessed 20 May 2022)

Woelk J (2020) La gestione della pandemia da parte della Germania: '*Wir schaffen das!*'. DPCE online 43(2):1713–1741. http://www.dpceonline.it (website last accessed 20 May 2022)

Parliamentarism in the Pandemic: Contemporary Challenges

Heike Merten

Abstract Parliamentary democracy has been stress-tested in the COVID-19 pandemic. The Parliament, as the representation of the people, must be able to work and make unpopular decisions to protect society. Only in a transparent and legitimate decision-making process is it possible to win the support of the people. Parliamentarism in the pandemic must function effectively and safely. Also important is a legally secure election of the parliament in times of crisis to have a legislator legitimised by the people. In times of crisis, a functioning parliamentary system is particularly important for a democracy.

1 Introduction

The Coronavirus has hit the world and, of course, Germany hard. The state had to make quick and drastic decisions to protect the health of the population. This was accompanied by massive restrictions on the citizens' liberties. The state is only allowed to restrict civil liberties as far as it is necessary to protect health. But what is necessary and who decides how? To clarify these questions is not always easy for decision-makers. It requires public discussion, also to create trust in and strengthen the enforceability of the necessary measures.

In a parliamentary democracy, the present MPs usually have these discussions publicly in parliamentary sessions. It is here where all the essential decisions must be taken. However, the pandemic in Germany, and not only here, has shown that governments alone take many essential decisions. The Parliament has lost a lot of power at the beginning of the pandemic. At the same time, the acceptance of the measures in the population has decreased. The role of political parties has also changed significantly during the pandemic.

This gives reason to take a closer look at parliamentarism in pandemic times. Have parliaments lived up to their key constitutional role in the pandemic? Is

H. Merten (✉)
Party Research Institute, Heinrich Heine University Düsseldorf, Düsseldorf, Germany
e-mail: heike.merten@hhu.de

K. Chrysogonos, A. Tsiftsoglou (eds.), *Democracy after Covid*,
https://doi.org/10.1007/978-3-031-13901-7_4

parliamentary will-formation and decision-making also possible in a virtual parliament? How can democratic elections be held remotely in a legally-secure manner? Is an exclusively postal vote possible? How can MP candidates be nominated in pandemic times? Is there a shift of power towards the executive? These are questions that will continue to occupy us in the future, as there is no end in sight to the pandemic and it is already clear that we will have to reckon with new pandemics and other crises in the future, for example as a result of natural disasters.

In a crisis such as a pandemic, the state needs to be able to act and be assertive. The Parliament, which directly represents the will of the people, must play a central role in this.

2 Constitutional State of Emergency?

"The Federal Republic of Germany, indeed the whole world, is in a state of emergency due to the Corona pandemic. Citizens are being deprived of their liberties". This is how news reports, interviews, blog posts, talk shows, but also editorials and scientific articles describe the special situation, which has now lasted for over two years, especially in the waves of the pandemic. From a constitutional point of view, the paraphrases reproduced in these articles must initially be irritating. They suggest the temporary abrogation of the law by the state,[1] by granting the executive such far-reaching decision-making powers. This is negatively connotated as a reminiscence of the so-called emergency article (Art. 48 (2)) from the Weimar Reich Constitution of 1919, which enabled the Reich President to suspend individual fundamental rights to restore public safety and order.

In purely factual terms, unlike in other countries, the law in the Federal Republic of Germany has never been suspended.[2] All pandemic-related measures have been adopted on a constitutional basis and through the procedures laid down for this purpose. Fundamental rights have not been suspended either. The measures to combat the pandemic restricted fundamental rights. The Federal Constitutional Court ruled in a landmark decision at the end of 2021 that this restriction of fundamental rights was constitutional.[3] The Court outlined a framework for the legislator of measures to combat the pandemic. It found the legally enacted contact restrictions, curfews and school closures to be consistent with the Constitution. When adopting the Act, the legislator based its assessment that there was a danger to life and health and a danger to the healthcare system on authoritative factual knowledge. So far, neither the Constitutional Court nor the Higher Administrative

[1] On the suspension of law in a state of emergency see already Schmidt (1934), p. 19; For a more in-depth look see Hoffmann (2005), pp. 171 et seq.

[2] See also Dreier (2021), pp. 229 et seq.

[3] BVerfG, Beschluss des Ersten Senats vom 19. November 2021 – 1 BvR 781/21 – and – 1 BvR 971/21 –.

Courts have assumed a violation of the Constitution due to a breach of the parliamentary assessment prerogative.[4] Even at the height of the Corona pandemic, the Constitution claims unrestricted validity. It is, on the one hand, the reason and, on the other hand, the limit for any exercise of state sovereignty, also and especially in this challenging special situation.[5] Parliamentarism, in which the centre of political decision-making powers lies with the Parliament, has been subjected to a stress test under pandemic conditions.[6] Such a test always reveals strengths but also weaknesses that need to be examined more closely. The insights gained must be used to make parliamentarism crisis-proof and future-proof.

3 Sovereignty and Decision-Making Power

The fundamental authority to act in a representative democracy lies with the parliament. Parliament is the only organ of state directly legitimised by the people in a democratic election. It, therefore, has a particularly high level of legitimacy for its actions. In addition to other important functions, such as the election of the Head of Government and the control of the Government, it also carries the legislative power—a function concretising the rule of law. In the parliamentary system of government of the Basic Law, the Parliament, as the representative of the democratic sovereign within the meaning of Article 20 (2) (1) of the Basic Law, is the central constitutional organ of the Federal Republic of Germany. It takes the most important decisions for the state and, thus, gives the state the ability to act in the first place. State law doctrine and state practice have so far unanimously assumed a physical presence of the deputies in the plenary chamber.

The ability of a Parliament to act is fundamental in a pandemic or crisis where rapid and drastic measures need to be taken. Even and especially in such a situation, the parliamentary business must be maintained and restrictions of parliamentary work must be prevented. A Parliament like the Bundestag, with 736 members meeting for plenary debates and committee meetings in the Reichstag building, where social distancing cannot be kept for spatial reasons, is exposed to a high risk of infection. In addition to the health risk for the Members of Parliament and the employees in parliamentary business, the functioning of the parliamentary system of government as a whole is at stake. To establish the distance and hygiene rules, the Bundestag could have held its plenary sessions on (much) larger premises. The location of the sessions is not specified by Constitutional Law. The Swiss Parliament

---

[4] However, most of the decisions of the constitutional and administrative courts have so far only been issued in interim relief proceedings. In these summary proceedings, the courts have generally objected to measures and statutory instruments with reference to the limits of the authorisation, the principle of equality and the principle of proportionality.

[5] Affirming Heining et al. (2020), pp. 861 et seq.; similarly Kersten and Rixen (2020), pp. 27 et seq., 33 et seq.; Michl (2020), pp. 507 et seq.; Dreier (2021), pp. 229 et seq.

[6] See also Marschall (2020), pp. 11 et seq.

(although also much smaller in number) has chosen this route and met in a convention centre in Bern.[7] The possibility of holding parliamentary sessions online was discussed out of necessity and with a critical eye during the pandemic. At the same time, however, it was seen as an opportunity to modernise parliamentarism and make it fit for the future. The call for "digital or virtual parliamentarism" became loud.[8] The European Parliament[9] and the British House of Commons went down this path and met in a "hybrid session".[10] In Germany, there was a controversial debate among constitutional lawyers as to whether the Constitution requires the physical presence of Members of Parliament and, thus, whether a constitutional amendment was necessary for virtual presence. The Scientific Service of the German Bundestag is of the opinion that the Basic Law does not permit meetings by videoconference from its very wording.[11] Among constitutional lawyers, the views are divided.[12]

The President of the German Bundestag has also raised the question of whether an emergency Parliament, i.e. a numerically greatly reduced plenum, should be introduced through an amendment to the Basic Law to ensure the functioning of the Bundestag in a pandemic or other times of crisis. State law doctrine,[13] but also the parliamentary groups of the German Bundestag,[14] have met this proposal with rejection.

During the pandemic, the Bundestag, therefore, preferred a pragmatic solution to ensure its ability to work. Based on voluntary agreements, fewer members attended the sessions and ballot boxes could also be used to cast votes outside the plenary chamber. In addition, the Rules of Procedure were amended for a limited time. This particularly concerned the rule on the quorum of the Parliament. Normally, the Bundestag has a quorum if at least half of its members are present (Sec. 45 (1) GOBT). The Bundestag lowered this quorum by a resolution on the Rules of Procedure, which introduced the provision of § 126a GOBT on the "Special Application of the Rules of Procedure due to the General Impairment by COVID-19".[15] Under this provision, the Bundestag has a quorum if at least

[7]KEYSTONE-SDA-ATS AG (2020).

[8]Roßmann (2020a).

[9]See Lenz and Schulte (2020), p. 748 on digital sessions of the Bundestag; see also European Parliament (2020). on the virtual plenary session of the European Parliament in April 2020.

[10]Marschall (2020), pp. 14 et seq.; See also House of Commons (2020); Borger (2020).

[11]Deutscher Bundestag (2020a). Proposed is, among other things, an amendment to Art. 39 (3) (1) of the Basic Law, according to which the Bundestag not only the end and restart of the sessions, but also the nature of their Implementation to be determined.

[12]Lenz and Schulte (2020), pp. 744 et seq.; Kersten and Rixen (2021), pp. 207–234.

[13]Möllers (2020); Brüning (2021), pp. 2727 et seq.; Schönberger and Schönberger (2020).

[14]Roßmann (2020b).

[15]The provision of Section 126a GOBT was introduced by resolution of the German Bundestag of 25 March 2020 (Der Präsident des Deutschen Bundestages (2020a)) and was to be limited in its effect to 30 September 2020 (Sec. 126a (5) GOBT old version) (Deutscher Bundestag (2020b), pp. 3, 5). The German Bundestag extended the validity of section 126a GOBT until 31 December 2020 by resolution of 17 September 2020 (Der Präsident des Deutschen Bundestages (2020b)) and

one-quarter of its members are present. The same applies to the quorum of the committees, whereby only here participation via electronic means of communication was made possible (Sec. 126a (2) GOBT). This lowering of the quorum only ensures the functioning of the Bundestag if the majority ratios of the parliamentary groups are also reflected in the Bundestag "reduced in size". This can in principle be achieved through a so-called pairing procedure.[16] The parliamentary groups agree that only so many of their deputies participate in the "reduced" Parliament that the parliamentary majority ratios are reflected in it. This presupposes the agreement of all Members and political groups for all Members of Parliament have, as an expression of their free mandate (Article 38 (1) (2) of the Basic Law), the right to participate at all times in meetings, debates, and votes of the Bundestag.[17] For a certain transitional period, such an approach is constitutional. However, the result is the informal introduction of an emergency Parliament, which in the long run hardly lives up to the parliamentary principle of representation (Article 38 (1) (2) of the Basic Law).

To protect the ability of Parliaments to work and to protect deputies, a mask mandate in Parliament was issued. The State Constitutional Court of Lower Saxony did not consider this to conflict with the constitutional rights of the deputies.[18] At the peak of the pandemic, proof of vaccination or recovery or a negative test was additionally required. There is some debate among scholars about the constitutional permissibility of these measures. Members of Parliament who refuse vaccination and testing can no longer exercise their parliamentary rights. The Federal Constitutional Court will decide whether this restriction is constitutional or not.

4 The Parliament's Scope of Action

The Parliament is the legislative body and, thus, in purely factual terms, it does not lack the power to act. The reservation of the law (*Vorbehalt des Gesetzes*), as the core of the principle of the rule of law, requires a legal basis for all restrictions of civil liberties by the state. The executive branch, which has been acting more intensively in the pandemic, requires explicit prior legal authorisation to be able to restrict civil rights. For the special case of executive law-making, the general legal obligation of the Government in Article 20 (3) of the Basic Law finds a concretisation in Article 80 of the Basic Law. Legislative decrees must remain within the framework of statutory provisions. This constitutionally founded

until 31 March 2021 by resolution of 17 December 2020 (Der Präsident des Deutschen Bundestages (2021a)) until the end of the legislative period by resolution of 24 June 2021 (Der Präsident des Deutschen Bundestages (2021b).

[16] On the pairing procedure see Klein and Schwarz (2021), Art. 38, para 235.

[17] BVerfGE 140, 115 (150 et seq. with further references).

[18] Niedersächsischer Staatsgerichtshof, Beschluss vom 27. September 2021 – StGH 6/20 –.

hierarchy of norms was often shaken by pandemic legislation. In many cases, the executive branch was empowered to fall back on a large number of laws and to modify them, i.e. either to repeal the claim to validity by means of differently worded provisions in ordinances or to amend them.[19] However, only the Parliament, which is directly legitimised by the people, is authorised and called upon to restrict the fundamental rights through measures to combat the pandemic. The Parliament has to debate the drastic restriction of civil rights in plenary and to come to a decision in a transparent and confidence-building procedure. Citizens' trust is the foundation of parliamentarism.

A look at the neighbouring country Austria has shown that continuous legislative activity is also possible in the field of pandemic legislation, where the parliament can be the decisive factor.[20]

5 Elections as the Foundation of Parliamentarism

The regular and lawful holding of elections is the foundation for a functioning democracy and, thus, also for parliamentarism. Elections to the people's representatives on federal, Land and municipal levels must, therefore, also be held in times of pandemic. Under Article 20 (2) of the Basic Law, the people, as the subject of legitimation, exercises its state power "in elections". The people, thus, provides the elected Parliament with the necessary democratic legitimacy. Through its legislative activity and its own elections, the Parliament, thus, provides the special legislative, executive, and juridical organs with their legitimacy, which in this way can be traced back to the people. Elections are, therefore, the fundamental processes of legitimation. In the conduct of elections, the principle of democracy, therefore, imposes requirements on the nomination of candidates and on the electoral campaign, as well as on the actual act of voting, which must also and especially be observed during a pandemic, crisis, or natural disaster.

5.1 Postponement of Elections

Postponing upcoming elections until after a pandemic or natural disaster and, thus, extending current election periods is not a realistic option.[21] Generally, it is not possible to predict when the crisis will be over; nor do the Constitutions provide for such postponements of elections from a current legislative period to protect democracy.

[19]Wollenschläger (2021), pp. 654 et seq.

[20]Dreier (2021), p. 242 with further references.

[21]Merten (2021a), pp. 61 et seq.; Merten (2021b), pp. 26 et seq.

The periodicity of elections is one of the necessary components of a democracy, which can only ever be a "temporary rule".[22] This core element of the principle of democracy, which is resistant to change (Article 79 (3) of the Basic Law), also applies in Germany to the Länder via Article 28 (1) of the Basic Law. It ensures that the legitimation of office bearers is renewed at regular intervals by the people appointed for this purpose. The duration of the regular legislative period of the Parliaments is therefore constitutionally fixed and a change is only possible by way of a constitutional amendment. A shortening or extension of the current electoral period by the Parliament in office by way of a constitutional amendment is excluded by the predominant opinion in jurisprudence, in contrast to a change of the duration of future electoral periods.[23] The deputies of precisely this current electoral period lack the necessary democratic legitimacy to extend their term of office, which was only conferred for the duration determined at the time of the elections.

If it, therefore, is not possible to postpone federal and state elections, the preparation and conduct of elections in times of pandemic and crisis must be examined more closely.

5.2 Candidate Listing

The first fundamental step in preparing for the election is the act of nominating candidates, because, without candidates, no election can be held. The nomination of candidates is an indispensable prerequisite for the conduct of the election and must also comply with democratic principles. Under the respective electoral laws, the nomination takes place in meetings of members or delegates among those present.[24] In times of pandemic, such physical meetings can pose a considerable risk to the health of the participants. To ensure the proper conduct of the September 2021 federal election, the Parliament amended the Federal Elections Act (BWahlG). Section 52 (4) of the BWahlG empowered the Federal Ministry of the Interior, and thus the executive branch, to deviate from the statutory provisions on standing candidates among those present by issuing a statutory order for the event of a natural disaster or similar event. The enactment of the statutory instrument also requires the consent of the Bundestag, which must first determine that it is impossible to hold the physical events in whole or in part. This necessary determination was made by the Bundestag on 14 January 2021 and the Federal Ministry of the Interior subsequently issued—with the required approval of the Bundestag—the so-called COVID-19 Election Candidate Nomination Ordinance.[25]

[22] BVerfGE 119, 247, para 47.

[23] Hahlen (2017), Sec. 16 para 10 with further references.

[24] Merten (2019), pp. 119 et seq.

[25] Der Bundesminister des Innern, für Bau und Heimat (2021).

This amendment to the law has received considerable criticism.[26] The concrete shaping of such essential electoral concerns must not be left to the executive. The Parliament must regulate these fundamental questions of the listing of election candidates according to the principle of parliamentary reservation (*Parlamentsvorbehalt*) itself.[27] Although after the authorisation-triggering determination of the impossibility of assemblies by the Bundestag, the latter must still agree to the subsequently issued statutory instrument of the executive. Why the legislature chose this three-step procedure and did not immediately amend the law itself is, however, incomprehensible. It also remains questionable how the Bundestag can determine the impossibility of carrying out assemblies if this impossibility cannot occur at all in purely factual terms. A meeting is, naturally, possible. However, it bears a health risk that can be reduced through protective measures in a pandemic as well. Thus, there is no case of impossibility, but only a health and constitutional policy weighing decision. In purely legal terms, election assemblies, for good reasons, cannot be so easily banned. Therefore, the necessary party meetings are always excluded from the Corona protection ordinances of the federal states. The—nevertheless determined by the Bundestag—(actual) impossibility can, therefore, not exist. Additionally, the determination of the content of the ordinance authorisation is also quite debatable.

The Federal Ministry of the Interior has made use of its relatively broad scope. The ordinance makes it possible to deviate from the obligation to hold face-to-face meetings to elect candidates and to hold meetings by means of electronic communication. Parties can also reduce the minimum number of participants stipulated in their statutes without amending the statutes to ensure a quorum. The final vote on candidates, lists, and representatives for the representative assemblies must continue to be held by ballot paper, postal vote, or as a combination of the two. Nominators are free to decide whether and how to use the COVID-19 Election Candidate Nomination Ordinance options. They may also continue to hold physical meetings.

The transfer of the meetings and, thus, also the pre-selection of candidates and list placement into the digital space is not entirely unproblematic from a democratic point of view.[28] This is only permissible within very narrow limits, for example for compelling reasons of health protection. The constitutional requirements are even more restrictive with regard to the formation of will through democratic means. Also, for the pre-selection of candidates as an essential and pre-decisive preparatory act for the election, the standard for state elections established by the Federal Constitutional Court and, thus, the principle of democracy, as well as the electoral principles of Article 38 of the Basic Law apply.[29] Accordingly, all essential steps of

---

[26]See on the whole already Merten (2021a), pp. 61 et seq.; Merten (2021b), pp. 26 et seq.

[27]Michl (2021a), von Notz (2020); S Schönberger (2021), pp. 22 et seq.; Michl (2021b), pp. 29 et seq.

[28]C Schönberger (2016), p. 486 et seq.; S Schönberger (2021), pp. 22 et seq.

[29]BVerfGE 89, 243 (251 et seq.).

the election must also be subject to public review.[30] Such verifiability of the determination of the result, which must be able to be carried out by the party members in case of the nomination of candidates in parties, is, however, lacking in a purely digital election. In the case of electronic voting systems, the concrete voting situation cannot be reconstructed. For this reason, candidate nominations that are essentially carried out via such electronic voting systems are particularly problematic from a constitutional point of view. For this reason, the Ordinance also provides that, in any case, the final binding vote on an election proposal on the candidate chosen by the majority in the electronic voting procedure is only permissible by means of a written vote of those entitled to vote, to be carried out in secret using ballot papers. However, this fails to recognise that the "non-binding preselection" by digital means already has such a significant influence on the final binding vote that it is difficult to disregard the principle of the public nature of the election there as well.

In addition, the equality of participation in the internal party candidate selection, which is rooted in the principle of democracy and electoral equality, must be ensured by a practically binding (pre-)selection of candidates by digital means. All party members must be able to participate in a digital candidate selection in the same way, irrespective of personal abilities, the existence of private electronic terminals, or a powerful private Internet connection.

Some federal states, such as NRW, follow this dubious solution of the federal legislator and includes an ordinance authorisation in the state election laws.[31] But NRW still made a pandemic-related adjustments for the implementation of the local elections 2020 through a law. States such as Thuringia, for example, are fortunately taking the path of wanting to regulate the essential issues in law. Concerning the current nomination of constituency candidates, it can be gathered from the press that the parties are almost exclusively relying on pandemic-compliant face-to-face events, probably also to ensure a legally secure nomination of candidates.

5.3 Electoral Admission

After the candidates have been nominated, it is necessary to obtain official admission to the election for the election proposals that have come about in this way. For this purpose, parties and electoral groups that have not previously been represented in Parliament must provide so-called supporter signatures (e.g. Sec. 20 (2) (2); 27 (1) (2) BWahlG). The supporters must enter their personal data on the forms personally and by hand (e.g. Sec. 34 (4); 39 (3) BWahlO). The number of signatures to be provided by persons entitled to vote is staggered. This requirement of supporting signatures already impairs equality of opportunity and electoral law under regular electoral conditions. However, the restriction on admission under

[30] BVerfGE 123, 39 et seq.

[31] Landtag Nordrhein-Westfalen (2020).

electoral law is constitutionally justified since it is based on a compelling reason: Regulations that make the admission of an election proposal dependent on the provision of a minimum number of supporting signatures serve to ensure the seriousness of the election proposal, with the aim of ultimately also counteracting a fragmentation of votes and producing a representative of the people that is capable of acting. The legitimacy of this concern is fundamentally recognised in the Constitutional Court's jurisprudence.[32]

This fundamental constitutional admissibility of making participation in elections dependent on the provision of supporting signatures is, however, subject to the "justification" provision of actual feasibility, both in terms of time and organisation. It must be kept in mind that the legal regulation already assumes a rather high number of support signatures to be provided and demands a considerable organisational effort from the small parties.

If this already applies under "normal conditions", it is advisable, in times of crisis, to introduce significant mitigations with regard to the support signatures or to refrain from a signature clause altogether in the interest of preserving equal political opportunities.[33] For the election to the German Bundestag, the required support signatures were reduced to one quarter in each case.[34]

5.4 *Electoral Campaign*

The pandemic and the associated precautionary measures are leading to significant restrictions on campaign activities in the streets and on door-to-door campaigning. Information stands and leaflet distribution in pedestrian zones, as well as personal campaign visits, are not possible if certain infection or hospitalisation incidence is exceeded. This also applies to hall or stage events.

A critical examination of such de facto bans on electoral campaigns in the public sphere must start with the relevant constitutional provisions (Arts. 21 and 38 of the Basic Law) for the protection of election advertising.[35] Inseparably linked to the right to propose candidates is the right to campaign for one's own candidates in public. The right to campaign must, therefore, be granted equally to all holders of approved election proposals, while preserving equality of opportunity. This constitutional right to campaigning with equal opportunities can only be restricted to protect conflicting constitutional interests. Whether and in what way restrictions

[32] BVerfGE 81 (96 et seq.); 82, 353 (364); 114, 107, (115 et seq.).

[33] For example, the Constitutional Court of Berlin suggested a reduction to 20 to 30 percent of the level before the Corona crisis. Verfassungsgerichtshof des Landes Berlin, Beschluss vom 17. März 2021 – VerfGH 4/21 –, – VerfGH 20 –, – 20 A/21 –; Verfassungsgerichtshof für das Land Nordrhein-Westfalen, Beschluss vom 30. Juni 2020 – 63/20.VB-2 –, Verfassungsgerichtshof Rheinland-Pfalz, Beschluss vom 28. Januar 2021 – VGH O 82/20 –, – VGH A 83/20 –.

[34] Deutscher Bundestag (2021).

[35] Merten (2020).

are actually justified must then be weighed up in the individual case. The balancing of interests must particularly consider the principle of equality of opportunity.

In principle, however, a non-contact election campaign remains possible even in pandemic times,[36] for example through billposting, direct mail, social media or even flyers in mailboxes and through election advertising broadcasts on public radio. In cases of natural disasters, this form of contactless election campaigning is nearly impossible. But this applies equally to all parties. In recent years, electoral campaigns have increasingly shifted into the digital space. As far as electoral campaign activities are limited due to Corona, there are still numerous possibilities for contactless advertising, so that, in principle, an electoral campaign must remain possible. It is true that this gives an advantage to established parties over first-time candidates and also, in case of doubt, an advantage to incumbents. But this is not a specifically Corona-related problem. This imbalance in the chances of success of electoral advertising generally accompanies every electoral campaign. In any case, campaign restrictions imposed by pandemic measures affect all parties equally and ensure—albeit under more difficult conditions for all—an electoral campaign with equal opportunities.

5.5 *Electoral Act*

In the actual electoral act, the written principles of electoral law enshrined in Article 38 (1) (1) of the Basic Law, as well as the unwritten principle of electoral law of the publicity of the election developed by the Federal Constitutional Court, must be observed. Accordingly, all essential steps of the election must be subject to public scrutiny.[37] Compliance with all six principles of electoral law can be ensured without any problems in the polling station on election day in the case of the ballot box election, which is conceived as the rule. The Federal Constitutional Court, therefore, also speaks of the ballot box election as the "constitutional model".[38] However, a traditional ballot box election at the polling station does pose risks in times of a pandemic, and so the option of a general postal vote was considered.[39]

A postal vote, on the other hand, is a "privatised electoral act"[40] in which the public control of the vote, but also the freedom of choice and the secrecy of the ballot are withdrawn. The Federal Constitutional Court nevertheless considers it permissible by way of exception to "achieve the widest possible participation in the election

[36] Verfassungsgerichtshof für das Land Nordrhein-Westfalen, Beschluss vom 30. Juni 2020 – 76/20 para 57.

[37] BVerfGE 123, 39 et seq.

[38] BVerfGE 134, 25 para 16.

[39] Orlowski (2020); Orlowski and Pohlmann (2020), pp. 38 et seq.

[40] Hahlen (2017), § 36, para 4.

and, thus, to take account of the principle of the generality of the election".[41] For the admissibility of an exclusive postal vote, therefore, other constitutional interests of considerable weight must argue, in addition to the generality of the election, for a restriction of the principles of electoral law in conformity with the Constitution. The state's duty to protect the health of its citizens, which follows from Article 2 (2) (2) of the Basic Law, is cited in this connection. It is argued that the exclusion of infections with the Coronavirus during a public election is a constitutionally legitimate reason for holding an election as a general postal vote.[42] The aspect of the protection of health is, thus, added to the constitutional objective of the highest possible voter turnout.

However, it remains questionable whether health protection on election day can actually be ensured exclusively by an exclusive postal vote. As long as it is possible to ensure voting at the ballot box in compliance with the protection against an infection, the ballot box is constitutionally required to safeguard the principles of electoral law and an exclusive postal vote can hardly be justified in terms of constitutional law. This is because even if the ballot box is adhered to in principle, the option of a postal vote or an early ballot box is available as an alternative, especially for persons at risk.

The proportion of postal voters in federal elections has grown steadily over time, even irrespective of pandemic periods.[43] State elections held during the pandemic period have seen a significant increase in absentee voters, up to 66.5% for a state election on 14 March 2021[44] and 47,5 % for the federal election on 26 September 2021.[45] No distinction is made in the postal voter count between "true" postal voters and those who cast ballots by way of early ballot. Both are included in the postal vote quota. In the latter case, the "postal voter" applies for his or her voting documents in person at the municipality, fills them out directly on-site at the postal voting office and also drops them into the (postal) ballot box on site. This is possible within 4 weeks before the actual election date. In the case of the early ballot, there are no problems as described above. It is equivalent to a ballot box election. It is doubtful whether a constitutionally permissible exception will still be accepted by the Federal Constitutional Court in the future in the case of a high quota of "genuine" postal voters, where the public control of the vote, but also the freedom of choice and the secrecy of the ballot, is withdrawn.

---

[41] BVerfGE 134, 25 (para 13).

[42] Lindner (2020).

[43] The absentee ballot rate was 4.9% in 1957; 5.8% in 1961; 7.3% in 1965; 7.1% in 1969; 7.2% in 1972; 10.7% in 1976; 13% in 1980; 10.5% in 1983; 11.1% in 1987; 9.4% in 1990; 13.4% in 1994; 16% in 1998; 18% in 2002; 18.7% in 2005; 21.4% in 2009; 24.3% in 2013 and 28.6% in 2017.

[44] Absentee voting percentages in elections during the Corona pandemic: local elections NRW 13 September 2020 42.8%, state elections Baden-Württemberg 14 March 2021 51.5%, state elections Rhineland-Palatinate 14 March 2021 66.5%, state elections Saxony-Anhalt 06 June 2021 29.1%. See Ministerium des Innern des Landes Nordrhein-Westfalen (2022).

[45] Der Bundeswahlleiter (2021).

Within the framework of electoral regulations, a high level of protection against infection must be ensured: e.g. in the polling station, each voter should have his or her own writing utensil; polling booths and ballot boxes must be disinfected regularly and other hygiene and infection protection measures must, of course, be observed. The obligation to wear a mask also applies in the polling station, of course. The ban on the wearing of masks by electoral bodies, which is standardised in the electoral laws (e.g. Sec. 10 (2) (2) BWahlG), must be subject to an exemption for pandemic periods.

There were also exceptions to the electoral regulations in the flood disaster regions in Germany. Here, tents, containers or buses might also be used as voting rooms for the Bundestag election. This is permitted in the event that a designated voting room can no longer be used. Since many people in the flooded areas have lost their homes and, thus, their postal addresses, a special solution was also required with regard to registration in the electoral roll and the election notifications to be delivered. The State Election Commissioner recommended that, if necessary, the contents of the notifications could be made known to the public, for example by means of posters, via the Internet services of the municipalities, radio, television or newspapers. Applications for absentee ballots could also be submitted to the home municipalities or online without an election notification. This also applied to eligible voters who were unable to stay at their homes.[46]

6 Outlook

Pandemic times and natural disasters bring to light problems at the level of the organisation of Government action. The clear preponderance of Government action in times of crisis makes the already executive-heavy nature of many political decision-making processes even more apparent.[47] The countless rounds of the Minister-Presidents meeting with the Chancellor have produced countless state law decrees as the dominant regulatory instrument, in addition to the excessive power of some federal ministries to issue decrees. For long stretches of the crisis, the Parliaments were mere spectators. However, especially in times of crisis, the Bundestag and the State Parliaments must consistently exercise their responsibilities as legislators. Only in this way is it possible to create parliamentary transparency and win the trust of citizens for drastic governmental measures.

[46] See Ministerium des Innern des Landes Nordrhein-Westfalen (2022).

[47] See also Dreier (2021), pp. 229 et seq.

References

Borger S (2020) Corona sorgt im britischen Parlament für Modernisierungsschub. https://www.derstandard.de/story/2000117442541/corona-sorgt-im-britischen-parlament-fuer-modernisierungsschub. Accessed 31 May 2022

Brüning C (2021) Was wirklich nottut – Parlamentsroutine statt Notparlament. NVwZ 40:272–275

Der Bundesminister des Innern, für Bau und Heimat (2021) Verordnung über die Aufstellung von Wahlbewerbern und die Wahl der Vertreter für die Vertreterversammlungen für die Wahl zum 20. Deutschen Bundestag unter den Bedingungen der COVID-19-Pandemie (COVID-19-Wahlbewerberaufstellungsverordnung). Bundesgesetzblatt 2021/1:115–116

Der Bundeswahlleiter (2021) Bundestagswahl 2021: Anteil der Briefwählerinnen und Briefwähler bei 47,3%. https://www.bundeswahlleiter.de/info/presse/mitteilungen/bundestagswahl-2021/53_21_briefwahlbeteiligung.html. Accessed 31 May 2022

Der Präsident des Deutschen Bundestages (2020a) Bekanntmachung zur Änderung der Geschäftsordnung des Deutschen Bundestages. Bundesgesetzblatt 2020/1:764

Der Präsident des Deutschen Bundestages (2020b) Bekanntmachung zur Änderung der Geschäftsordnung des Deutschen Bundestages. Bundesgesetzblatt 2020/1:2067

Der Präsident des Deutschen Bundestages (2021a) Bekanntmachung zur Änderung der Geschäftsordnung des Deutschen Bundestages. Bundesgesetzblatt 2021/1:97

Der Präsident des Deutschen Bundestages (2021b) Bekanntmachung zur Änderung der Geschäftsordnung des Deutschen Bundestages. Bundesgesetzblatt 2021/1:2868

Deutscher Bundestag (2020a) Ausarbeitung WD 3 – 3000 – 084/20. https://www.bundestag.de/resource/blob/690270/07e7b1aff547a62bbc7477281574de2c/WD-3-084-20-pdf-data.pdf. Accessed 31 May 2022

Deutscher Bundestag (2020b) Beschlussempfehlung und Bericht des Ausschusses für Wahlprüfung, Immunität und Geschäftsordnung (1. Ausschuss). https://dserver.bundestag.de/btd/19/181/1918126.pdf. Accessed 31 May 2022

Deutscher Bundestag (2021) Parteien müssen weniger Unterstützungsunterschriften vorlegen. https://www.bundestag.de/parlament/bundestagswahl/parteien-unterschriften-848540. Accessed 31 May 2022

Dreier H (2021) Rechtsstaat, Föderalismus und Demokratie in der Corona-Pandemie. DÖV 74: 229–242

European Parliament (2020) How Parliament works during a pandemic. https://www.europarl.europa.eu/news/en/headlines/eu-affairs/20200408STO76807/how-parliament-works-during-a-pandemic. Accessed 31 May 2022

Hahlen J (2017) § 16 Wahltag. In: Schreiber W, Hahlen J, Strelen K (eds) Kommentar zum Bundeswahlgesetz unter Einbeziehung des Wahlprüfungsgesetzes, des Wahlstatistikgesetzes, der Bundeswahlordnung und sonstiger wahlrechtlicher Nebenvorschriften, 9th edn. Carl Heymanns Verlag, Cologne

Heining H et al (2020) Why Constitution Matters – Verfassungsrechtswissenschaft in Zeiten der Corona-Krise. JZ 75:861–872

Hoffmann H (2005) Souverän ist, wer über den Ausnahmezustand entscheidet. Der Staat 44:171–186

House of Commons (2020) House of Commons Chamber Proceedings during the COVID-19 pandemic. https://old.parliament.uk/about/how/covid-19-hybrid-proceedings-in-the-house-of-commons/. Accessed 31 May 2022

Kersten J, Rixen S (2021) Der Verfassungsstaat in der Corona-Krise, 2nd edn. C.H. Beck, Munich

KEYSTONE-SDA-ATS AG (2020) Auch im Juni tagt das Schweizer Parlament in der Bernexpo. https://www.parlament.ch/de/services/news/Seiten/2020/20200501175206575194158159041_bsd178.aspx. Accessed 31 May 2022

Klein H, Schwarz K (2021) Artikel 38. In: Dürig G, Herzog R, Scholz R (eds) Grundgesetz-Kommentar, 95th supplement. C.H. Beck, Munich

Landtag Nordrhein-Westfalen (2020) Drucksache 17/11681. https://www.landtag.nrw.de/portal/WWW/dokumentenarchiv/Dokument/MMD17-11681.pdf. Accessed 31 May 2022

Lenz C, Schulte H (2020) Sitzungen des Bundestags per Videokonferenz: Gehst du noch hin oder streamst du schon? NVwZ 39:744–749

Lindner JF (2020) Wahlen in Zeiten von Corona Teil 2: Infektionsschutzrecht bricht doch Wahlrecht? https://verfassungsblog.de/wahlen-in-zeiten-von-corona-teil-2/. Accessed 31 May 2022

Marschall S (2020) Parlamente in der Krise? Der deutsche Parlamentarismus und die Corona-Pandemie. APuZ 38:11–17

Merten H (2019) Nach der Wahl ist vor der Wahl. JöR 67:107–137

Merten H (2020) Wahlen auf Abstand, Rechtliche Fragestellungen zu den Kommunalwahlen 2020 in NRW unter Pandemiebedingungen, Kurzanalyse. https://regierungsforschung.de/wahlen-auf-abstand/. Accessed 31 May 2022

Merten H (2021a) Wahlen in Pandemiezeiten – ein juristische Risikogebiet. Z Politikwiss 31:61–69. https://doi.org/10.1007/s41358-021-00259-2

Merten H (2021b) Wählen in Zeiten der Pandemie – Herausforderungen und Probleme. APuZ 47–49:26–33

Michl F (2020) Der demokratische Rechtsstaat in Krisenzeiten. JuS 60:507–510

Michl F (2021a) Bundestag mach Unmögliches möglich: Aufstellung von Kandidaten für die Bundestagswahl. https://verfassungsblog.de/bundestag-macht-unmogliches-moglich/. Accessed 31 May 2022

Michl F (2021b) Anything goes! – Zur Aufstellung von Wahlbewerbern in der Covid-19-Pandemie. MIP 27:29–36

Ministerium des Innern des Landes Nordrhein-Westfalen (2022) Häufige Fragen. https://www.im.nrw/haeufige-fragen-2. Accessed 31 May 2022

Möllers C (2020) Über den Schutz der Parlamente vor sich selbst in der Krise. https://verfassungsblog.de/ueber-den-schutz-der-parlamente-vor-sich-selbst-in-der-krise/. Accessed 31 May 2022

Orlowski F (2020) Entvölkerte Wahllokale – Trotz oder wegen der Pandemie? Die Briefwahl ist zu Recht umstritten, kann aber in akuten Krisenzeiten eine legale Handlungsoption darstellen. Eine juristische Analyse. https://regierungsforschung.de/entvoelkerte-wahllokale-trotz-oder-wegen-der-pandemie/. Accessed 31 May 2022

Orlowski F, Pohlmann S (2020) Die Briefwahl: Ein scharfes Schwert im Kampf gegen Epidemien? Überlegungen anlässlich kommunaler "Zwangsbriefwahlen". MIP 26:38–43

Roßmann R (2020a) Wie der Bundestag virtuell tagen könnte. https://www.sueddeutsche.de/politik/virtueller-bundestag-corona-schaeuble-digitaler-1.4874777. Accessed 31 May 2022

Roßmann R (2020b) Ein Rettungspaket für den Bundestag. https://www.sueddeutsche.de/politik/corona-bundestag-schaeuble-1.4867460. Accessed 31 May 2022

Schmidt C (1934) Politische Theologie – Vier Kapitel zur Lehre von der Staatssouveränität. Duncker & Humblot, Berlin

Schönberger C (2016) Vom Verschwinden der Anwesenheit in der Demokratie. JZ 71:486–494

Schönberger C, Schönberger S (2020) Regiert bald ein Notausschuss? https://www.faz.net/aktuell/feuilleton/debatten/corona-pandemie-zur-bedeutung-des-bundestags-16696222.html. Accessed 31 May 2022

Schönberger S (2021) Zwischen Parteitag und Fernsehshow – Parteienrecht in Zeiten der Corona-Pandemie. MIP 27:22–28

von Notz A (2020). It's Democracy, Stupid! Von einem Gesetzgeber, der dem Bundesinnenministerium in Demokratiefragen mehr zutraut als den politischen Parteien. https://verfassungsblog.de/its-democracy-stupid/. Accessed 31 May 2022

Wollenschläger F (2021) Die COVID-19-Pandemie als Stunde der Exekutive und die parlamentarische Demokratie des Grundgesetzes – Möglichkeiten und Grenzen exekutiver Rechtssetzungsbefugnisse als Instrument der Pandemiebekämpfung in 50 Jahre Juristische Fakultät Augsburg (eds) Koch et al. Mohr Siebeck Tübingen, pp. 651–704

COVID-19 and the Federal State

The German Experience

Ekkehard Hofmann

Abstract After almost two years through the pandemic, COVID-19 has proven to be a considerable and specific challenge for liberal states such as the Federal Republic of Germany. Its constitution requires state actors on all levels to take action to protect its citizens against risks entailed by infectious diseases, but also to respect the rule of law and fundamental rights, data protection legislation and institutional arrangements, particularly the relationship between the central level ("Bund") and the states ("Länder"). As it turns out, this federalist structure does not provide for an adequate legal framework when it comes to global pandemics such as COVID-19.

1 Introduction

Liberal states that respect the rule of law are facing an enormous task when it comes to fighting the spread of infectious diseases such as COVID-19 and curb excess mortality, combat and alleviate economic consequences of lockdowns and ensuring access to education and providing daycare options for families all at the same time. Given the unique and never-experienced-before nature of the pandemic, its dimensions required states to turn to tentative, constantly amended measures, and the willingness to deal with the fact that drastic steps had to be taken that needed justification, in a political and a legal sense. [1] The analysis below suggests that in most cases, the legislature and the executive branch of government were able to provide sufficient legal justification, given the leeway the courts were willing to grant the authorities under the given abnormal circumstances. Political justification, however, appears to have vanished to an extent that may give rise to alarm, if one takes regard of the outcome of the German general election in September 2021.

[1] *Beckmann*, UPR (2021), pp. 241, 249.

E. Hofmann (✉)
Faculty of Law, University of Trier, Trier, Germany
e-mail: hofmann@uni-trier.de

K. Chrysogonos, A. Tsiftsoglou (eds.), *Democracy after Covid*,
https://doi.org/10.1007/978-3-031-13901-7_5

The following considerations observe that the anti-COVID-19 strategy in many countries including Germany rested on two pillars. In the first phase of 2020 and at the time of writing in some respects still ongoing, restrictions were imposed that were supposed to limit the number of contacts, by closing down shops, restaurants, and other venues including schools and daycare centers, putting into place a quarantine regime for people that run the risk of being infectious or being even positively tested for COVID-19, requiring the public to wear masks and keep their distance from each other wherever possible. The general approach was to put anti-COVID restrictions only as long in place as case numbers were so high the death rate was surging. Whenever the mortality rate seemed to be under control and case numbers went down, restrictions were lifted again. This lead to a yo-yo-shape of the case numbers. [2] A no-COVID strategy was put on the table by a group of scientists, [3] but never had a chance in the real world.

In the second phase, initiated by the availability of vaccines in spring 2021, the vaccination campaigns started, by which most countries in the EU tried to keep case numbers, hospitality and mortality rates down. If you do not wish to follow the Chinese example of drastically policing these sets of measures, both now overlapping approaches do fundamentally rely on the willingness of the public to readily embrace the mentioned policies and actively participate in the collective effort to bring the pandemic to a halt as soon as possible. Therefore, the response of liberal states to COVID-19 should establish a legal framework that presents itself as simple, accessible, comprehensible and coherent over time and place.

The German response, for the most part, did not fit that description. Legislators worked up an impressive amount of legal acts, full of technical wording, and only to some extent accessible to the public in a practical sense. Part of that choice is due to the fact that Germany is a federal country whose constitution gives the states a huge influence on how policies are put into practice even if the respective field of law concerns a national, even global issue such as a pandemic. The chapter, firstly, explains this particular constitutional structure (Sect. 2). Secondly, it will inquire into the inadequacies brought about during the course of the implementation of the Federal Infectious Diseases Act ("FIDA") (Sects. 3 and 4). It concludes with a summary and outlook (Sect. 4).

[2] *McKeever* (2020) https://www.cnbc.com/2020/11/06/why-germanys-coronavirus-strategy-doesnt-appear-to-be-working.html. Accessed 31 May 2022.

[3] For this proposal, see https://www.ndr.de/nocovid100.pdf. Accessed 15 March 2022; it argues along the lines of *Pueyo* (2021), s. https://tomaspueyo.medium.com/coronavirus-the-hammer-and-the-dance-be9337092b56. Accessed 31 May 2022.

2 Federalism Under German Constitutional Law

Under the German Constitution ("Grundgesetz", GG), legislative power stems, in principle and save other constitutional stipulations, from the states ("Länder"). Art. 70 GG reads:

> (1) The Länder shall have the right to legislate insofar as this Basic Law does not confer legislative power on the Federation. [4]

The GG does, however, confer legislative power on the Federation in multiple ways, in the first place by allowing the Federation to legislate on all matters included in the so-called "Exclusive legislative power of the Federation" (Art. 71 GG), and the vast list of matters that Art. 74 GG ("Matters under concurrent legislative powers") features. Taken together, the GG endows the Federation with the power to make laws in the overwhelming majority of legal fields. As far as the Federation passes legislation, it overrules any provisions on the level of the states. Making things somewhat complicated, this does not imply that the Federation is also in charge of the implementation of all the areas in which it has legislative powers. Quite on the contrary, it is the main task and power of the states to execute legal acts, may they be of state or federal origin. This arrangement presents a substantial limitation of the powers of the Federation since most acts fall under the administrative competence of the *Länder*, who are in charge of implementing their own acts and the acts of the Federation as their sole responsibility, i.e. without having to answer to the Federation, as Art. 83 GG puts it:

> The Länder shall execute federal laws in their own right insofar as this Basic Law does not otherwise provide or permit. [5]

Only a few exceptions to this rule exist (e.g. Art. 84 Sec. 1 sentence 5 GG). These exceptions are interesting (s. below Sect. 3.1.1), but as a result of this general division of labor, it is the *Länder* that are in charge of the implementation of most legislative acts in Germany. The legislation on the protection against infectious diseases includes the Federal Infectious Diseases Act (FIDA, Infektionsschutzgesetz), which had been amended numerous times during the pandemic. [6] Its provisions preclude any state legislation. However, matters that are not (fully) addressed within the meaning of the stipulations of the federal act, are subject to the states' legislative authority pursuant to the above-mentioned Art. 70 GG.

---

[4] https://www.gesetze-im-internet.de/englisch_gg/englisch_gg.html#p0321. Accessed 31 May 2022.

[5] https://www.gesetze-im-internet.de/englisch_gg/englisch_gg.html#p0321. Accessed 31 May 2022.

[6] Gesetz zur Verhütung und Bekämpfung von Infektionskrankheiten beim Menschen (Infektionsschutzgesetz – IfSG, G. v. 20.7.2000 BGBl. I S. 1045; last amended by Article 8 G. v. 27.09.2021 BGBl. I S. 4530. Essential Parts of the FIDA have been approved by the German Federal Constitutional Court (Bundesverfassungsgericht), judgment dated 19 November 2021, 1 BvR 781/21, http://www.bverfg.de/e/rs20211119_1bvr078121.html. Accessed 31 May 2022.

3 The Federal Infectious Diseases Act ("FIDA", "Infektionsschutzgesetz") and Its Implementation

3.1 The "Federal Emergency Brake" and State Regulations

To exemplify, the Federal Infectious Diseases Act (FIDA) has its constitutional basis in Art. 74 Sec. 1 No. 19 GG that entitles the Federation to pass legislation on

> measures to combat human and animal diseases which pose a danger to the public or are communicable. [7]

The FIDA, in the form of one of its various current amendments, regulated how the public authorities should respond to the disease whenever the number of COVID-19 cases as a seven-day average per 100,000 people exceeds 100 (Sec. 28b FIDA, applicable between 23 April 2021 through 30 June 2021, and whenever the Federal Parliament (Bundestag) declares an epidemic emergency of national dimension (Sec. 5 Subsec. 1 sentence 1 FIDA), but no later than 30 June 2021), it does not answer the question as to what they should do whenever the number is below 100. This is the realm of Sec. 28a FIDA, as long the state of emergency pursuant to Sec. 5 Sec. 1 FIDA endures, but not accompanied by case numbers above the threshold of 100 cases per 100,000 people, and state legislature, of which 16 different variants exist. [8] As a result, the amount of applicable law gets multiplied by 16 whenever and wherever federal law does not preclude the enactment of state law.

But even if federal law exists, and the states are in charge of implementing it, 16 different variants of interpretation are not the exception, they are the rule, resulting in a vast number of cases before the courts of justice. In Bavaria alone, courts had to rule on 70,000 cases concerning COVID-19 related fines, in addition to roughly 25,000 cases of subsidy fraud in the Federal Republic. [9] This creates a vast number of legal substance. That is why the German constitution established Federal Courts of Justice that are supposed to harmonise, if necessary, diverting interpretations of federal provisions. But this process regularly takes years until Federal Courts have a final chance to clarify the meaning of federal statutes. Moreover, federal law can be extensive, too. Sec. 28b FIDA alone comprises 2461 words. Its provisions include the schooling sector, detailing the requirements for face-to-face classes in certain and different types of schools (Sec. 28b Sec. 3 FIDA). This is remarkable since without the declaration of an epidemic emergency of national dimension, school law is a matter for which the states have exclusive legislative powers. On the other hand, Sec. 28b FIDA does not extend to the areas of political

---

[7] https://www.gesetze-im-internet.de/englisch_gg/englisch_gg.html#p0321. Accessed 31 May 2022.

[8] *Lang* et al. (2021) https://www.twobirds.com/de/news/articles/2021/germany/covid-19-verordnungen-und-verfuegungen-bl. Accessed 31 May 2022.

[9] *Steiner*, DVP (2021), p. 257.

demonstrations and religious gatherings (Sec. 28b Subsec. 4 FIDA) which transfers the responsibility for these matters back to the states. [10]

Given that 16 different state courts of justice have the power to accept or set aside COVID-19 related restrictions such as mask wearing obligations, opening hours and conditions of use for shops, restaurants and bars, it is quite obvious that a multitude of norms apply and demand obeyance. They particularly address social distancing rules, how many people are allowed to gather in apartments, in private and public buildings, and for what purposes, which kind of sports are allowed, the details of overnight curfews, who is subject to quarantine for which duration, what the conditions for shortening the duration of quarantines are, which public authority to inform and in which manner if you enter the Federal Republic of Germany (and one of its states), the status of vaccinated, recovered and tested people, and so on. These provisions were subject to frequent amendments that contributed to a chaotic and obscure as frequently changing legal framework. In North-Rhine Westphalia alone, parliament and state executive issued 45 ordinances within the course of 15 weeks—e.g. three per week. [11]

In sum, German lawmakers produced an impressive amount of law, rendering the applicable legal framework quite complex, particularly because of the high degree of variety in details relevant to the implementation.

3.1.1 Direct Federal Implementation in Emergency Cases?

At least in theory, it would mitigate the issue of variety, if a federal norm would be implemented by federal public authorities. The German Constitution recognises such a solution, and embraces it by granting the Federation the power to regulate the administrative procedure:

> "In exceptional cases, owing to a special need for uniform federal legislation, the Federation may regulate the administrative procedure with no possibility of separate Land legislation", Art. 84 Sec. 1 Sentence 5 GG. [12]

It also empowers the Federal Government, with the consent of the Bundesrat, to issue general administrative provisions (Art. 84 Sec. 2 GG). The German Constitution also grants the Federal Government the power to exercise oversight to ensure that the Länder execute federal laws in accordance with the law (Art. 84 Sec. 3 sentence 1 GG). These options, however, do not include federal implementation by adjudication as a single-case (Sec. 35 Sentence 1 Verwaltungsverfahrensgesetz, Administrative Procedure Act, Verwaltungsakt) or general provision that deal with a delineated situation (Sec. 35 Sentence 2 Verwaltungsverfahrensgesetz, Allgemeinverfügung). But this is exactly what federal lawmakers added to the

---

[10] Art. 125a Sec. 1 GG; *Steiner*, DVP (2021), p. 258.

[11] Figures according to *Behnke*, APuZ (2020), p. 13.

[12] https://www.gesetze-im-internet.de/englisch_gg/englisch_gg.html#p0321. Accessed 31 May 2022.

FIDA by allowing the federal Ministry of Health to issue "Anordnungen" (administrative acts, Sec. 5 Subsec. 2 No. 1, 2, and 6 FIDA) for a number of different reasons. Since unwritten executive powers are also not available, the said provisions FIDA were deemed to be unconstitutional, [13] and in the meantime amended, revoking Nos. 1 and 2 of Sec. 5 Subsec. 2 FIDA.

3.1.2 Reducing Complexity by Coordination?

Sec. 28a FIDA comprises a comprehensive list of possible measures that could be put into place in a cumulative manner. To coordinate the measures nationwide, the states occasionally held meetings with the federal level. This was supposed to encourage a coordinated response to a global health threat. Most of these meetings ended with conclusions the majority of members agreed upon. However, frequently the states added reservations and other dissenting opinions. Even if they did not do that in a formal way, they acted differently, deviating from the general consent found in the meetings. As to the obligation to wear a mask in public, a meeting of that kind was held on 15 April 2020, discussing that topic, and in the aftermath of which some states introduced such a legal obligation, while others did not. Some of them even put a fine on not wearing a mask, some of them did not. The same goes for night-time curfews, which some states put into law, others relied upon government appeals and the willingness of people to voluntarily act responsibly and refrain themselves from going out.

3.1.3 Immigration Procedures Under COVID-19 as a Field of Reference

3.1.3.1 Restrictions: Quarantine

As these events created, in sum, a chaotic and complex framework of norms, their implementation entailed another issue that calls for further inquiry, i.e. the accessibility of norms. Consider the field of immigration procedures. If traveling to Germany, you have to register online if you come from a country that is declared to be a risk area. [14] At the same time, when you enter the Federal Republic of Germany, you also enter one of the 16 states, and hence, into the territory of another legislator, a state ("Land"), that is responsible for regulating the issues of who, if, how long and under which circumstances you might be required to quarantine yourself. These ordinances are only available in German. Even if you speak German, it helps if you are a legal professional, if you want to obtain the answers to these

[13] *Dreier*, DÖV (2021), pp. 229, 240; *Kersten and Rixen* (2020), p. 121; *Ritgen*, ZG (2021), pp. 1, 13; Wissenschaftliche Dienste des Deutschen Bundestags, Staatsorganisation und § 5 IfSG, Ausarbeitung v. 2.4.2020, WD 3 - 3000 -080/20, 10.

[14] https://www.einreiseanmeldung.de. Accessed 31 May 2022.

questions. To exemplify, the consolidated ordinance of the State of Hesse, dated 22 June 2021, updated by 25 September, 21, comprises 26 pages. [15] It includes stipulations on the obligation to wear a mask, restrictions to entry regarding certain sensitive areas such as hospitals and daycare institutions, and about the duration of quarantine. The regular word for quarantine in German is "Quarantäne", which you might know, albeit the ordinance uses the word "Absonderung". So even if know that the Federation and the State have different regulations that apply to your process of entering the country, you would have to be quite fluent in German, capable of tracking down the pertinent ordinances, and aware of the fact that quarantine is called "Absonderung" to find the relevant sections of said ordinance (e.g. Section 7). Section 7 of the said Hessian ordinance has eight subsections and a word count of more than 5,500 words. This is more than this chapter has. The picture is only slightly mitigated by the fact that some of the most important rules are explained and summarised, in German language of course, on a well laid-out webpage. [16]

To exacerbate the experience, it gets more complicated if you enter one of the states but only to travel to another place in Germany that may be situated in a different state. So even if you speak German, wish to follow the rules and are capable of tracking down information on your obligation to quarantine yourself (typically for 10 days after arrival), you would still need to find out if your 10-day-self-isolation could be shortened up (typically down to five days), if you provide for a second negative COVID-19 test result. In May 2021, this was the regular applicable legal framework in many German states. It would require you to identify the competent authorities (which are the local, communal ones, of course), then you would have to contact them and get this kind of information. The webpages of the communal health authorities typically did not provide you with the details of which kind of test you would have to take (PCR, PoC-PCR, rapid test, quick test?), where (yourself, any doctor, only at certain test centers?), and in which way to communicate the test results back to the local authorities. Sometimes, calling them on the phone by using their switchboard number would not work as they would have to refer to you a "Corona-Hotline", and calling the "Corona-Hotline" would only reveal the information that a PCR-test would suffice, which would entail a 75-Euro-bill and a waiting time for the return of the results for at least one day. In contrast, a rapid test was at that time for free (at least for German citizens) and available within one hour after the smear. You could, however, finally get your answer if you wrote an email to the competent health authority, and hope to receive a reply from them within hours informing you that a rapid test is sufficient, and the results should be sent to a specified email-address to which you should also attach the PDF of your first negative COVID-test result you needed before entering the plane you took for flying to Germany. If you travelled by car or on foot, there is no parallel way of ensuring that this procedure would work.

[15] https://hessen.de/sites/hessen.hessen.de/files/2021-10/lf_coschuv_stand_25.09.21.pdf. Accessed 31 May 2022.

[16] https://www.hessen.de/Handeln/Corona-in-Hessen. Accessed 31 May 2022.

3.1.3.2 Vaccination Campaign

In the ensuing phase of anti-COVID measures, getting people vaccinated is of utmost importance to keep fatalities down. To allocate the vaccines where they are needed most, the Federal vaccination regulation prioritised certain groups of the population. If you work for a qualified employer such as the state administration, they could certify that you work in a particularly important position. [17] This would prioritise you for a vaccination appointment. It is unclear whether your employer in, for example, in Rhineland-Palatinate, could issue a valid prioritisation certificate for your vaccination appointment that is made in the state of your residence, which does not need to be in Rhineland-Palatinate but could be elsewhere. It could be even in a foreign country, given the geographical situation of Germany, effectively precluding you from any prioritisation issued by a foreign employer with regard to your German place of residence. And if you registered your wish to be vaccinated with your local public authorities of residence, in the hope they would recognise your prioritisation, you would receive a message that confirmed your registration, giving you no further information whatsoever.

It might have been useful at that point of time to be enlightened about where you would be vaccinated, if certain medical conditions could exclude you from becoming vaccinated you could take care of in the meantime, or when, given as an estimate based on the current rate of vaccinations, you could expect to get your appointment. Once you receive that message ("Subject: Your Vaccination Appointment" (in German)), you would, in the case of Hesse, not find the date of your appointment in the text section of that message, but on page 3 in one of the four PDF-files that are attached to the message. It is hard to imagine that anyone of retirement age or older would have been easily able or willing to follow that procedure.

3.2 Tentative Conclusions

Of course, these observations are mostly anecdotal and restrained to the perspective of people travelling to Germany from abroad, but if you add the practice of state Prime Ministers one day after having had a meeting with all their colleagues and the Federal Ministries, announcing that they would not adhere to the conclusions of the meeting as to the current COVID fighting measures, because apparently the situation in their state was different compared to the others, it is not that surprising that a considerable portion of the populace was not thrilled by the political responses to the pandemic. However, Germany got through the pandemic seemingly as well or even better as other European countries, if you compare key indicators including the

[17] Sec. 4 Subsec. 1 No. 5 Coronavirus-Impfverordnung – CoronaImpfV, 31.3.2021, BAnz AT 01.04.2021 V1.

fatality rate, case numbers and the numbers of ICU patients. [18] A more coordinated and transparent response might have helped to even perform better, [19] given the fact that even countries such as Spain, Portugal and Chile have a higher rate of people fully vaccinated by October 2021 than Germany. [20] Considering this mediocre score, and if the above observations have some truth to them that could be generalised, the suspicion seems to be warranted that there is a worrisome inadequacy between modern challenges such as COVID-19 as a global disease, the use (or failing of use) of technological and scientific methods (digitalisation and genetic engineering), and the means and ways German public authorities addressed them.

4 The Inadequacy of the German Approach

The general supposition one could take from the observations above could be that the highly bureaucratic approach mainly chosen by government bodies in Germany focused on elaborating extensive legislation in the hope of covering all cases one could think of, limited by the territorial boundaries of each legislative body. Although highly embedded in a constitutional framework that rests on the rule of law and on sovereignty emanating from the states ("Länder") and their federation, this is a nineteenth-century approach applied to a twenty-first-century problem. A situation that calls for a globally coordinated, swift, effective, reasonable and comprehensible state response should be met accordingly. The German response falls short of that in many respects, partly because of its federalist constitution.

4.1 Federal Constitutions to the Rescue?

In defense of federalist structures, many observers argue that a federalist system is (i) a safeguard to civil liberties and (ii) a resilient and flexible design that is able to address health issues on a regional or even local level. [21] With regard to COVID-19, these features and preconditions are not necessarily present. SARS-CoV-2 is a global disease that does not fit the main features of the problems that were guiding the fathers and mothers of the German Grundgesetz and therefore does not meet the

[18] https://ourworldindata.org/explorers/coronavirus-data-explorer?zoomToSelection=true&time=2020-03-01..latest&facet=none&pickerSort=desc&pickerMetric=total_cases&hideControls=true&Metric=Confirmed+cases&Interval=7-day+rolling+average&Relative+to+Population=true&Align+outbreaks=false&country=GBR~DEU~FRA~GRC. Accessed 31 May 2022.

[19] *Giesberts* et al. NVwZ (2020), pp. 417, 418.

[20] https://ourworldindata.org/covid-vaccinations. Accessed 31 May 2022.

[21] *Kloepfer*, VerwArch (2021), pp. 169, 199; *Kersten and Rixen* (2021), p. 115; *Dreier*, DÖV (2021), pp. 229, 231.

adequacy conditions for finding solutions. In the nineteenth century, and mostly also 1949, health issues were of local, maybe regional nature, and they were not at the center of the debates. The Spanish flu was almost forgotten and creating a new German state after the holocaust and the Second World War was for sure not mainly interested in establishing a structure that would be able to deal with a global health crisis. The typical outbreak of measles in a school or in a hotel was much more like the guiding image these structures were made for. [22] The whole FIDA is designed to combat already known diseases, not a new one. [23] Its main features assume that the outbreaks of infectious diseases remained quite local and were of temporary nature. COVID-19 is none of that. [24]

However, advocates of German federalism hold that even with regard to COVID-19, the constitutional entitlement to follow different approaches allowed for a competition in search for the best solution. [25] This variety is deemed to represent a flexible instrument that allows for reacting adequately to local circumstances. [26] If necessary, states could ask for the help of other public entities including other states and the Federal Armed Forces. [27] Moreover, if one of the states sets up a strategy that turns out not to be not working, at least this failure would not extend to the other states. [28] This is true, but could be remedied even within a more federal concept, if it included deviations from the main, national strategy, allowing some of the regions or even states to try out other approaches under supervision and scientific monitoring.

It should be worth noting, nonetheless, that the assumption that a separation of power between states ("Länder") among themselves and the central level fosters checks and balances by putting any restrictive approach under observation and control by other competing entities, is hard to prove, maybe even impossible. [29] As far as political control is concerned by voting decisions, it is difficult to imagine that voters could be driven by an evaluation of their own state's COVID-19 policies in comparison to others. Not many of them would have a chance to assess the approach of a different state. They almost certainly would not leave their state of residence because of frustration in such a single issue. In contrast, as described above, a federalist approach certainly creates a multitude of transaction costs yet that undermine the efficacy of the measures. [30] It also does not help, if equally or

[22] *Dreier*, DÖV (2021), pp. 229, 231.

[23] *Lepsius*, Recht und Politik (2020), pp. 258, 268.

[24] *Papier*, APuZ (2020), pp. 4, 8.

[25] *Kloepfer*, VerwArch (2021), pp. 169, 199; *Kersten and Rixen* (2021), p. 115; *Behnke*, APuZ (2020), pp. 9, 12; *Lepsius*, Recht und Politik (2020), pp. 258, 264; *Gusy*, Recht und Politik (2020), pp. 139, 141.

[26] *Ritgen*, *ZG* (2021), pp. 1, 10.

[27] *Ritgen*, ZG (2021), pp. 1, 1.

[28] *Kloepfer*, VerwArch (2021), pp. 169, 199.

[29] *Behnke*, APuZ (2020), pp. , 9, 14.

[30] *Gusy*, DÖV (2021), pp. 757, 761.

comparably incompetent public bodies compete and present equally not effective approaches. They are only multiplying the errors.

4.2 *State Public Health Authorities: Under-Staffed, Under-Equipped*

To allow for powerful, resilient and sustainable efforts to combat COVID-19, public authorities need sufficient manpower, for example for tracing positive test results, and up to date technology for transferring test result data. State public health authorities in Germany may have been able to deal with a "normal" public health situation, but they have proven not to be adequately equipped in both areas given the magnitude of COVID-19. [31] In the last five decades, the German states, not being capable of amply funding the implementation of the ever increasing number of executive tasks given to them by state and federal legislation, took to the option of shifting the responsibilities of the specialised public health authorities to the "general police" to economise on personnel. [32] Some states merged public health authorities for the same reason. This procedure, however, creates greater physical distances to their "battle grounds", which somewhat contradicts the general idea of how a public administration should be organised at the bottom level. [33]

On top of the dire issue of staff and equipment, the outlined approach that puts a lot of effort into devising legally unimpeachable legislation and acts of implementation, takes away from skillfully addressing the matter of communication. If both pillars of anti-COVID-19 measures, decreasing contacts by restrictions, and the vaccination campaign, rely upon the willingness of the public to participate in these collective efforts, the measures should be understandable, the justifying reasons easily accessible and the norms on which they are based quickly available. This is not the case with German COVID-19 politics, and if you add the need for developing a coherent and comprehensible strategy in Europe and hopefully the world, the picture gets even more alarming.

[31] Although advocates for a federalist system, *Kersten and Rixen* (2021), p. 119, admit this; s. also *Steiner*, DVP (2021), pp. 257, 259.

[32] *Kersten and Rixen* (2021), p. 120.

[33] *Kersten and Rixen* (2021), p. 121.

5 Summary and Outlook

In a globalised world, international travel and commerce are woven into the fabric of the economy and as well as the widespread cultural expectation of multilateralism. [34] Open borders and free trade as conceptual pillars are not undisputed but have proven to provide for a peaceful and sound development in many parts of the world. Now if you look at COVID-19 abatement regimes that differ not only from country to country, but from state to state and even from region to region, legal complexity transforms into a substantial obstacle to trans-border commerce and trade, to ignorance even by the willing and informed, and even to some degree straightforward rejection towards the restrictions put upon the citizenry. These consequences should not be taken lightly. The ultra-right wing "Alternative für Deutschland, AfD" gained the majority of votes in some parts of Germany in the general election of 2021, which of course cannot be attributed to the state response to the pandemic alone. But responding let us say in town A in a certain way, and in town B based on a different strategy, resulting in an incompatible or at least incoherent other way, certainly encouraged some voters to suspect that public authorities did not follow a scientifically valid and effective concept but were led by other motives or even did not really know what they were doing. Both suspicions have the power to undermine the functioning of a liberal parliamentary democracy.

References

Beckmann M (2021) Das Bundesverfassungsgericht, der Klimawandel und der "intertemporale Freiheitsschutz". UPR 2021:241–251

Behnke N (2020) Föderalismus in der (Corona-)Krise? In: bpb (ed), Corona-Krise, APuZ (70) 35-37/2020, 9-15.

Dreier H (2021) Rechtsstaat, Föderalismus und Demokratie in der Corona-Pandemie. DÖV 74(2021):229–243

Giesberts L, Gayger M, Weyand P (2020) COVID-19 – Hoheitliche Befugnisse, Rechte Betroffener und staatliche Hilfen. NVwZ 39(2020):417–423

Gusy C (2020) Grundrechte unter Quarantäne? Recht und Politik 56(2020):139–141

Gusy C (2021) Pandemien als Stresstest der Demokratie. DÖV 74(2021):757–766

Hofmann H (2021) Das "Corona-Recht" – Zwischen verfassungsgemäßer Rechtsetzung unioperativ-notwendiger Krisenreaktion. ZG 36(2021):109–129

Kersten J, Rixen S (2020) Der Verfassungsstaat in der Corona-Krise, 2020, pp 111–133

Kloepfer M (2021) Verfassungsschwäche durch Pandemiebekämpfung. VerwArch 112:169–204

Lang M, Büscher T, Holtermann A (2021) COVID-19: Übersicht der Verfügungen und Verordnungen von Bund und Ländern, https://www.twobirds.com/de/news/articles/2021/germany/covid-19-verordnungen-und-verfuegungen-bl. Accessed 31 May 2022.

Lepsius O (2020) Grundrechtsschutz in der Corona-Pandemie. Recht und Politik 56(2020): 258–281

---

[34] Also *Hans Hofmann*, ZG (2/2021), pp. 109, 129.

McKeever V (2020) Why Germany's coronavirus strategy doesn't appear to be working this time around, https://www.cnbc.com/2020/11/06/why-germanys-coronavirus-strategy-doesnt-appear-to-be-working.html. Accessed 31 May 2022.

Papier H-J (2020) Verfassungsrechtliche Perspektiven. In: bpb (ed), Corona-Krise, APuZ (70) 35-37/2020, 4-8

Pueyo T (2021) Coronavirus: The Hammer and the Dance. https://tomaspueyo.medium.com/coronavirus-the-hammer-and-the-dance-be9337092b56. Accessed 31 May 2022.

Ritgen K (2021) Gesetzgebung in Krisenzeiten – die Entwicklung des Infektionsschutzrechts während der Corona-Pandemie. ZG 35:1–24

Steiner U (2021) Regieren in der Pandemie. DVP 72:257–259

The COVID-19 Pandemic in Cyprus: A Problematic Legal Regime, and the Potential of Rule of Law in Emergencies

Costas Stratilatis

Abstract In the first part of this chapter, we shall argue that the legal regime under which most of the COVID-19 measures were adopted in Cyprus is problematic both from the standpoint of the democratic principle and from the standpoint of the meta-principle of rule of law. In the second part, in the context of an analysis of the path that the Republic of Cyprus did not follow, i.e. a Proclamation of Emergency under Art. 183 of the Constitution, we shall see how a "compulsion of legality" (Dyzenhaus) was incorporated into the emergency doctrine upon which the operation of the constitutional order of Cyprus has been based since 1964. The doctrine of necessity in Cyprus illustrates the potential of the rule of law even in emergencies. The "compulsion of legality" which animates the Cypriot version of the doctrine of necessity affirms the importance of legislative action and of judicial review. At least on COVID-19 measures, this compulsion should orient courts away from constructions (such as the doctrine of "*actes de gouvernement*") which insulate executive action from judicial scrutiny.

1 Introduction

Cyprus remains a divided island as the Turkish army continues occupying more than one third of its territory—the occupied part of the island is administered by the "Turkish Republic of Northern Cyprus",[1] an illegal entity[2] recognised only by

I would like to thank Professor Achilles Emilianides for his crucial (as always) suggestions.

[1] See European Court of Human Rights (Grand Chamber), *Loizidou v. Turkey*, judgment of 18 December 1996, app. no. 15318/89, paras 52–56.

[2] Ibid. paras 19–23, 42, 44 (citing the relevant resolutions of the United Nations Security Council and other international documents).

C. Stratilatis (✉)
School of Law, University of Nicosia, Nicosia, Cyprus
e-mail: stratilatis.c@unic.ac.cy

K. Chrysogonos, A. Tsiftsoglou (eds.), *Democracy after Covid*,
https://doi.org/10.1007/978-3-031-13901-7_6

Turkey. As the European Court of Human Rights has found, this state of affairs entails continuing violations of the human rights (a) of missing persons and of their relatives (rights to life and to personal liberty on account of the failure of Turkish authorities to conduct effective investigation, right of relatives not to be subjected to inhuman treatment); (b) of the misplaced persons (right to return to their homes, property rights); and (c) of those Greek Cypriots who keep living in Northern Cyprus (religious freedom, freedom of expression, right to education, respect for their private and family life, respect for their correspondence, respect for their home, property rights, right not to be subjected to discrimination amounting to degrading treatment).[3] The pandemic exacerbated these, and some other relevant, human rights problems, mostly as a result of the closure of the crossing points across the Green Line which separates the two parts of the island.[4] The pandemic had a negative impact upon the work of the twelve bicommunal technical committees (some of which relevant with the protection of human rights), but the United Nations Peace-keeping Force in Cyprus (UNFICYP) was able to facilitate exchanges of medication and medical equipment, and the crossing of patients for medical treatment across the Green Line.[5] On the level of the peace process, despite the efforts of the UN Secretary-General Guterres to revitalise it, the result of the informal meeting of the leaders of the two communities and of representatives of the three guarantor powers (the UK, Greece and Turkey) in Switzerland in April 2021 was disappointing. In July 2021, the authorities in Northern Cyprus announced the further reopening of a part of the fenced-off Varosha area, an act which the UN Security Council condemned as violating previous resolutions.[6]

The measures that were adopted in the "free part" of the island (i.e. the part that is controlled by the Republic of Cyprus) included general and local lockdowns; curfews and other limitations upon free movement; social distancing and use-of-mask rules; travel restrictions to and from Cyprus including bans on flights for certain periods; prohibitions of gatherings and a ban on public assemblies and demonstrations; the closure of schools and of universities for certain periods; restrictions on church mass and other religious worship activities; measures intending to protect students as they returned to schools and employees as they returned to their workplaces; and the temporary suspension of court activities.[7] The constitutionality of the COVID-19 measures has so far been reviewed only by lower courts, for the most part in interim measures judgments.[8]

---

[3] See European Court of Human Rights (Grand Chamber), *Cyprus v. Turkey*, judgment of 10 May 2001, app. no. 25781/94.

[4] UN High Commissioner (2021).

[5] Ibid.

[6] Statement by the President of the Security Council, 23 July 2021, UN document S/PRST/2021/13, referring to UN Security Council resolutions 550 (1984) and 789 (1992).

[7] FRA (2020). A collection of many relevant decrees translated in English can be found at: https://www.pio.gov.cy/coronavirus/eng/categories/decrees (last accessed 24 May 2022).

[8] See e.g. District Court of Nicosia, *Savvides et al.* v. *Attorney-General et al.*, lawsuit no. 1498/2021, interim judgment of 9 July 2021.

In part 2 of this chapter, we shall present and then criticise the legal basis for the adoption of the COVID-19 measures, focusing on problems relevant with the powers of the executive to introduce restrictions on fundamental rights through secondary legislation. We shall also see how the inactivity of the parliament, in combination with a problematic court judgment, has created a legal context which poses dangers for rule of law in Cyprus. In part 3, we shall analyse the constitutional complications of the path that the Republic of Cyprus did not follow, i.e. a Proclamation of Emergency under Art. 183 of the Constitution. In this context, we shall see that the operation of the constitutional order of the Republic has been based on an emergency doctrine, the doctrine or law of necessity, since 1964. Thus, the activation of Art. 183 for the purposes of confronting the pandemic would in essence be an emergency within the emergency. Although this path was not followed, the analysis shall give us the opportunity to argue that even an emergency regime with no explicit constitutional foundation can be conditioned upon, and can operate in accordance with, principles stemming from rule of law.

2 Restrictions on Rights Introduced by Secondary Legislation

2.1 The Quarantine Law

Cyprus did not declare an official state of emergency as a considerable number of other European states did.[9] Nor did the House of Representatives, the parliament of Cyprus, pass any special law with the view to establish procedures for the drafting and for the enforcement of the measures that would be deemed necessary for mitigating the negative effects of the pandemic. The vast majority of COVID-19 related measures were introduced by means of decrees issued by the Minister of Health based on the authorisation granted by an old, arguably outdated,[10] colonial law.[11]

Indeed, the Quarantine Law, Cap. 260, was enacted back in 1932, when Cyprus was a British Colony. As is the case with other colonial legislation, the Quarantine

[9] FRA (2021), pp. 11–12.

[10] Kombos (2020, 2021).

[11] In autumn 2021, the government submitted to the House of Representatives a bill which, if adopted, will replace the colonial Quarantine Law, on which most COVID-19 measures have so far been based. Apart from a more detailed description of the measures that the executive may enforce in case of pandemics, the draft new law follows the philosophy of the colonial legislation (and, in many parts, it simply repeats the wording of the colonial law), i.e. it grants vast authority to the executive, uncontrolled by the parliament and/or by means of procedural guarantees involving experts in the decision-making process. Thus, most of (although not all) our critical remarks in part 2 apply to the draft law as well. We shall be noting possible differentiations of our critique in footnotes.

Law continues to be in force by virtue of the transitional provisions of Art. 188 of the Constitution of 1960, subject to their compatibility with the Constitution. Section 3 of the Quarantine Law authorises the Council of Ministers (originally, the Governor) to declare, by notification in the Official Gazette, any disease to be a dangerous infectious disease. Section 4 of the Quarantine Law authorises the Council of Ministers (originally, the Governor) to declare any "local area", whether within or without the Republic, to be an infected local area, with the result being that all passengers and goods therefrom shall be subject to the regulations made under the Law. Section 6 of the Quarantine Law authorises the Council of Ministers (originally, the Governor in Council) to issue regulations, by means of decrees published in the Official Gazette to prevent the introduction of any dangerous infectious disease into the colony, or the transmission of such disease therefrom, or the spread of such disease from one area within the Republic to another; to prescribe the powers and duties of such officers as may be charged with carrying out the regulations; to fix the fees and charges to be paid for any matter or thing to be done under the regulations, and to prescribe the person by whom such fees and charges shall be paid; to carry out the purposes and provisions of the Law and of the regulations made thereunder, and of any sanitary convention to which the Republic has acceded or may accede; and (after an amendment of the Law in 2003) to create an official network which shall follow and analyse data relevant with infectious diseases.

2.2 *Conflict with the Case Law of the Supreme Constitutional Court*

On 10 March 2020, the Council of Ministers decided to delegate its powers under the Quarantine Law, including the power to issue decrees, to the Minister of Health.[12] Such sub-delegation was based neither on the enabling law nor on the Constitution itself, but on an organic law dating back to 1962, the Law on the Delegation of the Exercise of Powers Derived from Any Law, Law 23/1962. The Cypriot government makes regular use of this law, and the Cypriot courts take it as constitutional. Nevertheless, in the case of COVID-19 measures, the use of Law 23/1962, and, more generally, the way in which the government of Cyprus made use of its power to issue secondary legislation, should be considered as unconstitutional, since the delegated powers in question *introduced* (they did not merely specify) extensive, in fact sweeping, restrictions on numerous constitutional rights at the same time.

[12] The draft law on pandemics that is pending in the parliament grants explicitly the authority to issue decrees both to the Council of Ministers and to the Minister of Health individually. However, it remains the case that the measures that are prescribed therein introduce exceptionally wide restrictions on a series of fundamental rights.

This view finds support in the case law of the Supreme Constitutional Court,[13] as affirmed by the case law of its successor, the Supreme Court of the Republic of Cyprus.[14] Particularly, back in 1962, the Supreme Constitutional Court invoked the democratic principle to check the power of the parliament to delegate its legislative authority to organs of the executive in matters involving restrictions on fundamental rights. It is worth quoting the opinion of the Cypriot court at some length:

> It is only the people of a country themselves, through their elected legislators, who can decide to what extent its fundamental rights and liberties, as safeguarded by the Constitution, should be restricted or limited and this principle is inherently contained in all constitutions, such as ours, which expressly safeguard the fundamental rights and liberties and adopt the doctrine of the separation of powers.
>
> In the opinion of the Court, therefore, the expression "imposed by law" in paragraph 3 of Article 23, the expression "prescribed by law" in paragraph 2 of Article 25 and like expressions in other Articles of Part II of the Constitution, mean, in so far as laying down and defining the extent and framework of the particular restriction or limitation is concerned, a law of the House of Representatives. This does not however, prevent the House of Representatives from delegating its power to legislate in respect of prescribing the form and manner of, and the making of other detailed provisions for, the carrying into effect and applying the particular restriction or limitation within the framework as laid down by such law, e.g. *the addition of further items or instances falling within the restriction or limitation in question*. Such a course is presumed to be included in the will of the people as expressed through the particular law of its elected representatives.[15]

The Quarantine Law did not prescribe particular measures other than a possible imposition of fines.[16] The Law did prescribe the general aims of the secondary legislation, but in other respects the authorisation could be characterised as a blanket one. From this viewpoint, Kombos correctly notices that, being part of the colonial legislation, the Quarantine Law "disregards the existence of the Constitution as the supreme source of law, as well as any contemporary understanding of human rights protection".[17] Besides, the extent and the depth of the restrictions on fundamental rights which were introduced by the decrees under the Quarantine Law were certainly without precedent. Considering the case law of the Supreme Constitutional Court,[18] we may conclude that those decrees were issued in repugnance to the Constitution; even more so since the authority of the Council of Ministers, itself a collective organ, was delegated to one of its members, the Minister of Health,

---

[13] *The Police and Hondrou*, 3 RSCC 82. To be noted that the President of the Court was the famous German professor (and student of notorious Carl Schmitt) Ernst Forsthoff.

[14] *Spyrou and others (No. 2)* v. *The Republic (Licensing Authority)* (1973) 3 CLR 627. See also Emilianides (2019), p. 72.

[15] *The Police and Hondrou*, at 86 (our emphasis).

[16] The new draft law has taken positive steps in this direction, i.e. it prescribes possible measures in some detail.

[17] Kombos (2021).

[18] To be noted that in Cyprus, the case law of the Supreme Constitutional Court and of its successor, i.e. the Supreme Court, is binding for lower courts, not least in administrative law, which in other respects follows the continental system. See Hatzimihail (2013), pp. 91–92.

without explicit authorisation by the enabling law. Indeed, if the aforementioned jurisprudence were ever to be applied and lead to the invalidation of the relevant by-laws, this should have been the case with the COVID-19 measures.

2.3 *The Inactivity of the Parliament*

Things would have been different if the parliament of Cyprus had intervened to determine the kind of measures which were to be taken in response to the pandemic, as well as to prescribe special procedures for the introduction of such measures and for their revision in time (e.g. prior consultation with stakeholders and with experts).[19] In fact, the House of Representatives intervened but only marginally, so as to amend the provisions of the Quarantine Law which were relevant with the penalties for violations of the regulations, with the powers of police authorities, and with the judicial procedure to be followed for the suspension of the economic activities of the enterprises which would be found to have violated the regulations under the Law. What the legislator did not do was to enumerate the prohibitions and other measures which formed the substantive part of these regulations, and to prescribe a procedure involving experts and stakeholders.

Alternatively, the House of Representatives could have intervened to approve, reject or modify the regulations themselves while exercising its powers under the Law on the Submission to the House of Representatives of Regulations Issued After a Legislative Delegation, Law 99/1989.[20] Section 3 of this Law provides that, irrespective of the provisions of any other law,[21] whenever a law grants to the Council of Ministers or to a member thereof the power to issue regulations, those regulations shall be submitted to the House of Representatives for approval. If the House does not modify or annul the regulations within sixty days, then the regulations shall be published in the Official Gazette as they have. If the House modifies the regulations, wholly or partially, then the regulations shall be published in the Official Gazette as they have after the modifications. Although not part of the

[19] This last defect, i.e. the absence of procedural guarantees, remains in place in the new draft law.

[20] In one of the interim measures judgments that have been issued so far with regard to the COVID-19 measures, the District Court of Nicosia responded to this allegation by arguing that Law 99/1989 applies only to regulations, not to decrees. See District Court of Nicosia, *Kosta et al.* v. *The Attorney-General et al.*, lawsuit no. 1322/2021, interim judgment of 27 July 2021. This argument runs contrary to the letter of the Quarantine Law, Art. 6, which authorises the Council of Ministers to issue regulations by means of decrees. And so did the Minister of Health (after the sub-delegation of such authority), who issued regulations by means of decrees. To justify the distinction between decrees and regulations, the District Court appealed to the Law on Interpretation, Cap. 1, and to two Supreme Court judgments, but neither this Law nor the judgments guarantee the distinction. Not surprisingly, the new draft law mentions only decrees, not regulations. But the substance of the problem, i.e. the absence of parliamentary approval, remains in place.

[21] This is another argument that rebuts the distinction between decrees and regulations, as introduced by the District Court of Nicosia (see previous note).

Constitution, the rules of Law 99/89 are well-suited to serve the democratic principle under a presidential system as that of Cyprus. On the other hand, in not few cases, the Supreme Court has ruled that certain matters of an administrative nature (e.g. the appointment or termination of appointment of public service personnel, the regulation of fishing methods, the determination of working hours for shops, etc.) fall within the exclusive competence of the executive.[22] However, the COVID-19 measures as such could hardly be considered as falling under this case law.

What could and should have been delegated to the executive was (a) the specification and (b) the revision of the measures in time, (c) subject to parliamentary scrutiny.[23] Admittedly, in the case of the COVID-19 measures the type of parliamentary scrutiny that the Law 99/89 prescribes would be inappropriate. The Regulations had to be put into force immediately, not after lengthy parliamentary deliberation or after the lapse of the 60 days deadline in case of parliamentary inactivity. Thus, one may argue that the Parliament should have only the power to amend or reject particular measures for the future, not retrospectively. This type of scrutiny presupposes either an amendment of Law 99/89 (introducing an exceptional procedure of parliamentary scrutiny in cases of public health and other emergencies) or, even better, an amendment of the Quarantine Law (introducing the procedures and the substantive measures of a public health emergency).[24] However, a more energetic stance on the part of the House of Representatives was certainly required from the standpoint of the democratic principle, as specified in the jurisprudence of the Supreme Constitutional Court on the issue of delegated legislation. Even if the parliament did not have the time to deliberate on the initial measures that were taken as a response to the pandemic, it certainly was in a position to proceed into the necessary legislative action at a later stage.

The lack of parliamentary deliberation on the COVID-19 measures was also an aggravating factor for the quality of the legal regime from the viewpoint of the requirements under the fundamental principle of rule of law.[25] Lack of transparency regarding the justification of the measures, combined with uncertainty regarding both the substance of these measures and the involvement of experts and of stakeholders in the decision-making process, are problems which could have been alleviated only through the legislative introduction of procedural and of substantive requirements, including an enumeration of the kinds of measures which the executive could take.[26] The government would then have had the power to activate, specify, revise or deactivate these measures according to changing circumstances, following a procedure that would be more efficient, more comprehensive and more

[22] For a summary of this case law, see Emilianides (2019), pp. 61–66.

[23] The draft new law on pandemics has addressed only point (a), not points (b) and (c) of our critique.

[24] For a discussion on the necessity for introducing a special regime for public health emergencies in France, see Gelblat and Marguet (2020).

[25] See Kombos (2021).

[26] The draft new law on pandemics did nothing to alleviate these concerns.

transparent, enhancing thus the acceptability of the measures. To be sure, the powers of the executive in emergencies are unavoidably extensive, but this does not necessarily entail a decrease in the ability of parliaments to design procedures and to stipulate substantive safeguards in correspondence with rule of law principles such as transparency, adequate justification and participation of experts and of affected parties in the decision-making process.

2.4 A Problematic Court Ruling

The deficiencies of the legal regime in Cyprus will be aggravated further if the Supreme Court ever adopts the reasoning of a ruling of the Administrative Court which classified one of the decrees that introduced the COVID-19 measures into the category of "*actes de gouvernement*", exempting them thus from judicial scrutiny.[27] The measure in question in this interim measures judgment was the limitation of free entrance to the Republic: The relevant decree permitted such entrance only to those persons who would procure a health certificate issued by a state laboratory or by a laboratory which would have agreed with the state from which the interested person would depart that it will be conducting the relevant examinations. The applicant, a Cypriot student in a university of England, argued that it was not possible for her to obtain such a certificate at the material time (March 2020), since no such certificates were issued by British authorities. Thus, the measure in question effectively amounted to a deprivation of her constitutional right to enter the Republic. On the other hand, Art. 14 of the Constitution of Cyprus reads as follows: "No citizen shall be banished or excluded from the Republic *under any circumstances*" (our emphasis). Notably, there is no other clause in the Constitution providing for limitations upon constitutional rights in general. We cannot address here the interesting issue of whether there can exist absolute constitutional rights. Suffice it to notice that the issue becomes all the more interesting in the context of the right not to be excluded from the territory of a state (here: Cyprus) because this right is effectively a political one (i.e. a right intrinsically connected with citizenship), whereas the discussion on absolute rights has so far focused almost exclusively on the human right that is derived from the prohibition of torture and of other inhuman or degrading treatment.[28] Be that as it may, the Cypriot court responded to the substantive allegation of the applicant that she was deprived of her right under Art. 14 of the Constitution only through an *obiter dictum* (according to which the Republic had only regulated the right in question), and only after the application had been dismissed on the grounds, first, that the decree in question was a regulatory, not an individual, administrative

[27] *Patsalidi* v. *Republic of Cyprus*, case no. 301/2020, judgment of 16 April 2020, ECLI:CY:DD:2020:188.

[28] See e.g. Mavronicola (2012, 2017); Smet (2013); Greer (2011, 2015, 2018); Biggar (2020), pp. 167–189; Gewirth (1981).

act, not being susceptible to the power of the Administrative Court to void administrative acts as per Art. 146 of the Constitution; and, second, that the same decree was in any case an "*acte de gouvernement*", with the result being again that it escapes judicial control under Art. 146 of the Constitution.

The immunity of regulatory administrative acts ("normative", according to the terminology of continental Administrative Law, which Cypriot courts follow) does not extend to the incidental review of their constitutionality in the context of applications for the annulment of the individual administrative acts that are based on the regulatory act.[29] Thus, the non-susceptibility of regulatory acts to the power of the Administrative Court to annul administrative acts creates a gap in the judicial protection of fundamental rights, but this is a problem that can be alleviated, albeit with non-negligible difficulty—one has to provoke the issuance of an individual administrative act, which in most cases cannot be anything else than a fine imposed on him/her after he/she has violated one of the COVID-19 measures.

Even more serious is the gap that is created by the classification of (at least some of) the COVID-19 decrees into the category of "*actes de gouvernement*". The relevant case law of the Supreme Court has justified the doctrine of "*actes de gouvernement*" through reference to French and to Greek jurisprudence, and has defined such acts as ones "patently" related to the discretion of the Government over political matters such as the relations between the executive and the legislature, international relations, and decisions concerning the internal and external safety of the state.[30] The Supreme Court of Cyprus has recognised that the classification of an administrative act into *actes de gouvernement* cannot be decided otherwise than on an *ad hoc* basis. It has also recognised that there is a tendency not to enlarge this category, but rather to restrict it. Contrary to this tendency, perhaps influenced by the climate surrounding the pandemic at an early stage, the judge of the Administrative Court justified his decision to classify the decree whereby entrance to the Republic was restricted into *actes de gouvernement* through the argument that this was an "extremely important act directly linked with the protection of public health, the limitation of the spread of the coronavirus pandemic, prevention of the collapse of the public health system, and protection of human life itself" (our translation).[31] However, even if the pandemic is taken as posing a danger for the safety of the state (in our view, this is hardly the case), nothing necessitates granting the government

---

[29] In the Greek legal order, a source of the case law of Cypriot courts on administrative law issues, regulatory acts are clearly susceptible to the power of administrative courts to annul administrative acts. The difference between the Cypriot and the Greek legal order in this respect could find an explanation to the fact that the system of government in Cyprus is presidential, whereas in Greece it is parliamentary.

[30] *Louca* v. *The President of the Republic* (1983) 3 CLR 783, followed, inter alia, by *Karaliota v. The Republic* (1985) 3 CLR 2053; *Loizou et al.* v. *The Republic* (1992) 4 CLR 2643 (in Greek); *Hatziandreou* v. The Republic (2001) 3 CLR 352 (in Greek); *Kyriacou* v. *The Republic*, case no. 692/2012, judgment of 26 November 2012.

[31] *Patsalidi* v. *Republic of Cyprus*, case no. 301/2020, judgment of 16 April 2020, ECLI:CY:DD:2020:188.

carte blanche as regards the measures taken as a response to this particular danger, in contrast to other cases (e.g. the dissolution of the parliament or the replacement of a minister) on which the judicial branch would find difficult if not impossible to pass a judgement without paralysing or unduly frustrating the constitutional powers of the executive, creating thus a novel source of power inimical to all the others—this was at least part of the rationale behind the adoption of the rule that exempted "*actes de gouvernement*" from judicial scrutiny back in 1849 in France.[32]

In our view, there is nothing inherent in the drafting of the measures that intend to address a public health emergency—as contrasted perhaps to the proclamation of the emergency itself, in the rare cases wherein this is assigned to the executive alone—which would dictate the abstention of courts from controlling the relevant legislative and administrative acts. In the case of emergencies, the tendency to restrict the scope of "*actes de gouvernement*" goes hand in hand with the rationale behind Art. 15 ECHR, which has left to national authorities' considerable discretion as to whether a public emergency exists, submitting however the measures taken as a response to such emergency to the scrutiny of the Strasbourg court based on the principles of necessity and of proportionality. The ruling of the Administrative Court is hardly compatible with the increased emphasis of international and of national courts worldwide to uphold the requirements stemming from rule of law, including substantive judicial review, even in the face of emergencies.[33] As we shall see in the next section, this observation holds true no less in the Republic of Cyprus.

3 An Emergency Within an Emergency

3.1 The Cypriot Version of the Doctrine of Necessity

The most interesting aspect of the legal regime in Cyprus has to do with the path that was not followed, that is, an official declaration of a state of emergency. Article 183 (1) of the Constitution of Cyprus provides that: "In case of war or other public danger threatening the life of the Republic or any part thereof, the Council of Ministers shall have power, by a decision taken in this respect, to issue a Proclamation of Emergency". Such a decision is subject to a veto by the President and/or by the Vice-President, and may suspend several, specified in paragraph 2 of Art. 183, articles of the Constitution, all safeguarding fundamental rights. After its publication in the Official Gazette of the Republic, the Proclamation "shall be laid forthwith before the House of Representatives. If the House of Representatives is not sitting it must be convened as soon as possible for this purpose" (Art. 183 par. 4).

---

[32] See Laferrière (2020).

[33] For a rebuttal of the view that courts should play a minimal role in issues of contentious public policy such as national security issues, including discussion on the political questions doctrine (the American analogue of the French doctrine of "*actes de gouvernement*"), see Greene (2018): chap. 4.

The House of Representatives may either reject or approve the Proclamation of Emergency. During the Emergency, the Council of Ministers, if satisfied that immediate action is required may, subject to the right of veto of the President and/or of the Vice-President, make any ordinance strictly connected with the state of emergency, having the force of law.

Not for lack of real emergencies, no such Proclamation has been issued in the lifetime of the Republic of Cyprus. Nevertheless, after the withdrawal of the representatives of the Turkish Cypriot community from state organs in early 1964, the existence of the Constitution itself has been based on an emergency doctrine, the doctrine or law of necessity, as constructed by the Supreme Court in the case of *Ibrahim*.[34] The basic articles of the Constitution, unamendable by virtue of the Zurich Agreement between Greece and Turkey, to which the existence of the Republic of Cyprus is owed, enshrine the cardinal principle of bi-communalism, i.e. the necessary cooperation of the two communities, Greek Cypriot and Turkish Cypriot, for the operation of the Republic. In 1964, instead of proceeding to a revolutionary act such as the amendment of the basic constitutional articles (this would be tantamount to making a new Constitution), the Greek Cypriot leadership chose to continue governing Cyprus under the Constitution of 1960, excusing the unavoidable deviations from the constitutional provisions that required the participation of Turkish Cypriot officials in state organs by means of appealing to the doctrine or law of necessity. The latter was constructed not as a supra-constitutional principle, but as one inherent in the constitutional order, particularly as a principle qualifying the supremacy of the Constitution. This principle gives priority to the survival of the state and to the implicit constitutional duty of state organs to govern and to deliver justice as against strict observance of particular constitutional rules (even those which determine the constitution of state organs), whenever exceptional circumstances, as the ones that the Republic was facing at the time (and which had subverted the foundation of the constitution, i.e. the cooperation of the two communities in exercising political power and in delivering justice), dictated so. Above all other organs, the legislature, acting on behalf of the people of Cyprus, shall adopt the necessary measures. The deviations from the relevant constitutional provisions shall be considered justified, provided that, subject to the scrutiny of the Court (which shall examine the relevant cases on an *ad hoc* basis), the following prerequisites are satisfied: (a) "an imperative and inevitable necessity or exceptional circumstances" are present; (b) "no other remedy to apply" exists; (c) the measure taken is "proportionate to the necessity"; and (d) the measure is "of a temporary character limited to the duration of the exceptional circumstances".[35]

Greek Cypriot jurists have convincingly contrasted the use of the doctrine of necessity in Cyprus to *coups d' État* or other forms of upheaval in government,

---

[34] *The Attorney-General of the Republic* v. *Mustafa Ibrahim and others* (1964) CLR 195. For the doctrine or law of necessity in Cyprus, see Polyviou (2015); Kombos (2015); Emilianides et al. (2016).

[35] *Ibrahim*, at 265 (Josephides, J.).

where necessity and/or the contiguous, supposedly Kelsenian, "principle of effectiveness" were invoked by courts so as to affirm the abrogation of a Constitution in favor of a new one, or so as to condone executive action in direct defiance of the Constitution with the aim of replacing it.[36] Indeed, the Cypriot version of the doctrine of necessity differs significantly from such cases. The justification of the doctrine of necessity in *Ibrahim* privileges legislative instead of executive action, and the application of the doctrine is made dependent upon specific criteria, stated in advance, which incorporate a proportionality test, while the final word on each and every case belongs to the Court. One could thus argue that, at least in principle, the use of the doctrine of necessity in Cyprus obeys to what Dyzenhaus has called the "compulsion of legality", i.e. "the perceived necessity to have a legal authorization for state action because legally unauthorized action is widely considered illegitimate".[37] If an emergency regime claims something more than a mere cloak of legality, the compulsion of legality must set in motion a "virtuous cycle", whereby "the institutions of legal order cooperate in devising controls on public actors that ensure that their decisions comply with the principle of legality, understood as a substantive conception of rule of law".[38]

Considering the unique features of the Cypriot version of the law of necessity, we may stipulate that, perhaps paradoxically, it is an emergency doctrine serving, instead of undermining, the separation of powers, legality and, more generally, the rule of law.[39] As the Supreme Court of Canada has indicated, reading *Ibrahim* in view of a very different problem:

> . . . a Court may temporarily treat as valid and effective laws which are constitutionally flawed in order to preserve the rule of law. The [*Ibrahim*] case stands for the proposition that under conditions of emergency, when it is impossible to comply with the Constitution, the Court may allow the government a temporary reprieve from such compliance in order to preserve society and maintain, as nearly as possible, normal conditions. The overriding concern is the protection of the rule of law.[40]

The major difference of the case of Cyprus from cases as the one which occupied the Canadian court is the indefinite (as it came to be) extension of the emergency. While the attempts to resolve the Cyprus problem had been failing one after another,

[36] See Kombos (2015); Polyviou (2015); *contra* Özersay (2004).

[37] Dyzenhaus (2012), p. 451.

[38] Dyzenhaus (2012), p. 452.

[39] For the defense of legality in emergencies, see inter alia, Dyzenhaus (2006a); Greene (2018). The relationship between liberal-democratic institutions and emergency powers is more complex outside the context of the "western world". See in this regard the excellent treatise of Ramraj (2009). In our view, the Cypriot version of the doctrine of necessity sits uncomfortably both with the "western" typologies of emergency powers (e.g. Gross and Ní Aoláin (2006); Ferejohn and Pasquino (2004); Dyzenhaus (2012) and with the types of cases to which Ramraj refers.

[40] *Reference re Language Rights under the Manitoba Act 1870* [1985] 1 RCS, 763. For a discussion of the use of *Ibrahim* in the *Manitoba Language* cases and in other court judgments from various countries (most of them addressing upheavals in government), see Polyviou (2015), chap. 7; Kombos (2015), chap. 3.

the constitutional order of Cyprus had to operate based on the doctrine of necessity. Thus, in numerous cases, the Supreme Court of Cyprus condoned laws, and some administrative acts, which deviated from the letter of the Constitution. The doctrine of necessity was also used as the justificatory ground for the amendment of non-basic articles of the Constitution of Cyprus in the absence of the Turkish Cypriot members of the House of Representatives, that is, in contravention of the procedure that is prescribed in Art. 182 par. 3 of the Constitution which requires separate two-thirds majority decisions on the part of the Greek Cypriot and of the Turkish Cypriot members of the House of Representatives, respectively. It was on the grounds that the requirements of the doctrine of necessity were not met that the Supreme Court blocked in 1986 the first attempt of the House of Representatives to pass a law amending non-basic articles of the constitution in the absence of the Turkish Cypriot representatives.[41] The second attempt in 1989 was met with a split five to five judgment which permitted the amendment law to enter into force only on account of the "presumption of constitutionality", i.e. the presumption that all laws are considered valid unless declared not to be or unless repealed.[42] The judges which found the constitutional amendment impermissible in the absence of the Turkish Cypriot members of the House of Representatives argued that, by its own nature, the doctrine of necessity allows only temporary deviations from the Constitution, while constitutional amendments have by their own nature permanent character. The opposite opinion was based on the thought that constitutional amendments serve the adjustment of the Constitution to changing social circumstances without introducing a rupture in law. According to this opinion, if it were accepted that the Constitution cannot be amended before the Turkish Cypriot members of the House of Representatives return, the non-basic articles of the Constitution would be transformed into basic, i.e. unamendable, ones, with the result being detrimental to the smooth functioning of the material constitution and to the democratic principle. Based on this opinion, in 1997 the Court opened properly the door to constitutional amendments in a case which was decided by a majority of nine to five judges.[43] What remained to be seen was whether the doctrine of necessity could also condone a Proclamation of Emergency under Art. 183 of the Constitution.

3.2 *Could Article 183 Have Been Activated Based on the Doctrine of Necessity?*

In response to this interesting albeit hypothetical question, we should first notice that the wordings of Art. 183 on the substantive prerequisites for a Proclamation of Emergency are identical to those of Art. 15 ECHR (as is the case with most other

[41] *President* v. *House of Representatives* (1986) 3 CLR 1439.

[42] *Nicolaou* v. *Nicolaou* (1992) 1 CLR 1338.

[43] *Kouloumtis and other* v. *House of Representatives* (1997) 1 CLR 1026.

provisions of part II of the Constitution of Cyprus). We shall not address the discussion on the applicability of Art. 15 ECHR in the context of the COVID-19 crisis.[44] For present purposes, we shall simply assume that Art. 15 ECHR is applicable. Accordingly, Art. 183 of the Constitution of the Republic of Cyprus, interpreted in accordance with Art. 15 ECHR, could have been activated as a response to the COVID-19 crisis—the question whether this would have been appropriate under the circumstances is a different issue.[45]

Then, on possible appeal to the doctrine of necessity to excuse the implementation of Art. 183 in the absence of a Turkish Cypriot Vice-President, also in the absence of the Turkish Cypriot members of the House of Representatives, we should notice that, in contrast to the requirements of the amendment procedure, Art. 183 does not require separate decisions of the Greek Cypriot and of the Turkish Cypriot members of the House of Representatives, respectively. This is a reason which favors the use of the doctrine of necessity so as to implement Art. 183. To be sure, this eventuality would present us with a quite strange condition, i.e. the use of an emergency doctrine to enable the Cypriot executive and legislator to activate the constitutional procedure for a Proclamation of Emergency. Yet, this oddity would not be strictly impermissible—at least not, if one subscribes to the reasoning of the Supreme Court which justified the deviation from the (stricter) procedural rules on constitutional amendments, given that the latter introduce permanent changes into the Constitution, while an Emergency justifies only temporary deviations therefrom.

There is, however, another reason which, at least *prima facie*, obstructs the activation of Art. 183 by appealing to the doctrine of necessity. In *Ibrahim*, i.e. the judgement which constructed the doctrine of necessity, the respondents argued that, in the absence of a Proclamation of Emergency as provided in Art. 183, "no state of emergency can exist in Cyprus; and therefore no 'necessity' to justify departure from constitutional or statutory provisions".[46] Although not cited in *Ibrahim*, the essence of this argument coincides with a previous ruling of the Supreme Constitutional Court (President Forsthoff, and the Turkish Cypriot Judge Munir, were in the majority, whereas the Greek Cypriot Judge Triantafyllides was in the minority) in the all-important municipalities case (the most important controversy among the ones which had led the Republic to the constitutional paralysis in 1963), namely that:

> . . . under a written Constitution, such as that of the Republic of Cyprus, which expressly provides for extraordinary competences to overcome certain defined situations of emergency, there can be no implied power, outside of such express constitutional provisions, of any organ of the Republic to override, in a case of "necessity", competences of other organs, and to step beyond the limits of its own competences or to act without the basis of a law, even though such a basis would normally be required for its actions.[47]

---

[44] For positive views, see inter alia, Greene (2020); Jovičić (2021).

[45] For a skeptical view, based on considerations relevant with rule of law, see Emilianides 2020. Cf. Kombos (2020), arguing that "the proclamation of a state of emergency was not constitutionally possible".

[46] *Ibrahim* at 215.

[47] *The Turkish Communal Chamber* v. *The Council of Ministers* (1963) 5 RSCC 59, at 77.

The three Greek Cypriot Judges in *Ibrahim* (among them, Judge Triantafyllides, who had been a member of the Supreme Constitutional Court in the municipalities case) did not attempt to respond to the aforementioned ruling, in order to then reverse it, as they should have done under normal circumstances. The judges of *Ibrahim* merely rejected the argument of the counsel of the respondents on the grounds that Art. 183 was "completely inadequate to meet the present emergency".[48] Then, the Court moved a step further: the Greek Cypriot judges argued that the emergency clauses of the Constitution were themselves establishing, "in a very convincing manner, how far from reality some of our constitutional provisions can now be found; and how badly our Constitution requires injections of the doctrine of necessity to keep some of its parts alive".[49]

The inadequacy or unworkability of the Constitution was one of the three argumentative pillars (the other two being the rigidity of the Constitution and the fact that it had not originally been the product of the constituent power of the people, but it had been imposed) on which the construction of the doctrine of necessity was premised. But if while constructing the doctrine of necessity the Court took Art. 183 as an indication of the unworkability of the Constitution, one might legitimately ask: How could we now use the doctrine of necessity *in order to* activate Art. 183?

An answer to this question might start from the argument that, even if the finding of the Supreme Court on the unworkability of Art. 183 was not valid, this does not necessarily entail that the wider argument about the unworkability of the Constitution of 1960 was not valid as well. Besides, nothing in *Ibrahim* precludes a future use of Art. 183, this time premised on the doctrine of necessity so that the supposed obstacle before 1963, i.e. a possible refusal of the Turkish Cypriot representatives or a veto on the part of the Turkish Cypriot Vice-President, would have been removed. The major problem with the implementation of Art. 183 based on the doctrine of necessity does not lie in the reference of the Supreme Court to Art. 183 in *Ibrahim*, but in the ruling of the Supreme Constitutional Court as cited above; that is, the argument that, under a written constitution which contains clauses for the proclamation of emergencies, the relevant procedure cannot but be exclusive.

3.3 Neither Black Nor Grey Holes, But Only an Irony

This argument points to the heart of the problem of emergencies in/under constitutional law: the Schmittian suspicion that a constitution cannot (efficiently) regulate (all kinds of) emergencies. Indeed, the *scope of application* of Art. 183 in Cyprus was totally unsuitable for the purposes of confronting the real emergency of 1964. This is so because, as we saw, the provisions that may be suspended under Art.

[48] *Ibrahim*, at 215 (Vassiliades, J.).

[49] Ibid. See also *Ibrahim*, at 225–226, 234 (Triantafyllides, J.), and 265–266 (Josephides, J.).

183 all safeguard constitutional rights, while the emergency of 1964 affected exclusively the structural part of the Constitution, i.e. the part which regulates the composition and the functioning of state organs after the withdrawal of Turkish Cypriot representatives. But notwithstanding the original gap, the Cypriot judges did not allow the creation of either a legal black hole (i.e. a lawless void introduced by the political organs and sanctioned by the courts) or a legal grey hole (i.e. a legal space in which there are some, but only insubstantial, constraints on executive action).[50] On the contrary, they designed the doctrine of necessity so as to uphold the rule of law as much as possible, constraining the holders of political power within the confines of the Constitution in all issues except for the participation of Turkish Cypriot representatives in constitutional organs and procedures.

The construction of the doctrine of necessity in Cyprus signifies the attempt of Greek Cypriot jurists to internalise and, hence, regularise the exception within the boundaries of constitutional law. It may be the case that the "compulsion of legality" (Dyzenhaus), as exhibited in the original construction of the doctrine, was not always successful in limiting the permissible deviations from the Constitution only to issues relevant with the absence of the Turkish Cypriot representatives from state organs. It may also be the case that the proportionality test which was incorporated into the doctrine was not always implemented as strictly as required (this observation applies no less to *Ibrahim* itself). Nevertheless, *Ibrahim* could hardly be taken as an insubstantial barrier to executive and/or legislative discretion—much less when the deviations did not affect constitutional rights but only marginally.

It is therefore ironical—paradoxical according to Kombos[51]—to see that, when facing an emergency affecting many (one could even say: most) constitutional rights, a Cypriot court chooses a model of deference to the executive (an unjustified and unsustainable expansion of the doctrine of "*actes de gouvernement*" into the decrees that regulate the public health emergency) rather foreign to the compulsion of legality that characterises the doctrine of necessity. Interestingly, the main jurisprudential source of the doctrine of "*actes de gouvernement*" in Cyprus, the judgement *Louca* of the Supreme Court, was in essence a contrast of the doctrine of necessity to the doctrine of "*actes de gouvernement*". Delivering the judgment of the Court, Triantafyllides, J. (one of the "fathers" of the doctrine of necessity in Cyprus), upheld the measure in question (the termination of the services of a member of the Public Services Commission based on a law that had previously been found to have been justified by the doctrine of necessity) on the grounds that "it would be entirely incompatible with the precept of the Rule of Law requiring the exercise of judicial control in connection with the application of the 'law of necessity' to hold that [the relevant decision of the

[50] For the concept of black and of grey holes, see Dyzenhaus (2006b); also Greene (2018). Dyzenhaus (2006b) considers grey holes more harmful to the rule of law than black holes, since the limited protection that grey holes provide cloak the lack of substantial protection, and equip the executive with some constitutional legitimacy, whereas in the case of black holes, it is at least apparent that the executive moves outside the contours of the Constitution.

[51] Kombos (2021).

President] [...] escapes judicial control, to an appropriate extent, under Article 146 of the Constitution, because such decision is an 'act of Government'".[52]

If the COVID-19 measures had been adopted based on the doctrine of necessity, they would have been cast into judicial scrutiny based on the principle of proportionality, and the Court would even have to consider whether the measures should have been adopted by the legislature, considering that the doctrine of necessity prioritises legislative instead of executive action. The doctrine of "actes de gouvernement" precludes such a kind of judicial control,[53] and creates a "grey hole", that is, lack of substantial protection corroborated by the courts. We hope that, when the case (or some other comparable case) that led the Administrative Court to remember the doctrine of "*actes de gouvernement*" reaches the Supreme Court, the latter will not follow this path.

4 Conclusions

The initial problems of the legal regime under which the COVID-19 measures were drafted and enforced in Cyprus (a constitutionally problematic (sub-)delegation, deficits in democratic legitimacy and in correspondence with rule of law principles such as transparency and procedural propriety) need not be aggravated by an unjustifiable deference of courts to the executive as per the doctrine of "*actes de gouvernement*". This is in keeping with the long history of "emergency law" in Cyprus, which, at least *prima facie*, illustrates the potential of the rule of law even when deviating from the Constitution, even under harsh circumstances, as the ones that the Republic of Cyprus faced in 1963–1964 (and once again in 1974). A legal culture upholding the "compulsion of legality" (Dyzenhaus) needs to be preserved not only for the sake of orderly, legitimate and fair governance in the present contingency, but also as a constitutive and, thus, indispensable feature of the Cypriot constitutional order.

If the first pillar of the "compulsion of legality" is judicial review, the second is the commitment to parliamentary procedures, at least when it comes to restrictions on fundamental rights so deep and so extensive as the ones that the COVID-19 emergency entailed. We may have become accustomed to subscribing to the traditional constitutional imaginary according to which parliaments are not fit for addressing emergencies. Perhaps it is now time to overcome the taboo of traditional parliamentary deliberation in the physical presence of MPs, and to take seriously the technological developments which make possible parliamentary deliberation without sacrificing the timeliness and the efficiency of the measures that need to be taken as a response to (public health or other) emergencies.

[52] *Louca*, op. cit.

[53] Kombos (2021).

The doctrine of necessity in Cyprus illustrates the potential of the rule of law in emergencies. The "compulsion of legality" which animates the Cypriot version of the doctrine of necessity affirms the importance of legislative action and of judicial review. At least on COVID-19 measures, this compulsion should orient courts away from constructions (such as the doctrine of "*actes de gouvernement*") which insulate executive action from judicial scrutiny.

References

Biggar N (2020) What's wrong with rights? Oxford University Press, Oxford

Dyzenhaus D (2006a) The constitution of law: legality in a time of emergency. Cambridge University Press, New York

Dyzenhaus D (2006b) *Schmitt v. Dicey*: are states of emergency inside or outside the legal order? Cardozo Law Rev 27:2005–2039

Dyzenhaus D (2012) States of emergency. In: Rosenfeld M, Sajó A (eds) The Oxford handbook of comparative constitutional law. Oxford University Press, New York, pp 442–462

Emilianides AC (2019) Cyprus. In: Alen A, Haljan D (eds) International Encyclopedia of laws: constitutional law. Alphen aan den Rijn, Kluwer Law International

Emilianides AC (2020) Proclamation of Emergency and Article 183 (in Greek). Blog *Δικαιοσύνη* 26.3.2020. https://dikaiosyni.com/katigories/arthra/kirixi-ektaktis-anagkis-kai-arthro-183 (last accessed: 27 May 2022)

Emilianides AC, Papastylianos C, Stratilatis C (2016) The Republic of Cyprus and the law of necessity. Sakkoulas Publications (in Greek), Athens-Thessaloniki

Ferejohn J, Pasquino P (2004) The law of the exception: a typology of emergency powers. Int J Const Law 2(2):210–239

FRA (European Union Agency for Fundamental Rights) (2020) Coronavirus pandemic in the EU – Fundamental Rights Implications – Country: Cyprus

FRA (European Union Agency for Fundamental Rights) (2021) Fundamental Rights Report – 2021. Publications Office of the European Union, Luxemburg

Gelblat A, Marguet L (2020) État d'urgence sanitaire: la doctrine dans tous ses états? La Revue des droits de l'homme [Online], Actualités Droits-Libertés. https://doi.org/10.4000/revdh.9066

Gewirth A (1981) Are there any absolute rights? Philosophical Q 31:1–16

Greene A (2018) Permanent states of emergency and the rule of law: constitutions in an age of crisis. Hart Publishing, Great Britain

Greene A (2020) States should declare a State of Emergency using Article 15 ECHR to confront the Coronavirus Pandemic. Strasbourg Observers Blog, April 1, 2020

Greer S (2011) Should police threats to torture suspects always be severely punished? Reflections on the Gäfgen Case. Human Rights Law Rev 11(1):67–89. https://doi.org/10.1093/hrlr/ngr001

Greer S (2015) Is the prohibition against Torture, Cruel, Inhuman and degrading treatment really 'Absolute' in international human rights law? Human Rights Law Rev 15:101–137. https://doi.org/10.1093/hrlr/ngu035

Greer S (2018) Is the prohibition against torture, cruel, inhuman and degrading treatment really 'Absolute' in international human rights law? A reply to Graffin and Mavronicola. Human Rights Law Rev 18:297–307. https://doi.org/10.1093/hrlr/ngy013

Gross O, Ní Aoláin F (2006) Law in times of crisis: emergency powers in theory and in practice. Cambridge University Press, New York

Hatzimihail NE (2013) Cyprus as a mixed legal system. J Civ Law Stud 6:37–95

Jovičić S (2021) COVID-19 restrictions on human rights in the light of the case-law of the European Court of Human Rights. ERA Forum 21:545–560. https://doi.org/10.1007/s12027-020-00630-w
Kombos C (2015) The Doctrine of necessity in constitutional law. Sakkoulas Publications, Athens-Thessaloniki
Kombos C (2020) Covid-19 and the cypriot example: a constitutional paradox, UK. Const Law Blog (7th May 2020)
Kombos C (2021) Constitutional Improvisation and Executive Omnipotence: the Cypriot Handling of the Pandemic, VerfBlog, 2021/3/02, https://doi.org/10.17176/20210302-154130-0
Laferrière E (2020) Chapitre II – Actes de gouvernement. Revue générale du droit on line 2020, numéro 52399 (www.revuegeneraledudroit.eu/?p=52399)
Mavronicola N (2012) What is an 'absolute right'? Deciphering absoluteness in the context of Article 3 of the European convention on human rights. Human Rights Law Rev 12(4):723–758. https://doi.org/10.1093/hrlr/ngs020
Mavronicola N (2017) Is the prohibition against Torture and Cruel, Inhuman and degrading treatment absolute in international human rights law? A reply to Steven Greer. Human Rights Law Rev 17(3):479–498. https://doi.org/10.1093/hrlr/ngx019
Özersay K (2004) The excuse of State necessity and its implications on the Cyprus conflict. Perceptions 9(4):31–70
Polyviou PG (2015) The Case of *Ibrahim*, the Doctrine of necessity and the Republic of Cyprus. Chryssafinis & Polyviou, Nicosia
Ramraj VV (ed) (2009) Emergencies and the limits of legality. Cambridge University Press, New York
Smet S (2013) Conflicts between absolute rights: a reply to Steven Greer. Human Rights Law Rev 13(3):469–498. https://doi.org/10.1093/hrlr/ngt020
United Nations High Commissioner for Human Rights (2021) Question of human rights in Cyprus, 11 February 2021, A/HRC/46/23

Part III
Balancing and Judicial Scrutiny in a Pandemic

American Lessons: The COVID-19 Pandemic and the US Supreme Court

Anna Tsiftsoglou

Abstract Ever since the outbreak of the COVID-19 Pandemic in America in March 2020, several US states imposed harsh measures to combat the pandemic. Such state measures have at times seriously violated human rights, such as freedom of religion or freedom of movement. This chapter attempts to look at how the US Supreme Court has responded to the pandemic and reviewed several state measures over the past couple of years through selected cases on freedom of religion and compulsory vaccinations. We particularly look at its views on the role of the judiciary during the crisis, the scrutiny applied on human rights violations, as well as whether changes in the Court's composition during the Trump Era have in fact influenced its judicial reasoning. Overall, has the COVID-19 pandemic had an impact on judicial review and the Court's role? If so, how?

1 The COVID-19 Pandemic and the US Supreme Court

In March 2020, the COVID-19 Pandemic hit the United States of America.[1] It was only a few months before the 2020 Presidential Elections when former US President Trump declared a national emergency on COVID-19, and things had started to really heat up in the country. States had to respond to this crisis fast.

Presidential Elections aside, the pandemic hit the US Supreme Court at a turning point in its history. During the course of his one-term presidency, Trump had managed to appoint three conservative justices in a row (Neil Gorsuch, Brett Kavanaugh, and Amy Coney Barrett),[2] the latter only weeks before Election Day.[3] This resulted in an expanded conservative majority (6:3) for the Roberts court, which

[1] Washington Post (2020a).

[2] US Supreme Court (2022).

[3] Washington Post (2020b).

A. Tsiftsoglou (✉)
Faculty of Law, Aristotle University of Thessaloniki, Thessaloniki, Greece
e-mail: atsif@law.auth.gr

K. Chrysogonos, A. Tsiftsoglou (eds.), *Democracy after Covid*,
https://doi.org/10.1007/978-3-031-13901-7_7

has since struggled to reach consensus on critical COVID-related cases affecting a broad array of human rights,[4] from abortion rights and freedom of religion to prisoner rights and compulsory vaccinations. Newly confirmed Justice Ketanji Brown Jackson, the first Black woman in the history of the Court, while a liberal appointment[5] shall not likely alter this cemented republican majority.

Most—if not all—of this "COVID case law" was literally created "in the shadows." That is, it constituted part of the Supreme Court's *shadow docket*, which refers to all the non-merits decisions—emergency orders the Court issues, such as injunctions or stays without oral argument and, often, without any explanation or legal justification.[6] Many times, in these decisions it is hard to tell which judge agreed with the ruling, unless there is a written dissent or concurring opinion. Compared to the merits docket, the shadow docket usually has received much less attention until recently, when the great bulk of the Court's COVID case law and related litigation "lurked in the shadows"[7] during the pandemic.

This chapter examines a series of COVID-related cases included in this shadow docket that concerned freedom of religion claims as well as the issue of compulsory vaccinations against COVID-19 in public and private workplaces.

2 The First Amendment: Freedom of Religion Cases

The First Amendment to the US Constitution is one of the cornerstones of American democracy. In this 230-year-old article, adopted in 1791 as one of the Ten Amendments constituting the American Bill of Rights,[8] some of the most vital fundamental rights such as freedom of religion, as well as freedom of speech have been protected as emblems of the American Revolution:

> Congress shall make no law **respecting an establishment of religion, or prohibiting the free exercise thereof**; or abridging **the freedom of speech, or of the press**; or **the right of the people peaceably to assemble**, and to petition the Government for a redress of grievances.

Freedom of religion, under the First Amendment, enjoys a twofold protection: (a) through the so-called *Establishment Clause* ("Congress shall make no law respecting an establishment of religion"), which prohibits government from encouraging or promoting religion in any way (due to the separation between Church and the State in America, compared to other states)[9] and (b) through the *Free Exercise Clause* ("..or prohibiting the free exercise thereof"), which prohibits the government to interfere with one's religious belief and, within limits, religious worship. The two

[4]Wermiel (2020).

[5]White House (2022).

[6]Baude (2015), pp. 1, 3–5.

[7]Wermiel (2020).

[8]Chemerinsky (2006), p. 12.

[9]Sajo and Uitz (2013), pp. 909–912.

clauses are complementary as they protect different aspects of the same right, but in tension.[10]

Several applications for injunction to the US Supreme Court concerned COVID-19 measures imposed by a variety of states, such as California, Nevada, and New York, particularly during the first and second waves of the pandemic (Spring-Fall 2020) that allegedly violated the *Free Exercise Clause*. Due to problems inherent on the interpretation of this clause[11] many of such claims were unsuccessful.

Meanwhile, the leading reference point for respondent states and the Court during the pandemic turned out to be an over-century-old precedent, the *Jacobson* case.[12] According to the latter, states have the "police power" to regulate over matters of their jurisdiction, with considerable discretion, involving public health matters. States also have the authority to enforce compulsory vaccination laws, as well as other public health and safety measures, as long as they are deemed "reasonable."[13] Nevertheless, the *Jacobson* precedent, despite not addressing a First Amendment violation, became a misleading precedent when it was applied, over a century later, in the context of the COVID-19 pandemic, as it has been revealed in practice.[14]

2.1 *The First Wave of the Pandemic Cases (Summer 2020)*

When the first wave of the COVID-19 pandemic hit the States in Spring 2020, several litigants challenged State-imposed public health measures at state courts, also filing applications for injunctions at the US Supreme Court. The first two cases decided by the highest court concerned COVID-19 measures imposed in California and Nevada, on emergency applications filed by two religious groups from the same states.

In *South Bay I,*[15] concerning limitations on the free exercise clause on public health grounds by the State of California, the Court denied the application for injunction. Justice Kagan referred the matter to the Court and it denied it without explanation. Chief Justice Roberts, concurring in denial of the application, considered such measures limiting attendance at places of worship[16] as *reasonable*, since

[10] Chemerinsky (2006), p. 1182.

[11] Note (2021), pp. 1782–1783.

[12] Jacobson v Massachusetts, 197 US 11 (1905) (concerning an individual's challenge to a state regulation mandating compulsory vaccination against smallpox in Massachusetts).

[13] As held, "The police power of a state embraces such reasonable regulations relating to matters completely within its territory, and not affecting the people of other States, established directly by legislative enactment, as will protect the public health and safety." Jacobson, 11.

[14] Parmet (2020), pp. 118–119.

[15] South Bay United Pentecostal Church v Newsom, 590 US _ (2020) ("South Bay I").

[16] California state regulations in effect at that time limited attendance at places of worship to 25% of building capacity or a maximum of 100 attendees. See South Bay I, p. 1–2.

similar restrictions had been imposed to *comparable secular* gatherings, such as theater shows or movie screenings, where large crowds gather in internal spaces for extended periods of time. Particularly, Roberts stressed *the States' broad police power*, citing the century-old *Jacobson* precedent, to regulate matters of public health as deemed fit, especially in critical times as in the COVID-19 pandemic, as long as they were reasonable. Moreover, the Chief Justice stressed the fact that such matters should be decided by elected officials only, exercising their broad power, who both have the relevant expertise and are accountable to the people:

> The precise question of when restrictions on particular social activities should be lifted during the pandemic is **a dynamic and fact-intensive matter subject to reasonable disagreement.** [. . .] Where those broad limits are not exceeded, ***they should not be subject to second-guessing by an "unelected federal judiciary,"*** which lacks the background, competence, and expertise to assess public health and is not accountable to the people.[17]

Conservative Justice Kavanaugh, with whom Justices Thomas and Gorsuch joined, dissented, supporting the view that under the Court's jurisprudence, restrictions to the free exercise clause should be subject to *strict judicial scrutiny*. Particularly, States should not treat religious institutions less favorably than comparable secular ones, *unless shown that such rules are justified by a compelling public interest and that they are narrowly tailored to advance that interest*.[18] However, as Justice Kavanaugh noted, such justification had not been provided hereby by California. Instead, the 25% occupancy gap imposed on religious organizations had not been imposed on secular businesses and such unjustified discriminatory treatment against religion violated the Free Exercise Clause, under the First Amendment.

A similar case, originating from another religious organization in Nevada,[19] concerned again the discriminatory COVID-19 treatment of churches compared to secular businesses in Nevada. Specifically, a 50-person maximum capacity had been imposed on religious organizations, whereas secular businesses such as the gigantic Las Vegas casinos could admit up to 50% of their maximum occupancy, thus allowing thousands of patrons at the same time.[20] Again, the Court denied the application presented to liberal Justice Kagan without any explanation at all.

Decided only two months after *South Bay I*, and despite the similarity of the cases, *Calvary Chapel* provoked this time four loud dissents from the conservative branch, three justices of which had expressed concerns in *South Bay I*, too, albeit not in such a prolonged fashion. Justices Alito and Kavanaugh were particularly caustic.

Justice Alito, with whom Justices Gorsuch, Thomas, and Kavanaugh joined, emphasized that the Court has *"a duty to defend the Constitution, and even a public health emergency does not absolve us of that responsibility."*[21] Moreover, Alito underlined the *time factor*: the pandemic may justify restrictions to human rights,

[17] South Bay I, Roberts concurring, p. 2.

[18] South Bay I, Kavanaugh dissent, p. 2.

[19] Calvary Chapel Dayton Valley v Sisolak, 591 US _ (2020) ("Calvary Chapel").

[20] Calvary Chapel, Alito dissent, p. 1.

[21] Calvary Chapel, Alito dissent, p. 1.

even unprecedented ones, *at the dawn* of the emergency, *but not forever*. Measures enacted at the outbreak of COVID-19 by States exercising their police power in matters of public health may have gone virtually unchecked by Courts, for reasons of shortage of time, lack of information, and expertise. Nevertheless, the pandemic, as long as it may last, does not offer a limitless *carte blanche* to States:

> **But a public health emergency does not give Governors and other public officials *carte blanche* to disregard the Constitution for as long as the medical problem persists.** As more medical and scientific evidence becomes available, and as States have the time to craft policies in light of that evidence, courts should expect policies that more carefully account for constitutional rights.[22]

The *time factor*, when applied to cases like *Calvary Chapel*, which concerned measures enacted *two months already after* former President Trump's declaration of national emergency, defies any "unbounded police power" for their enactment. Thus judicial deference such as the one exhibited in *South Bay I* could not be an option, and restrictive measures like the debated ones had to withstand judicial review. Pronounced vividly by Justice Kavanaugh, overly judicial deference during crises may prove costly particularly in First Amendment issues, as the Court's history can tell. Justices need to stand up especially during emergencies to prevent arbitrariness in cases concerning restrictions on the sensitive freedoms of religion and speech:

> **COVID-19 is not a blank check for a State to discriminate against religious people, religious organizations and religious services.** There are certain **constitutional red lines** that a State may not cross even in a crisis. (...) This Court's history is **littered with unfortunate examples of overly broad judicial deference to the government when the government has invoked emergency powers and asserted crisis circumstances to override equal treatment and free speech principles.** The court of history has rejected those jurisprudential mistakes and **cautions us against an unduly deferential judicial approach,** especially when questions of racial discrimination, religious discrimination or free speech are at stake.[23]

Both dissenting Justices Alito and Kavanaugh stressed *the importance of strict scrutiny*. Freedom of religion is not an absolute right, but subject to restrictions. Although according to the Court's jurisprudence, any restrictions to the Free Exercise clause that are "not neutral" and "of general applicability" must survive strict judicial scrutiny.[24] The criteria of neutrality and general applicability may often be complex to apply, given the difficulties inherent in *comparison by analogy*. Free exercise analogies, such as the ones applied in *Calvary Chapel* and in other COVID-related cases, often lead to ad hoc analogizing. Comparing praying at synagogues with gambling in casinos, for instance, may not lead to objective balancing.[25]

When resorting to analogy, judges such as dissenting Justice Kavanaugh, compare presumably comparable values (i.e., churches with casinos and gyms), based on

[22] Calvary Chapel, Alito dissent, p. 3.

[23] Calvary Chapel, Kavanaugh dissent, p. 10.

[24] Chemerinsky (2006), p. 1252; Sajo and Uitz (2013), pp. 919–920.

[25] See particularly the analysis provided in Note (2021), p. 1803.

their own subjective views (i.e., on people's interactions in close proximity in both spaces), placing secular and religious activities randomly on the same balance.[26] With this analogical approach, *applicants* bear the burden of proof to show that seemingly comparable or "analogous" activities received differential treatment without justification.[27] Instead, it might have been safer, as suggested by theory,[28] if justices replaced this kind of free-exercise analogizing with *a burden-shifting approach*, where the *respondent States*, instead of the applicants, would bear the burden of showing that any discriminatory measure was in fact *justified* or *face strict scrutiny* for such disparate treatment. Shifting the burden of proof from the applicants to the State may have resulted in more objective reasoning.

2.2 The Second Wave of the Pandemic Cases (2020 October Term)

The wave of COVID litigation continued as the crisis deepened. On the eve of Thanksgiving Day in November 2020, a New York case,[29] decided *per curiam*, signified a change of course for the Court on Free Exercise claims during the pandemic. In *Roman Catholic Diocese*, which concerned two different religion applicants (Catholic and Jewish), the Supreme Court granted both relief by enjoining the enforcement of a NY State regulation that enforced severe restrictions on attendance at religious services in areas classified as "red" or "orange" zones.[30] Particularly, the 5:4 conservative majority, which included newly appointed Barrett, held that such Free Exercise restrictions were not narrowly tailored to serve the compelling state interest of public health protection. In fact, the NY measures were tighter than those imposed in other states such as California. The majority exclaimed:

> **Members of this Court are not public health experts**, and we should **respect** the judgment of those **with special expertise and responsibility** in this area. But **even in a pandemic, the Constitution cannot be put away and forgotten**. The restrictions at issue here (. . .) strike **at the very heart of the First Amendment's guarantee of religious liberty.**[31]

Interestingly, the majority granted partial relief despite the fact that the challenged regulation was no longer in place when the ruling was issued. Rejecting the mootness of the matter, the majority held that relief was still needed since applicants

---

[26] See for example, Calvary Chapel, Kavanaugh dissent, p. 12.

[27] See for example, Calvary Chapel, Kavanaugh dissent, pp. 8–9.

[28] See particularly the arguments in Note (2021), p. 1796.

[29] Roman Catholic Diocese of Brooklyn v Cuomo, 592 US _ (2020) ("Roman Catholic Diocese").

[30] A cap of 10- and 25- person occupancy at red and orange zones, respectively.

[31] Roman Catholic Diocese, Per Curiam Opinion, p. 5.

remained under a constant threat that the debated area could be reclassified as red or orange and be subject, again, to tight attendance restrictions.

As in *Calvary Chapel* and *South Bay I*, the demand of strict judicial scrutiny of such discriminatory measures imposed on religious organizations was not shared by all the members of the Court. Two powerful concurring opinions of Justices Gorsuch and Kavanaugh again reminded that the Constitution cannot be sidelined in emergencies and justices must intervene when fundamental rights are in danger:

> Government is not free to disregard the First Amendment in times of crisis. At a minimum, that Amendment prohibits government officials from treating religious exercises **worse than comparable secular activities**, unless they are pursuing **a compelling interest** and using **the least restrictive means available**. Yet recently, during the COVID pandemic, certain States seem to **have ignored these long-settled principles.**[32]

And justices should not stay passive, or, in the words of Justice Kavanaugh,

> Federal courts therefore must afford **substantial deference** to state and local authorities about **how best to balance competing policy considerations during the pandemic.** But **judicial deference in an emergency or a crisis does not mean wholesale judicial abdication, especially when important questions of religious discrimination, racial discrimination, free speech or the like are raised.**[33]

Dissenting justices Roberts, Breyer and Sotomayor highlighted, on the other hand, inter alia, the need to respect *Jacobson*, thus the States' police power, as well as medical experts' decisions. Justices should not try to substitute such expertise with their own,[34] or, as Justice Sotomayor put it, "play a deadly game in second guessing the expert judgment of health officials (. . .)"[35] Again, as in *Calvary Chapel* and *South Bay I*, the Court does not refrain from free exercise analogies in this case, too, which, as already noted above, rather lead to subjective and irrational balancing. At any rate, *Roman Catholic Diocese*'s legacy might be considered the "dethroning of Jacobson,"[36] since it was not a free-exercise case and such precedent could not justify a boundless police power of States in matters of public health forever.

The Court changed course with *South Bay II*,[37] granting partial relief to the applicant. What is interesting here, which *inter alia* concerned the ban of singing in religious services for public health reasons, is how deference to the political branches has started to vanish in the Court's reasoning. With only one loud dissent in the case (of liberal Justice Kagan), it is evident that the Court is beginning to modify its former adherence to the *Jacobson* precedent and strictly scrutinize State mandates for their neutrality and narrow tailoring. Again, medical expertise is treated as a factor justices cannot put aside or the "Court will inject uncertainty into an area

---

[32] Roman Catholic Diocese, Gorsuch concurring, p. 1.

[33] Roman Catholic Diocese, Kavanaugh concurring, p. 3.

[34] Roman Catholic Diocese, Breyer dissent, pp. 4–5.

[35] Roman Catholic Diocese, Sotomayor dissent, p. 3.

[36] Parmet (2021), referring to the leading Jacobson precedent.

[37] South Bay United Pentecostal Church v Newsom, 592 US _ (2021) ("South Bay II").

where uncertainty has human costs."[38] Justice Kagan reminds us of the tough role of justices who, in the midst of a crisis, need to stay vigilant while reviewing crisis measures. Still, while unelected and not accountable, the judiciary cannot give a carte blanche to the States to violate the Constitution indefinitely or as long as the pandemic lasts.

In *Tandon*[39] decided in April 2021, the Court's change of course was solidified. With this *per curiam* order, which was followed this time only by a two-page dissent of the liberal branch (Kagan, Breyer, and Sotomayor), the Court's former deference seems to have completely vanished, and strict scrutiny was applied. For the fifth time since the COVID-19 outbreak, the Court rejected the Ninth Circuit's findings in California and maintained that *strict scrutiny* remained the standard applied in such cases.

Particularly, the justices stressed the fact that said measures, which prohibited more than three households gathering together at a time for any in-home prayer and Bible studies, for public health and safety reasons, were not neutral and generally applicable. Since religious organizations, like the applicant church, were treated less favorably than comparable secular institutions, *strict scrutiny* had to be satisfied. The Court emphasized that the State of California had the burden to satisfy this standard by showing that less restrictive means would not prevent COVID infection or that religious activities were more dangerous than secular businesses. Finally, the issue of mootness came up again in this case, since states such as California or New York constantly changed their COVID regulations while litigation was pending at Courts. The Court ruled that given the possibility of States enforcing harsher regulations, they could not moot pending cases simply by changing their regulations.

3 The Compulsory Vaccination Cases (2021 October Term)

Besides the freedom of religion case law in the pandemic, another interesting group of cases involved the controversial issue of compulsory vaccinations in workplaces. The 2021 October Term saw the surge of such cases, with the first ones decided in October and December 2021, on Maine[40] and New York[41] state mandates.

Does v Mills and *Dr v Hochul* both concerned the compulsory vaccination of healthcare workers against COVID-19, in Maine in New York States, respectively. Both applications for injunctive relief were denied. In the Maine Case, Justice Barrett supported the view that the applicants were not likely to succeed on the merits. Interestingly, freedom of religion again came up as a claim in both cases, since both State regulations did not include any exemptions *on religious grounds*,

---

[38] South Bay II, Kagan dissent, p. 6.

[39] Ratesh Tandon v Newsom, 593 US _ (2021) ("Tandon").

[40] John Does et al. v Janet Mills, 595 US _ (2021) ("Does v Mills").

[41] Dr A et al. v Kathy Hochul, 595 US _ (2021) ("Dr. A v Hochul").

except for *medica*l reasons. Again, any free exercise clause restriction like the one claimed demanded *strict scrutiny*, as highlighted by the Conservative majority in both cases.

Conservative Justice Gorsuch authored two long dissents in both cases, scrutinizing the measure in detail. In the Maine case, he pointed to the fact that the State had not shown that its rule represented the least restrictive means available, when over 85% of health workers in the State of Maine had already been vaccinated and whether denying exemptions to religious objectors would be essential to achieving thresholds. He also emphasized that things had already changed, since by that time America had had wide access to COVID vaccines, in contrast to a year ago, and COVID could not be regarded as wide a risk as before the availability of vaccines.[42] Accordingly, in the New York case, Justice Gorsuch stressed the absence of statistics on behalf of the State to show the numbers needed to achieve immunity in healthcare workers. He also pointed to the dangers of majoritarian thinking on freedom of religion and to the dangers of emergencies like the pandemic serving as excuses for arbitrariness and democratic backsliding. Judicial deference could not go on forever: *"As days gave way to weeks and weeks to months,* ***this Court came to recognize that the Constitution is not to be put away in challenging time,*** *and we stopped tolerating discrimination against religious exercises. (…) But* ***how many more reminders do we need that the Constitution is not to be obeyed or disobeyed as the circumstances of a particular crisis may suggest?"***[43]

Finally, in January 2022, the Court issued two more orders on the issue of compulsory vaccination, this time concerning public[44] and private[45] workplaces.

The Court blocked compulsory (vaccine-or-test) vaccinations for large private workplaces in the *OSHA* case[46] but green-lighted the vaccination mandate for public health care workers in the *Biden* case.[47,48] Both cases divided the Court. *Inter alia*, the vaccination mandate challenged the *nondelegation doctrine*, according to which Congress may not delegate its legislative power to administrative agencies; rather policy choices should be made by the politically accountable Congress and not by unelected administrative officials.[49] This doctrine, stemming from the principle of

[42] Does v Mills, Gorsuch dissenting, pp. 6–8.

[43] Dr. A v Hochul, Gorsuch dissenting, pp. 12–14.

[44] Joseph Biden, President of the United States et al. v Missouri, 595 US _ (2022) ("Biden").

[45] National Federation of Independent Business et al. v Department of Labor, Occupational Safety and Health Administration, 595 US _ (2022) ("OSHA").

[46] The OSHA mandate required all employers with 100 or more employees—roughly two-thirds of the US private sector—to compel those employees to either be fully vaccinated against COVID-19 or to be tested weekly and wear masks at work.

[47] The Department of Health and Human Services issued the rule, which applies to more than 10 million workers, that requires nearly all health care workers at facilities that participate in the Medicare and Medicaid programs to be fully vaccinated against COVID-19 unless they qualify for a medical or religious exemption.

[48] Howe (2022), pointing also to the record time in which these interim decisions were issued.

[49] Chemerinsky (2006), pp. 327–328; Barak (2006), p. 227.

separation of powers in America grants administrative agencies the power to implement the legislative will, but not the power to make grand policy choices, substituting the legislator. Nevertheless, modern democracy demands compromises and thus, this doctrine has been rather "clouded and infrequently applied"[50] by the US Supreme Court. Modern legislature should be the policymaker, and be accountable to the people, and not delegate this power to unelected administrators. OSHA, an administrative agency, could not have been authorized to issue such a mandate affecting millions of people.[51] Or, that should have been expressly said. Rather, major questions should have been addressed by the legislator alone.

4 Conclusions: Lessons from the US Supreme Court in the Pandemic

The US Supreme Court has undoubtedly grown stronger in the COVID-19 pandemic. It has assessed the risks, its institutional role and knew when to exercise deference.

The Court has been aware both of the health emergency and of the "police power" States have enjoyed on issues of public health in their territory for over a century. Such respect to a century-old precedent should not be considered as "passivity," but rather as *realism* by the judiciary, at least in the initial phases of the emergency. Adherence to precedent does not necessarily mean self-restraint.[52]

The three recent judicial appointments to the Court by former President Trump may have "cemented" the conservative majority, but this majority did not necessarily "define" the predicted outcomes.[53] Justice Barrett, for instance, herself a devout Catholic, has rejected several orders by religious groups at a number of the COVID cases examined. Justices Kavanaugh and Gorsuch, both Catholic, too, have been much louder in their dissents or concurring opinions.

Moreover, a new trend seems to have emerged during the pandemic. The Supreme Court has treated the shadow docket as an "agenda-setting" opportunity.[54] These "shadow" orders have revealed, surprisingly, plenty of the Court's thinking about its role in the pandemic, with long dissents about judicial deference, the role of the experts, the role of the States and the future of the First Amendment. Breaking with the past, this Court even gave the shadow docket a "merits" quality.

Judicial deference during the pandemic has changed over time. One could only applaud this change. Unelected justices, cautious of their institutional role,

---

[50] Barak (2006), p. 229.

[51] OSHA, Per curiam opinion.

[52] Barak (2006), p. 275.

[53] Epstein (2010), p. 488.

[54] Epstein (2010), p. 490.

particularly in times of crisis,[55] sided with the political branches for reasons of efficiency when the COVID pandemic broke in America. Also aware of the States' prerogative and police power on issues of public health, the majority of the US Supreme Court decided to refrain from strict scrutiny of human rights violations. But as the crisis grew deeper, and time passed, deference could not be sustainable. The Court gradually exercised stricter scrutiny on First Amendment violations, guided by its conservative majority.[56] When the issue of compulsory vaccinations affecting millions of Americans in private workplaces reached the US Supreme Court in January 2022, it intervened proactively, as was rather expected. After all, such a reaction could be considered another proof of today's "judicialization of politics."[57] Compulsory vaccinations, a controversial matter in America as well as elsewhere, was transferred from the political arena to the courts, somewhat successfully.

In the "age of human rights"[58] like the one we live in, the judge has gained a much- elevated role in well-functioning democracies. Particularly in times of an emergency, it is the judge's duty to stand up front, and defend human rights. Sometimes defending the Constitution can be the hardest game of all.

References

Barak A (2006) The judge in a democracy. Princeton University Press, Princeton

Baude W (2015) Foreword: the Supreme Court's Shadow Docket. N Y Univ J Law Liberty 9:1

Chemerinsky E (2006) Constitutional law: principles and policies, 3rd edn. Aspen, New York

Eisgruber C (2007) Constitutional self-government. Harvard University Press, Cambridge

Epstein L (2010) The U.S. Supreme Court. In: Whittington et al (eds) The Oxford handbook of law and politics. OUP, Oxford, pp 486–502

Hirschl R (2010) The judicialization of politics. In: Whittington et al (eds) The Oxford handbook of law and politics. OUP, Oxford, pp 119–141

Howe A (2022) Fractured court blocks vaccine-or-test requirement for large workplaces but green-lights vaccine mandate for health care workers. https://www.scotusblog.com/2022/01/fractured-court-blocks-vaccine-or-test-requirement-for-large-workplaces-but-green-lights-vaccine-mandate-for-health-care-workers/ Accessed 31 May 2022

Note (2021) Constitutional constraints on free exercise analogies. Harv Law Rev 134:1782–1803

Parmet W (2020) Rediscovering Jacobson in the Era of COVID-19. B.U. Law Rev Online 100:117–133

Parmet W (2021) Roman Catholic Diocese of Brooklyn v. Cuomo – the Supreme Court and pandemic controls. N Engl J Med 384:199–201

Sajo A, Uitz R (2013) Freedom of religion. In: Rosenfeld M, Sajo A (eds) The Oxford handbook of comparative constitutional law. Oxford University Press, Oxford, pp 909–927

Swenson D (2021) United States Supreme Court approach to first amendment freedom of religion in response to the COVID pandemic. Rev Eur Comp Law 46(3):237–261. https://doi.org/10.31743/recl.12707

[55] Eisgruber (2007), pp. 46, 78.

[56] Swenson (2021), p. 237.

[57] Hirschl (2010), p. 119.

[58] Barak (2006), p. 81.

US Supreme Court (2022) Current Members of the United States Supreme Court. https://www.supremecourt.gov/about/biographies.aspx. Accessed 31 May 2022
Washington Post (2020a) Trump Declares Coronavirus Outbreak a National Emergency. https://www.washingtonpost.com/world/2020/03/13/coronavirus-latest-news/. Accessed 31 May 2022
Washington Post (2020b) Senate confirms Barrett to the Supreme Court, cementing its conservative majority. https://www.washingtonpost.com/politics/courts_law/senate-court-barrett-trump/2020/10/26/df76c07e-1789-11eb-befb-8864259bd2d8_story.html. Accessed 31 May 2022
Wermiel St (2020) Symposium: Coronavirus litigation lurks in the shadows. https://www.scotusblog.com/2020/10/symposium-coronavirus-litigation-lurks-in-the-shadows/. Accessed 31 May 2022
White House (2022) The Senate Confirms Ketanji Brown Jackson to serve on the U.S. Supreme Court. https://www.whitehouse.gov/kbj/. Accessed 31 May 2022

The Rule of Law and Fundamental Rights in the Coronavirus Pandemic in Germany

Wolfgang Kahl and Konstantina-Antigoni Poulou

Abstract The coronavirus pandemic has been a great challenge for most constitutional states in many aspects. This will be illustrated in this contribution taking Germany as an example, with the focus lying mainly on the rule of law principle and fundamental rights, examined in light of the case law developed so far. Notably during the first lockdown, a lot of fundamental rights in Germany were massively curtailed. This is why this unprecedented situation was sometimes qualified as a "state of emergency" or a "corona-dictatorship", given that the breadth, depth and duration of the encroachments on fundamental rights were, and in some cases still are, exceptionally great. Nevertheless, the following contribution demonstrates that such an approach is misplaced. The German Basic Law ("Grundgesetz") does not provide for a state of emergency or any other exceptional provisions regarding the interventions in fundamental rights in times of crisis. The traditional model of the separation of powers has proven to be sufficiently flexible to meet the needs for even far-reaching encroachments on fundamental rights on the one hand, and to adequately control and react to these encroachments in accordance with the rule of law on the other.

1 Introduction

The coronavirus pandemic has been a great challenge for constitutional states in many aspects, foremost due to the unprecedented encroachment on fundamental rights in peacetime. Within a few days, whole sectors of our everyday lives were suddenly shut down in March 2020 and the economic, social and cultural activities came to a standstill. This is why some authors referred to this development as a

W. Kahl (✉)
Faculty of Law, Ruprecht-Karls-Universität, Heidelberg, Germany

Institute for German and European Administrative Law, Heidelberg, Germany
e-mail: wolfgang.kahl@jurs.uni-heidelberg.de

K.-A. Poulou
Faculty of Law, Ruprecht-Karls-Universität, Heidelberg, Germany

K. Chrysogonos, A. Tsiftsoglou (eds.), *Democracy after Covid*,
https://doi.org/10.1007/978-3-031-13901-7_8

"corona-dictatorship"[1] or a "state of emergency",[2] in which fundamental rights were suspended. One and a half years later, a great deal has been achieved but the pandemic is still away from being an unpleasant memory of the past.

The aim of this contribution is to take a sober and differentiated view in the form of a first interim report on the constitutional issues in Germany throughout the coronavirus pandemic.[3] It will first plead for the application of the Basic Law and all constitutional principles enshrined therein even in times of crisis. Second, it will elaborate on the state's duty to protect life and health (Article 2(2) sentence 1 of the Basic Law) and its judicial review. The third and main part of the contribution will analyse the encroachments on various fundamental rights during the coronavirus pandemic and inform on the respective case law of the administrative courts and the Federal Constitutional Court (hereafter: BVerfG). The fourth part will then touch upon the further components of the rule of law principle, namely the theory of materiality ("Wesentlichkeitstheorie") and the parliamentary reservation ("Parlamentsvorbehalt"). Finally, the contribution concludes with some final remarks and an overall assessment of the fight against the coronavirus in Germany under a constitutional law perspective.

2 The COVID-19 Pandemic As a "State of Emergency" Under the Basic Law?

Mainly during the first lockdown, numerous fundamental rights in Germany were massively curtailed. This is why some authors qualified this unprecedented situation as a "state of emergency" or a state of "suspension of fundamental rights",[4] given that the breadth, depth and duration of the encroachments on fundamental rights were, and in some cases still are, undisputedly exceptionally great. Nevertheless, the widespread usage of the terms "state of emergency" and even more of the term "suspension of fundamental rights" is misplaced, given that the Basic Law neither provides for a state of emergency or any other exceptional provisions regarding the

[1] Cf. Lepsius (2020b), *Verfassungsblog*; highly critical of using such a term Lieberknecht et al. (2021, March 11), p. 6.

[2] Kingreen (2021b, February 21), p. 6.

[3] On constitutional issues pertaining to the federal principle ("Bundesstaatsprinzip"), see the contribution of E. Hofmann in this book.

[4] Meinel and Möllers (2020, March 20), p. 9; some authors even warned of a "fascistoid hysterical hygienic state", Heinig (2020), *Verfassungsblog* and a "hygiene dictatorship", Lepsius (2020b), *Verfassungsblog*; Möllers (2020), *Verfassungsblog* considers the German response to the coronavirus pandemic as the most massive collective encroachment on fundamental rights in the history of the Federal Republic of Germany without adequate legal basis. Reporting Kersten and Rixen (2021), p. 57 et seq.

interventions in fundamental rights in times of crisis,[5] nor for areas not regulated by law. Articles 20(3) and 1(3) of the Basic Law clearly stand in the way of such an interpretation.[6] A constitutional state does not deal with the coronavirus pandemic in a state of emergency but on the basis and within the framework of the Basic Law, against which all laws, statutory orders and administrative acts are to be measured and have so far been measured in the context of numerous legal remedies.[7] The judicial proceedings on the constitutionality of laws under Section 47(1) of the Rules of Administrative Courts (VwGO) play a significant role with regard to statutory orders, especially since the administrative courts have the competence not to apply unconstitutional laws. In the context of the substantive review of the various state measures, the classic scheme of scope of protection – encroachment – justification, including especially the central principle of proportionality, comes into play, whereby a wide variety of civil rights and also Article 3(1) of the Basic Law are relevant as standards of review.

3 The State's Duty of Protection

Of particular interest is the question on the extent to which the state is obliged to take measures to combat the coronavirus pandemic. Fundamental rights in the German constitutional doctrine are not only perceived as subjective rights of defence against state intervention (*status negativus*) but also have an objective dimension, from which the state's duty of protection flows.[8] Fundamental rights constitute in this sense a deliberate, value-driven decision of the constitution.[9] The addressees of this duty are all holders of public authority. The violation of the state's duty of protection can be asserted by those affected by way of a constitutional complaint.[10] The question, however, as to how the state's positive duty to protect is to be attained

[5] Very clearly emphasised by Dreier (2021), p. 229; Häberle and Kotzur (2021), p. 134. Even in the case of defence (Article 115c(2) of the Basic Law) fundamental rights cannot be generally suspended but only allow for narrowly defined modifications, see BVerwG, judgment of 21.6.2005 – 2 WD 12/04; Schmitz and Neubert (2020), p. 668.

[6] Greve (2021), p. 28.

[7] Guckelberger (2020), p. 4; Kloepfer (2021), p. 175; neither can be spoken of a de facto suspension, see Goldhammer and Neuhöfer (2021a), p. 213.

[8] For an extensive overview of the state's duty of protection, see Klein (1989), pp. 1633–1640.

[9] BVerfG, order of 8.8.1978 – 2 BvL 8/77 para 109.

[10] See BVerfG, order of 25.2.1975 – 1 BvF 1, 2, 3, 4, 5, 6/74. For the inaction of the legislature with regard to regulations on a so-called "Triage" in case of exhaustion of medical capacities in the pandemic BVerfG (3. Chamber of the First Senate), order of 16.7.2020 – 1 BvR 1541/20; BVerfG (3. Chamber of the First Senate), order of 12.5.2020 – 1 BvR 1027/20. On the triage problem cf. also from a constitutional law point of view Lehner (2021), pp. 252–262.

and what regulatory measures must be met, remains complicated and controversial.[11]

3.1 Article 2(2) Sentence 1 of the Basic Law in Particular

In the context of the coronavirus pandemic, the focus regarding fundamental rights lies on the duty to protect life and health under Article 2(2) sentence 1 of the Basic Law. This includes the state's duty to protect and promote the lives of individuals and to protect them from injury to their physical integrity.[12] This duty of protection may even refer to precautionary measures before a danger or a risk for life or health arises. However, this duty of protection is not absolute. It must be weighed against any conflicting interests.[13] The legislator is granted a wide margin of appreciation in this respect. This prerogative of the legislator and, albeit more restrictedly, of the executive as well, has its roots in the principle of democracy and the separation of powers (Article 20(1 and 2) of the Basic Law). However, it is also supported by epistemological reasons and the probabilistic nature of the measures, given that regulators must counter a risk with protective measures without having firm scientific-empirical proof of the real risk at their disposal.[14] In this context, there are two possible ways, in which an encroachment on fundamental rights may occur: either the state acts in fulfilment of its duty to protect the right to life and health and therefore triggers the defensive dimension of other restricted fundamental rights (objective dimension) or it fails to fulfil its obligation to protect and the individuals affected file a constitutional complaint to demand protection (subjective dimension).[15] In the first case, the state's reaction to an emerging danger to fulfil its obligation to protect simultaneously constitutes the justification ground for the restriction of other fundamental rights.[16] In the second case, the subjective dimension of the right to life and health is triggered when a certain hazard level is exceeded, so that the exposure to danger can in effect be equated with the violation of a fundamental right.[17]

[11] Klein (1989), p. 1635.

[12] Murswiek (2021b), p. 506 notes that this duty of protection refers in principle to damages caused either by the state or by third parties and not by natural phenomena, such as a pandemic. In this regard, the state's obligation lies in protecting vulnerable people from getting infected by others.

[13] Greve (2021), p. 29. Similarly in the Italian constitutional order, see Scalia (2020), p. 98.

[14] BVerfG, order of 24.11.2010 – 1 BvF 2/05 para 142.

[15] Goldhammer and Neuhöfer (2021a), p. 215 et seq.

[16] BVerfG (3. Chamber of the Second Senate), order of 7.4.2020 – 1 BvR 755/20 para 11; BVerfG (2. Chamber of the First Senate), order of 9.6.2020 – 1 BvR 1230/20 para 19.

[17] Goldhammer and Neuhöfer (2021a), p. 215.

3.2 Judicial Control

When dealing with cases regarding the state's obligation to protect, the intensity of judicial control by the BVerfG is rather low, as indicated by the legal tests of manifest error ("Evidenzkontrolle") and prohibition of insufficient actions ("Untermaßverbot"). Above all, the protective measures must meet certain minimum requirements and be effective and suitable for the purpose pursued. However, as the BVerfG recently emphasised again in its seminal "Climate Change" order, a violation of the obligation to protect can only be established, if one of the following three conditions is met, namely if protective measures have not been taken at all, if the regulations and measures taken are obviously unsuitable or completely inadequate to achieve the required protection goal, or if they fall considerably short of the protection goal.[18] In this respect, the holders of public authority must always balance the legal interests that need to be protected; a right to a *specific* measure is, however, not granted. The right to life in this equation constitutes a high but not the highest value.[19] The status of the highest value is attributed only to human dignity (Art. 1(1) of the Basic Law).[20] In contrast to human dignity, the right to life is subject to balancing against other rights. However, it cannot be disregarded that life is the basis of human dignity and the prerequisite for all other fundamental rights.[21]

Against this background, the principles of practical concordance and proportionality ultimately play a key role in addressing potential conflicts of fundamental rights.[22] In cases, in which the state's preventive measures result in the encroachment on a fundamental right, the usual three-step control applies, whereby the suitability, necessity and proportionality stricto sensu of the ordered measures are examined.[23] In the context of the coronavirus pandemic, this practically means that the state is not limited to protecting people at risk solely by restricting their own freedom; rather, it may introduce regulations that also restrict the freedoms of presumably healthier and less vulnerable people. Otherwise, the people at risk would have to completely withdraw from everyday life and any form of social participation.[24] In view of the above, the BVerfG rejected the request for an interim order against preventive statutory coronavirus measures, which, according to the plaintiff, should only concern people that belong to high-risk groups. Such an approach would contradict the Basic Law's perception of man as a social being.[25]

---

[18] BVerfG, order of 24.3.2021 – 1 BvR 2656/18 paras. 154 et seq.; on the examination steps, see Manssen. (2021), para 64.

[19] BVerfG, judgment of 26.2.2020 – 2 BvR 2347/15 a.o.

[20] Richter (2021), p. 17.

[21] Richter (2021), p. 17.

[22] BVerfG (1. Chamber of the First Senate), judgment of 13.5.2020 – 1 BvR 1021/20 para 9.

[23] Further Murswiek (2021a), p. 3 et seq.

[24] BVerfG (1. Chamber of the First Senate), judgment of 13.5.2020 – 1 BvR 1021/20 para 9.

[25] See for example BVerfG, judgment of 20.07.1954 – 1 BvR 459, 484, 548, 555, 623, 651, 748, 783, 801/52, 5, 9/53, 96, 114/54 para 32.

In any case, the state has to strike a proportionate balance between the constitutionally protected freedoms on the one hand and the need for protection on the other.[26]

So far, the BVerfG has been reluctant to affirm a violation of the obligation to protect under Article 2(2) sentence 1 of the Basic Law with regard to the preventive statutory coronavirus measures. A prominent example constitutes the case of a 65-year-old man who filed a constitutional complaint, arguing that he belonged to the "high-risk group" as defined by the Robert Koch Institute.[27] He essentially complained that the easing of the COVID-19 preventive measures would violate his fundamental right under Article 2(2) sentence 1 of the Basic Law. The BVerfG argued that life and physical integrity are extremely important legal interests; it could even be assumed that the complete social isolation of the entire population would offer the best protection against infection. However, the legislative authority does not exceed its assessment prerogative when it permits social interaction under certain conditions. Only in this way could other constitutionally protected fundamental freedoms be also taken into consideration, such as the freedom of religion[28] and the freedom of assembly.[29] Similarly, the legislative authority could consider the social acceptance of the measures and consider a cautious or even drastic approach to be more appropriate, when considering a long-term effective protection of life and health. Besides, even from a scientific point of view, it is uncertain which easing of measures has a bigger effect on the prevention of infection. Against this background, the BVerfG did not consider the state's obligation to protect under Article 2-(2) sentence 1 of the Basic Law to have been violated.

3.3 Expert Knowledge and the Parameter of Time

The particularity of the coronavirus pandemic mainly lies in the fact that not only democratic decision-making[30] but also judicial control relies heavily on scientific expert knowledge,[31] especially with regard to the stages of suitability and necessity of the proportionality test.[32] Expert knowledge regarding the coronavirus pandemic is, however, in constant progress and sometimes controversial even among experts. New research findings lead to new insights, meaning that the constitutional assessment of measures restricting the fundamental rights suffers from a deficit of well-established facts. Any measures against the coronavirus pandemic must, therefore,

[26] BayVerfGH, judgment of 30.12.2020 – Vf. 96-VII-20 para 21.

[27] BVerfG, judgment of 12.5.2020 – 1 BvR 1027/20; for a critical assessment of the decision, see Muckel (2021), p. 264.

[28] BVerfG (2. Chamber of the First Senate), judgment of 10.4.2020 – 1 BvQ 28/20.

[29] BVerfG (1. Chamber of the First Senate), judgment of 15.4.2020 – 1 BvR 828/20.

[30] Cf. Gärditz (2021b), p. 511 et seq.

[31] Fundamental to this Münkler (2020).

[32] Goldhammer and Neuhöfer (2021b), p. 214.

always be open to revision and adjusted to the latest scientific-empirical findings,[33] otherwise they cannot pass the proportionality test.[34] The legislator's duty of monitoring ("Beobachtungspflicht") and duty of rectification ("Nachbesserungspflicht") are popular legal concepts of special significance in this respect. The parameter of time presents an additional challenge to the legislative authority, given that the latter must be granted with adequate flexibility and have the reflexes to adjust the preventive measures in time.[35] In addition, the limited duration of the restrictive measures may lead to a less intense intervention,[36] which is why the federal legislator explicitly introduced it as a concept in the new regulatory framework.[37] In the same vein, the BVerfG has attached particular weight to the time component in the context of the proportionality assessment to rule for or against the validity of a measure.[38]

4 Fundamental Rights and Judicial Review During the Coronavirus Pandemic

The vast majority of the measures ordered against the coronavirus pandemic were in form of statutory orders ("Rechtsverordnungen") by the German federal states ("Länder") on regional level and constituted the legal basis, upon which the encroachment on a number of fundamental rights was founded ("Gesetzesvorbehalt"). The legal instrument for their introduction was the German Infection Protection Act –IPA ("Infektionsschutzgesetzt – IfSG")[39] and more specifically Sections 28 et seq. thereof. In view of the proportionality requirements, the legitimate aim of the "coronavirus measures" consisted in the guarantee of an effective healthcare system and thereby in the protection of life and health of the

[33] VGH München, judgment of 30.3.2020 – 20 NE 20.632 para 63; VGH Kassel, judgment of 1.4.2020 – 2 B 925/20 para 21; Kersten and Rixen (2021), p. 275 et seq.; Schmitz and Neubert (2020), p. 668.

[34] Gärditz (2021a), p. 2764.

[35] Gärditz (2021a), p. 2764.

[36] Implicitly BVerfG (2. Chamber of the First Senate), judgment of 10.4.2020 – 1 BvQ 28/20 para 14; BVerfG, judgment of 10.4.2020 – 1 BvQ 31/20 para 16.

[37] For more details, see below under Sect. 5.

[38] On the limited duration of measures: BVerfG, (2. Chamber of the First Senate), judgment of 10.4.2020 – 1 BvQ 28/20 para 14; BVerfG, judgment of 10.4.2020 – 1 BvQ 31/20 para 16; BVerfG, order of 19.11.2021 – 1 BvR 781/21 para 233; on the time needed until the biggest part of the population is fully vaccinated BVerfG, order of 5.5.2021 – 1 BvR 781/21, a.o. para 53.

[39] This law is the key legal instrument ("universal weapon") in the entire response to the pandemic in Germany. Cf. critical, because of the marginalisation of the Basic Law, the disregard for the hierarchy of norms ("primacy of the constitution") and the issue of unconstitutional "law-representing ordinances" Dreier (2021), p. 235 at seq.

population.[40] Nevertheless, the statutory orders differed in their regulations among the federal states in that they flexibly addressed the needs of each state at the time of their introduction and thereby concretised the abstract conditions of the IPA according to the scientific and factual data at their disposal.[41]

Ever since the first lockdown in March 2020, many German citizens had recourse to administrative courts to seek interim relief against the restrictive regulations. Up to today, a plethora of cases has ultimately reached the BVerfG, mainly based on Section 32 of the Federal Constitutional Court Act (BVerfGG).[42] In the context of this procedure, the BVerfG may provisionally decide a matter by way of a preliminary injunction if this is urgently required to avert severe disadvantage, to prevent imminent violence or for another important reason in the interest of the common good. The decisions issued so far offer a wide overview of the BVerfG's perception of the room for manoeuvre as well as of the limits of the executive during a severe health crisis.

4.1 General Freedom of Action

Among the most common and worldwide spread measures against the coronavirus are the obligation to wear a mask in public spaces, to provide for a negative coronavirus test or be in quarantine, when requested, as well as the imposition of a curfew during night hours. These regulations primarily aim at slowing down the infection rate by reducing physical and social contact with people other than those of one's own household, although at the same time they directly infringe on the general freedom of action (Article 2(1) of the Basic Law) and the freedom of movement (Article 2(2) sentence 2 of the Basic Law).

With regard, first, to the obligation to wear a mask, it has been qualified as a minor encroachment on the general freedom of action and the general right of personality.[43] In view of the legitimate aim of the measure that lies in avoiding the exponential increase of the coronavirus cases and the irreversible consequences of such a development, in combination with the wide discretion of the legislative authority, the balancing exercise between the general freedom of action and the health protection leans in favour of the latter. Besides, not only is the imposition of this obligation of

[40] See new Section 28a of the IPA; BVerfG (2. Chamber of the First Senate), judgment of 10.4.2020 – 1 BvQ 28/20 para 13.

[41] BVerfG (2. Chamber of the First Senate), order of 3.6.2020 – 1 BvR 990/20 para 12.

[42] The applicant must, however, already have (unsuccessfully) sought interim relief (Section 47 para. 6 VwGO) before administrative courts according to the subsidiarity principle, see BVerfG (1. Chamber of the First Senate), order of 20.3.2020 – 1 BvR 661/20 para 4.

[43] OVG Hamburg, judgment of 1.4.2021 – 5 Bs 54/21 para 40; see also, BVerfG (1. Chamber of the First Senate), order of 27.6.2020 – 1 BvQ 74/20 para 3.

limited duration, it also does not apply to people with health problems, who are discouraged from wearing a mask.[44] In the same vein, the obligation to self-quarantine after visiting a place listed as a "risk area" is proportionate, since the restriction of the freedom of action and the freedom of movement is of limited duration and low intensity. The benefits of quarantine, namely the timely detection of new infections and the protection of the total population outweigh any downsides of the measure.[45]

More controversial seems to be the imposition of a curfew during night hours, now regulated under Sections 28a(1) and 28b(1) of the IPA.[46] When dealing with this issue in the context of interim proceedings, the BVerfG ruled that, should the application be successful at this stage but unsuccessful during the main proceedings, a powerful tool against the coronavirus pandemic would have been neutralised.[47] Given the low percentage of fully vaccinated people at that time, it could not be ruled out that in the absence of a curfew, the citizens would hold private meetings and disregard the social distancing rules. The imposition of a curfew functioned, therefore, as a control instrument during night-time in this regard.[48] The BVerfG ruled in the main proceedings in favour of the constitutionality of the measure in question, given that the legislator pursued constitutionally legitimate purposes, namely the interruption of the exponential growth of the virus to avoid overwhelming the healthcare system as a whole and to thereby ensure the provision of medical care nationwide.[49] Besides, the legislator's assessment at the time of the Act's adoption was based on authoritative factual knowledge, by entrusting the Robert Koch Institute with the evaluation of any relevant studies that appear worldwide as well as their preparation for the Federal Government and the general public.[50]

4.2 Freedom of Religion

During the first wave of the coronavirus pandemic, all kinds of church services were prohibited, meaning that the unconditionally granted freedom of religion under

[44] BayVGH, judgment of 15.5.2020 – 20 NE 20.1102 paras. 16 et seq.

[45] BVerfG (2. Chamber of the First Senate), order of 25.8.2020 – 1 BvR 1981/20 para 10. On the contrary, a general obligation to self-quarantine regardless of the current situation of the pandemic and the infection cases would be a disproportionate and therefore unlawful measure, see NdsOVG, judgment of 11.5.2020 – 13 MN 143/20 para 33.

[46] The former wording of Section 28 of the IPA did not meet the requirements of the principle of precision ("Bestimmtheitsgebot") on curfews, see Guckelberger (2020), p. 6 et seq.

[47] BVerfG, order of 5.5.2021 – 1 BvR 781/21 a.o. para 52.

[48] BVerfG, order of 5.5.2021 – 1 BvR 781/21 a.o. para 52. In favour of the proportionality of the measure, see Greve and Lassahn (2021), p. 667 et seq.; against the proportionality of the measure Boehme-Nessler (2021a), pp. 671 et seq.; Edenharter (2021), p. 571.

[49] BVerfG, order of 19.11.2021 – 1 BvR 781/21 paras. 167 et seq.

[50] BVerfG, order of 19.11.2021 – 1 BvR 781/21 paras. 177 et seq.

Article 4(1) and (2) of the Basic Law was essentially suspended. Religious people were practically unable to practice their religion in the sense of Article 4(2) of the Basic Law and therefore sought judicial relief. The BVerfG qualified the restrictive measure as a severe encroachment on the freedom of religion both for Catholics and Muslims with regard to the total prohibition to visit churches and mosques even during Easter time.[51] However, the justification of such a prohibition was possible in light of the state's obligation to protect under Article 2(2) sentence 1 of the Basic Law and the high risk of infection of the rest of the population, which could even result in a number of deaths.[52] The proportionality of the measure was further supported by its limited duration but it should be under constant review in light of the ongoing scientific and factual developments.[53]

Shortly afterwards, however, the BVerfG ruled that exceptions from such prohibitions should apply in coordination with the local public health department, as long as all necessary hygienic rules would be respected. A total prohibition to exercise the freedom of religion was therefore found disproportionate.[54] Even if churches and mosques did not hold any service on their own initiative, this did not affect the legitimate interest of religious people to take legal action, because their reopening could not be ruled out in case the regulation on the prohibition was judicially overturned.[55] A fair balance between the exercise of the freedom of religion, on the one hand, and the protection of life and health, on the other, was, therefore, ultimately struck.

4.3 *Freedom of Assembly*

All measures introduced on the basis of the IPA aimed at social distancing and the prevention of big crowds. As a consequence, the freedom of assembly under Article 8(1) of the Basic Law was essentially restricted, given that its realisation presupposes the physical presence of a group of people to defend a specific cause.[56] The freedom

[51] BVerfG, order of 10.4.2020 – 1 BvQ 28/20 para 11; BVerfG, order of 10.4.2020 – 1 BvQ 31/20 para 10; BVerfG (2. Chamber of the First Senate), order of 29.4.2020 – 1 BvQ 44/20 para 13.

[52] BVerfG, order of 10.4.2020 – 1 BvQ 28/20 para 13; BVerfG, order of 10.4.2020 – 1 BvQ 31/20 para 13.

[53] BVerfG, order of 10.4.2020 – 1 BvQ 28/20 para 14; BVerfG, order of 10.4.2020 – 1 BvQ 31/20 para 16.

[54] BVerfG (2. Chamber of the First Senate), order of 29.4.2020 – 1 BvQ 44/20 para 9; in the same vein Edenharter (2021), p. 572, according to which the possibility to watch a service through electronic devices is not an argument in favour of the proportionality of a total prohibition.

[55] BVerfG, order of 10.4.2020 – 1 BvQ 28/20 para 6. According to the administrative courts such a legitimate interest did not exist, because a potential success of the legal remedy would not have any factual or legal benefits on the applicants, BayVGH, judgment of 9.4.2020 – 20 NE 20.738 para 23; HessVGH, judgment of 07.04.2020 – 8 B 892/20.N para 25.

[56] Meinel and Möllers (2020, March 20), p. 9 speak of a suspension of the freedom of assembly.

of assembly is of great constitutional importance, since it is inherently linked to democracy and the active participation in the economic, political and social developments.[57] Its high value for a democratic state was recognised in the notorious *Brokdorf*[58] decision of the BVerfG. This is why the freedom of assembly should always be guaranteed, even during a pandemic. Nevertheless, the freedom of assembly is subject to restrictions prescribed by law: for *open air* assemblies, the written legal reservation in Article 8(2) of the Basic Law applies, whereas for *indoor* assemblies, unwritten reasons exist to justify the encroachment, the so-called "conflicting constitutional law" ("kollidierendes Verfassungsrecht").[59]

During the first lockdown,[60] almost all German federal states either prohibited gatherings completely or with a reservation with regard to granting permission.[61] The aim of the measure was to prevent people from getting infected because of the physical contact among the participants.[62] Despite the state's duty of protection under Article 2(2) sentence 1 of the Basic Law, the BVerfG underlined the importance of the freedom of assembly and clarified that the individual circumstances and possibility to apply hygienic rules, namely to keep minimum distances,[63] wear a facemask[64] or reduce the number of participants[65] must always be taken into consideration before permitting or refusing an assembly.[66] Otherwise, a general and total prohibition of gatherings could not be justified and was therefore disproportionate.[67] The cooperation obligation between the administrative authority and the participants does not mean, however, that a compromise must be reached to the detriment of life and health protection of the others if, for example, the administrative authority is not convinced of the exact number of participants or that the agreed rules will be respected.[68]

[57] Goldhammer and Neuhöfer (2021b), p. 642.

[58] BVerfG, order of 14.5.1985 – 1 BvR 233/81, 1 BvR 341/81.

[59] On the proportionality of the restrictive measures during the coronavirus pandemic, see Martini et al. (2020), p. 934; Sinder (2021), p. 106 et seq.

[60] For more details, see Kersten and Rixen (2021), p. 118 et seq. who divide the development of the freedom of assembly during the coronavirus crisis in three phases.

[61] The BVerfG left the question unanswered, whether prohibitions on gatherings with a reservation on granting permission are (un)constitutional, BVerfG (1. Chamber of the First Senate), order of 17.4.2020 – 1 BvQ 37/20 para 24. In favour of their constitutionality Greve (2021), p. 38; against their constitutionality VG Hamburg, judgment of 16.4.2020 – 17 E 1648/20 para 17; Kersten and Rixen (2021), p. 138.

[62] Greve (2021), p. 38.

[63] BVerfG (1. Chamber of the First Senate), order of 16.5.2020 – 1 BvQ 55/20 para 10.

[64] BVerfG (1. Chamber of the First Senate), order of 27.6.2020 – 1 BvQ 74/20 para 3.

[65] BVerfG (1. Chamber of the First Senate), order of 31.5.2020 – 1 BvQ 63/20 para 7.

[66] BVerfG (1. Chamber of the First Senate), order of 17.4.2020 – 1 BvQ 37/20 para 24; in the same vein BVerfG (1. Chamber of the First Senate), order of 15.4.2020 – 1 BvR 828/20 para 15.

[67] Edenharter (2021), p. 575; Martini et al. (2020), p. 934.

[68] In this respect VG München, judgment of 29.5.2020 – M 13 E 20.2351 paras. 22 et seq.; similarly, BVerfG (1. Chamber of the First Senate), order of 1.5.2020 – 1 BvR 1003/20 para 8.

In view of the above, the gatherings were gradually allowed, even if their aim was to demonstrate against the "coronavirus measures" and strategy. A prohibition to convene an assembly is, nevertheless, still possible if all proportionality requirements are met. This was the case with the so-called "Querdenken"-movement,[69] in which the competent administrative authority argued that it could not enforce any less restrictive measures.[70] Indeed, the BVerfG clarified that based on the experience with previous demonstrations defending a similar cause, during which the hygienic rules were totally disregarded, the permission of such a demonstration with approximately 20,000 participants would result in a real risk of infection and could therefore be denied.[71] Any restriction of the freedom of assembly must, however, abide by the strict proportionality requirements and correspond to the dynamic and volatile development of the pandemic.[72]

In light of these developments, the federal legislator reacted and introduced a specific provision on the freedom of assembly in Section 28a(2) sentence 1 No. 1 of the IPA. Under this provision, a prohibition of a gathering can be ordered on the condition that the containment of the coronavirus pandemic would be significantly jeopardised, although all other available protective measures have already been considered. This regulation basically constitutes an expression of the proportionality principle. The practical consequence is that the German federal states can henceforth restrict the freedom of assembly or order a prohibition by way of a general prohibition based on Section 28(1) in combination with 28a(1) No. 10, (2) sentence 1 No. 1 and (3) of the IPA or alternatively by way of a statutory order under Section 32 of the IPA.

4.4 Freedom of Occupation and Freedom of Property

The freedom of occupation under Article 12(1) of the Basic Law as well as the freedom of property constitute further rights that were significantly restricted during the pandemic by state orders that prohibited the opening of all kinds of shops. This meant specifically for business owners a twofold restriction, given that they could neither exercise their profession nor earn their living by exploiting their property.[73] Again, such drastic measures were introduced in view of the increasing infection cases and the state's duty to protect the health of individuals by guaranteeing an effective healthcare system. These measures were in principle qualified as

[69] See in detail Kersten and Rixen (2021), p. 124 et seq.

[70] BVerfG (1. Chamber of the First Senate), order of 21.11.2020 – 1 BvQ 135/20 paras. 6–7.

[71] BVerfG (1. Chamber of the First Senate), order of 5.12.2020 – 1 BvQ 145/20 para 8.

[72] BVerfG (1. Chamber of the First Senate), order of 30.8.2020 – 1 BvQ 94/20 para 16.

[73] Schmitz and Neubert (2020), p. 667. On the matter of the compensation of those affected, see Dolde and Marquard (2021), pp. 674–679; Kersten and Rixen (2021), p. 192 et seq.; Viessmann (2021), pp. 397–401.

proportionate by the administrative courts.[74] Although the courts acknowledged that the people affected would have to deal with irreversible economic losses or even wind up their business,[75] the irreversible consequences of an overloaded healthcare system on individuals and the society in total should be prioritised. Nevertheless, there were individual regulations, such as the closing time of the gastronomy sector, that were found unnecessary and therefore disproportionate.[76]

4.5 Right to Equality

Considering the wide range of the affected fundamental rights during the coronavirus pandemic and the different effects of the measures on different groups of people, special attention must be given to the right to equality under Article 3(1) of the Basic Law. Even during a pandemic, the fundamental rule applies that basically equal matters are to be treated equally, basically unequal matters unequally.[77] At the same time, the principle of coherence (consistency) must also be observed as part of the proportionality test.[78] The right to equality, however, is only binding for one and the same legislator. Therefore, it does not refer, for example, to the different measures introduced in the different German federal states.[79] Even so, unequal treatment is allowed within a single regulation, only if it can be justified on the basis of objective criteria.

As mentioned above, almost the entire economic activity was shut down during the coronavirus pandemic in Germany, except for certain branches, such as supermarkets and pharmacies. This unequal treatment was justified by the need to ensure the supply of the population with the necessary goods for their daily needs.[80] More exceptions were gradually regulated, according to the epidemiologic data and the basic needs of the population,[81] so that bookstores, bike stores as well as generally stores, whose facilities did not exceed an 800 m^2 surface and could guarantee the observance of hygienic rules, could reopen in April 2020 after the decline of

[74] SächsVerfGH, order of 14.5.2020 – Vf. 72-IV-20 (e.A.) paras. 15 et seq.; OVG Bremen, order of 9.4.2020 – 1 B 97/20 paras. 41 et seq.; OVG Lüneburg, order of 22.4.2020 – 13 MN 105/20 para 37; OVG Münster, order of 6.4.2020 – 13 B 398/20.NE paras. 51 et seq.; VGH München, order of 30.3.2020 – 20 CS 20.611 paras. 21–22.

[75] See for example BVerfG (2. Chamber of the First Senate), order of 28.4.2020 – 1 BvR 899/20 para 11; VGH Mannheim (1. Senate), order of 7.5.2020 – 1 S 1244/20 paras. 24, 28.

[76] See for example VG Berlin, order of 15.10.2020 – 14 L 422/20 para 26; VG Aachen, order of 22.10.2020 – 7 L 758/20 para 2; VGH Kassel, order of 29.10.2020 – 6 B 2634/20 para 22.

[77] BVerfG (3. Chamber of the First Senate), order of 18.7.2019 – 1 BvL 1/18, 1 BvL 4/18, 1 BvR 1595/18 para 92.

[78] See Erdmann (2020), pp. 1798–1802.

[79] Goldhammer and Neuhöfer (2021b), p. 645.

[80] See for example VG München, order of 20.03.2020 – M 26 E 20.1209 para 54.

[81] Schenk (2020), p. 799.

incidence rate. Were these differentiations justified and in compliance with the right to equality? The standard of review applied in such cases by administrative courts is oriented to the principle of proportionality – only without a three-step structure –, the content and limits of which cannot be determined in abstract but only according to the different factual and regulatory areas affected in each case.[82] With regard to the limit of 800 m^2 for example, the vast majority of administrative courts ruled in favour of the measure in view of the wide discretion of the regulator and the argument that in that way, the formation of big crowds in cities would be prevented.[83] In case that a measure is found incompatible with the right to equality,[84] the courts will simply not apply the unlawful distinctive law provision; they cannot introduce a different regulation on their own motion because this would interfere with the prerogative of the legislator.[85]

5 Rule of Law

Apart from the question whether fundamental rights were sufficiently warranted, another aspect of the rule of law ("Rechtsstaatsprinzip") plays a crucial role, when touching upon constitutional matters during the coronavirus pandemic, namely the constitutionality of the protective ordinances. As will be elaborated, particularly problematic were the measures ordered during the first wave of the pandemic in

[82] See BVerfG (3. Chamber of the First Senate), order of 18.7.2019 – 1 BvL 1/18, 1 BvL 4/18, 1 BvR 1595/18 paras. 91 et seq.

[83] See for example OVG Bautzen (3. Senate), order of 07.01.2021 – 3 B 424/20 paras. 65 et seq.; OVG Bremen, order of 23.4.2020 – 1 B 107/20 paras. 24-25; OVG Hamburg (5. Senate), order of om 30.04.2020 – 5 Bs 64/20 paras. 53 et seq.; OVG Koblenz, order of 18.1.2021 – 6 B 11642/20 paras. 25 et seq.; OVG Lüneburg, order of 29.4.2020 – 13 MN 120/20 para 10; OVG Saarlouis, order of 27.4.2020 – 2 B 141/20 paras. 31 et seq.; OVG Schleswig, order of 30.4.2020 – 3 MR 15/20 paras. 25 et seq. There were, however, some administrative courts that found the measure to be in violation of the right to equality, see VG Hamburg (chamber 3), order of 21.4.2020 – 3 E 1675/20VG paras. 24 et seq.; VG Regensburg (14. Chamber), order of 5.5.2020 – RO 14 E 20.783 para 23. Some administrative courts expressed their concerns also in relation to the opening of bookstores regardless of their surface, VGH München (20. Senate), order of 27.4.2020 – 20 NE 20.793 para 38; VerfGH Sachsen, order of 30.4.2020 – Vf. 61-IV-20 (e.A.), 62-IV20 (e.A.), 63-IV-20 (e.A.) 64-IV-20 (e.A.) para 30.

[84] This was the case with the closing of fitness studios, see VGH München (20. Senate), order of 12.11.2020 – 20 NE 20.2463 para 27.

[85] VGH München (20. Senate), order of 27.04.2020 – 20 NE 20.793 para 40; VerfGH Sachsen, order of 30.4.2020 – Vf. 61-IV-20 (e.A.), 62-IV20 (e.A.), 63-IV-20 (e.A.) 64-IV-20 (e.A.) para 27.

relation to the parliamentary reservation, the theory of materiality, as well as the principle of precision ("Bestimmtheitsgebot"[86]). According to the BVerfG's case law on the materiality theory, the parliamentary legislature must take all essential decisions, especially those referring to fundamental rights.[87] The theory of materiality functions in this respect also as a prohibition of delegation.[88]

In the first phase of the pandemic,[89] the central statutory provision for the adoption of protective measures to combat the pandemic, either in form of general orders ("Allgemeinverfügung") or of ordinances, was the general clause in Section 28(1) of the IPA.[90] It is admitted that general clauses are constitutionally permissible in principle and in compliance with the principle of precision, since legal norms need to be as specific as possible in view of the nature of the issues to be regulated and the objective of the norm.[91] It suffices in this respect that the provisions can be adequately interpreted according to the general rules of interpretation.[92] Particularly in the field of risk prevention, general clauses are designed precisely in that way, to be able to respond flexibly and effectively to risks that are difficult or impossible to foresee in advance. In this sense, encroachments on fundamental rights are acceptable for a transitional period on the basis of general clauses in risk prevention law until the legislature takes action, if necessary.[93] Otherwise, a very precise and detailed regulation would prove to be counterproductive and ineffective, especially in a dynamic situation of a pandemic that requires flexible reflexes.[94] In the context of the coronavirus pandemic, the BVerfG has implicitly referred to the constitutionality of the statutory provision of Section 28 of the IPA.[95] Some administrative courts expressed, however, concerns about the suitability of Sections 28 and 32 of the IPA as a legal basis by referring to the extensive and prolonged encroachment on a number of fundamental rights.[96]

---

[86] On ordinances, see the lex specialis in Article 80(1) sentence 2 of the Basic Law demanding a precise statutory provision ("Ermächtigungsgrundlage").

[87] Cf. BVerfGE 68, 1 (109); BVerfGE 98, 218 (251); BVerfGE 116, 24 (58); BVerfGE 136, 69 (114); BVerfGE 137, 350 (363 et seq.); BVerfGE 150, 1 (96 et seq.). This obligation of the federal Parliament cannot be substituted by laws enacted by the regional parliaments of the federal states, see Brocker (2020), pp. 1485–1488; Klafki (2020), p. 1722.

[88] Boehme-Nessler (2021b), p. 245; Kluckert (2021), p. 99.

[89] On the different phases of the pandemic, see Kingreen (2021a), pp. 2766–2771.

[90] Cf. Kingreen (2021a), p. 2767.

[91] BVerfG, order of 7.7.1971 – 1 BvR 775/66 para 33.

[92] BVerfG, order of 12.11.1958 – 2 BvL 4, 26, 40/56, 1, 7/57 para 139.

[93] BVerfG, order of 8. 11. 2012 – 1 BvR 22/12 para 25.

[94] Greve (2021), p. 33.

[95] BVerfG, order of 31.3.2020 – 1 BvR 712/20 para 17.

[96] VGH München, order of 27.4.2020 – 20 NE 20.793 para 45; VerfGH des Saarlandes, order of 28.8.2020 - Lv 15/20 para 136; the prevailing opinion in the literature is advocating the incompatibility of Section 28 of the IPA with the principle of precision and the theory of materiality, cf. e.g. Edenharter (2021), p. 558 et seq.; Lepsius (2021), p. 735; von Weschpfennig (2020), p. 474 et seq.

In the course of the pandemic, the cases of severe interference with fundamental rights increased and so did the stringent requirements for the observance of the parliamentary reservation.[97] Followingly, the parliamentary legislature made a number of amendments to the IPA and abided, albeit to a certain extent, by the materiality principle through the introduction of new regulations specifically addressing the coronavirus pandemic.[98] The new Section 28a of the IPA provides for a non-exhaustive catalogue of protective measures to contain the coronavirus, including mandatory facemasks, curfew and contact restrictions. In this respect, Section 28a of the IPA supplements the general clause of Section 28(1) of the IPA. In conjunction with Section 32 of the IPA, it henceforth constitutes the basic statutory provision for the legislative authorities. The latter must provide the grounds for the introduced protective statutory orders and also set a time limit for their duration. A further novelty is the so-called "emergency brake"-regulation of Section 28b of the IPA, which enables the automatic and uniform enaction of certain protective measures throughout Germany depending on the seven-day incidence, i.e. the number of infections per 100.000 inhabitants. It therefore constitutes a self-executing norm, in the sense that the entry into force and expiry of the measures occur automatically.[99]

With regard specifically to the constitutionality of Section 28b of the IPA, the BVerfG rejected the constitutional complaints regarding mainly the contact restrictions with their related fines and the curfews with the corresponding administrative offence in its recent decision.[100] The contact restrictions mandated by Section 28b (1) first sentence No. 1 of the IPA interfered with the right to family life and the freedom to shape one's marriage (Art. 6(1) of the Basic Law), and with the right to the free development of one's personality (Art. 2(1) of the Basic Law). However, these interferences met constitutional requirements both formally and substantively and were therefore justified under constitutional law. First, the interferences with these fundamental rights were formally constitutional since they fell within the Federation's concurrent legislative powers pursuant to Art. 74(1) No. 19 of the Basic Law.[101] In addition, they did not disregard the limits on the legislator's

[97] Dreier (2021), p. 232; Klafki (2021), p. 597; Volkmann (2020), pp. 3153–3160; von Weschpfennig (2020), pp. 478, 485.

[98] Greve (2021), p. 36; Kloepfer (2021), p. 188. Some authors take, however, a different view and consider the new Section 28a of the IPA to be still incompatible with the principle of precision and the materiality theory Boehme-Nessler (2021b), p. 250; Edenharter (2021), p. 560 et seq.; Gölzer et al. (2021), p. 929 et seq.; Kingreen (2021a), pp. 2768–2769; Kluckert (2021), p. 102; von Weschpfennig (2020), p. 483.

[99] The automatic imposition of a curfew was found constitutional by the BVerfG both in the interim measures procedure as well as the main proceedings, BVerfG, order of 5.5.2021 – 1 BvR 781/21 paras. 42 et seq.; BVerfG, order of 19.11.2021 – 1 BvR 781/21 para 198; sceptical Klafki (2021), p. 599; Lepsius (2021), p. 736 et seq.

[100] BVerfG, order of 19.11.2021 – 1 BvR 781/21.

[101] BVerfG, order of 19.11.2021 – 1 BvR 781/21 paras. 118 et seq.

discretion regarding its choice of action resulting from the principle of the separation of powers, nor did it violate the requirement of general applicability ("Allgemeinheitsgebot") arising from Art. 19(1) first sentence of the Basic Law.[102] Furthermore, the contact restrictions and the corresponding administrative offence were sufficiently specific.[103]

Second, the contact restrictions were proportionate. They served constitutionally legitimate purposes, which the legislator pursued to also fulfil its duties of protection arising from Art. 2(2) first sentence of the Basic Law. They were, according to constitutional standards, suitable and necessary to achieve these purposes and they were not disproportionate.[104] In this respect, both the legislator's assessment of the existence of a threat to the general public and the reliability of the foundations from which this assessment was or could be derived, are subject to review by the Court. However, the Constitution also gives the legislator a certain leeway with regard to both questions, which limits judicial review. Where scientific knowledge is tentative and the legislator's possibilities to draw sufficiently reliable conclusions are therefore limited, it is enough for the legislator to proceed on the basis of a context-appropriate and tenable assessment of the available information and evidence. This leeway is based on the legislator's responsibility to decide on conflicts between high-ranking and highest-ranking interests despite uncertainties – a responsibility that the legislator, with its unique form of democratic legitimation, is accorded by the Basic Law.[105] Given in particular the factual situation at the time when the Act was adopted, the legislator could rely on the assumption of a need to act with particular urgency to protect those interests.

Finally, the curfews imposed also interfered with various fundamental rights, such as the fundamental right to liberty under Article 2(2) second sentence in conjunction with Art. 104(1) of the Basic Law, the right to family life and the freedom to shape one's marriage arising from Art. 6(1) of the Basic Law and with the right to the free development of one's personality arising from Art. 2(1) of the Basic Law. These interferences were, however, likewise and formally and substantively constitutional and therefore justified. The Federation had legislative competence to issue this measure and the Act satisfied the requirements of legal clarity and specificity in legislation.[106] The challenged curfews were also proportionate in the specific situation. As part of an overall protection strategy, they served the constitutionally legitimate purpose of protecting life and health, they were, in the sense of constitutional law, suitable and necessary to pursue this purpose, and they were not disproportionate to that purpose.[107] More particularly, the legislator's assumption that it would be able to reduce the number of COVID-19 cases by means of the

[102] BVerfG, order of 19.11.2021 – 1 BvR 781/21 paras. 134, 151.

[103] BVerfG, order of 19.11.2021 – 1 BvR 781/21 paras. 153 et seq.

[104] BVerfG, order of 19.11.2021 – 1 BvR 781/21 paras. 167 et seq.

[105] BVerfG, order of 19.11.2021 – 1 BvR 781/21 para 171.

[106] BVerfG, order of 19.11.2021 – 1 BvR 781/21 para 253.

[107] BVerfG, order of 19.11.2021 – 1 BvR 781/21 para 274.

curfews mandated in Section 28b(1) first sentence No. 2 of the IPA was within the leeway it enjoys when assessing the suitability and necessity of a measure. Thus, in light of the findings regarding the effectiveness of the measures and the considerable danger to life and health, which were confirmed by expert third parties in these proceedings, the legislator's decision to opt for the challenged measures under the specific circumstances of the pandemic was based on sound reasons and was compatible with the Basic Law.[108] The reasoning of the BVerfG is to be welcomed,[109] especially because it respects the legislature's prerogative in assessing a complex issue, on which even virologists disagreed, and thus respects the limits of constitutional jurisprudence as well as the principles of separation of powers and, above all, parliamentary democracy.

In view of the above, it follows that the state initially had to improvise on the basis of very general statutory provisions in the fight against the pandemic. Later, for reasons linked to the principles of democracy and the rule of law, the federal legislature made some improvements to these statutory provisions in the IPA.[110] The fact, however, that the executive authorities are still granted with considerable leeway (e.g. Section 32 of the IPA) remains a cause for concern.[111] They can issue entirely new protective measures without the involvement of the Parliament; they have the power to define numerous open legal terms; they may extend the period of validity of the measures and thus the duration of the numerous, sometimes substantial encroachments on fundamental rights without any further justification.[112] It should be born in mind that the reservation of the law ("Vorbehalt des Gesetzes") in conjunction with the theory of materiality do not require any parliamentary law but rather place high requirements on the content, i.e. the regulatory density and precision of the law.[113] In this respect, the Parliament is not exempt from its duty to continuously improve and readjust the currently existing legal bases in a public and

[108] BVerfG, order of 19.11.2021 – 1 BvR 781/21 para 303.

[109] Similarly, Mayer (2021, December 17), p. 6.

[110] Cf. instructive on this, emphasising the different advantages of executive law-making (first phase [March to October 2020]) and of a more parliamentary legislation (second phase [beginning in November 2020]) Heinig (2021, August 21), p. 6.

[111] See Erdmann (2020), p. 1802.

[112] Boehme-Nessler (2021b), p. 246 et seq.; Dreier (2021), p. 236; von Weschpfennig (2020), p. 487.

[113] See Heinig (2021, August 21), p. 6, who, however, rightly points out the partial constitutional delineation of the relationship between parliament and government under the Basic Law on the one hand and to the potential advantages of executive lawmaking in the interest of effective and expeditious protection of fundamental rights in certain situations, such as a pandemic, on the other hand.

pluralistic legislative process.[114] In other words: it is time for a replacement of the current government-centred and administrative state by a more liberal and parliamentary state.[115]

6 Conclusion

The overall management of the coronavirus pandemic draws the attention to the core responsibilities and available options for action of the state within the framework of a liberal, democratic order. On the one hand, the democratic constitutional state reaffirms its value, even and especially in times of crisis, by effectively fulfilling a central task, namely ensuring the safety and primarily the life and health of its citizens. On the other hand, there is no such thing as life and health protection "above everything else".[116] The very considerable encroachments on fundamental rights, in some cases even being disproportionate or contrary to equality, must therefore not be overlooked or underestimated.

After all, has the coronavirus pandemic weakened the constitution as such, or even undermined the rule of law? The answer is clearly negative. The opposite is rather the case: the fight against the pandemic has so far been and will probably continue to be conducted on the basis of and within the framework of the traditional and highly developed German doctrine of constitutional law, with the rule of law principle playing a central role. The conventional model of the separation of powers has proven to be sufficiently flexible to meet the needs for even far-reaching encroachments on fundamental rights and to adequately control and react to these encroachments in accordance with the rule of law.[117] There was no need for an "emergency law"[118] in this regard, nor would it be compatible with Germany's self-understanding as a constitutional state governed by the rule of law, not only in good times, but also and especially in difficult times.[119] Perhaps the executive authorities should have acted sooner, and the legislature should have actively participated more quickly.[120] But it should be born in mind that this situation was unprecedented and caught all state authorities off guard. In any case, one thing is certain: the experience gained during the pandemic (much of which still has to be closely examined and

[114] On the advantages of this process, especially in times of pandemic, Gärditz (2021b), p. 521; Kersten and Rixen (2021), p. 95 et seq., 106 et seq.

[115] Same as here Dreier (2021), p. 242; Mehring (2021), p. 751.

[116] Heinig et al. (2020), p. 864.

[117] It is therefore wrong to argue that there was a failure of judicial control due to a failure of the principle of proportionality in the pandemic; but so argues Lepsius (2020a, December 20), p. 11.

[118] In general, rightly in favour of a strict separation between normal and exceptional situations under security law, with the latter also requiring legal (constitutional) containment, Barczak (2021).

[119] The rule of law proves its value especially in times of crisis (so did it during the pandemic crisis), cf. Müller (2020, December 20), p. 10.

[120] Kingreen (2021a), p. 2768; Kloepfer (2021), p. 196.

analysed in retrospect[121]) is not only valuable for virologists and epidemiologists, but also teaches us as lawyers an important lesson for future challenges of a comparable nature, which we hope will not take place for at least the next hundred years.

References

Barczak T (2021) Der nervöse Staat, 2nd edn. Mohr Siebeck, Tübingen

Boehme-Nessler V (2021a) Ausgangssperren zur Pandemiebekämpfung? Neue Zeitschrift für Verwaltungsrecht:670–674

Boehme-Nessler V (2021b) Das Parlament in der Pandemie. Die Öffentliche Verwaltung:243–251

Brocker L (2020) Exekutive versus parlamentarische Normsetzung in der Corona-Pandemie. Neue Zeitschrift für Verwaltungsrecht:1485–1488

Dolde K-P, Marquard M (2021) Ausgleichspflicht für pandemiebedingte Betriebs- und Tätigkeitsverbote. Neue Zeitschrift für Verwaltungsrecht:674–679

Dreier H (2021) Rechtsstaat, Föderalismus und Demokratie in der Corona-Pandemie. Die Öffentliche Verwaltung:229–243

Edenharter A (2021) Grundrechtseinschränkungen in Zeiten der Corona-Pandemie. Jahrbuch des Öffentlichen Rechts der Gegenwart 69:555–581

Erdmann M (2020) Kohärenz in der Krise? Neue Zeitschrift für Verwaltungsrecht:1798–1802

Gärditz KF (2021a) Grundrechtsschutz in der Pandemie. Neue Juristische Wochenschrift:2761–2766

Gärditz KF (2021b) Freie Wissenschaft als Gelingensbedingung der politischen Willensbildung in der Pandemie. Jahrbuch des öffentlichen Rechts 69:505–534

Goldhammer M, Neuhöfer S (2021a) Grundrechte in der Pandemie – Allgemeine Lehren. Juristische Schulung:212–217

Goldhammer M, Neuhöfer S (2021b) Grundrechte in der Pandemie – Freiheit und Gleichheit. Juristische Schulung:641–646

Gölzer S, Fischer-Uebler A, Schaub A (2021) Die ungenutzte Macht der Parlamente in der Covid-19-Pandemie. Neue Zeitschrift für Verwaltungsrecht:928–935

Greve H (2021) Grundrechtsschutz und Grundrechtseingriff im Zuge der Coronavirus-Pandemiebekämpfung. Zeitschrift für Gesetzgebung:25–42

Greve H, Lassahn P (2021) Die bundeseinheitliche "Notbremse" – Verfassungsfragen zum Vierten Bevölkerungsschutzgesetz. Neue Zeitschrift für Verwaltungsrecht:665–670

Guckelberger A (2020) Ausgangsbeschränkungen und Kontaktverbote anlässlich der Corona-Pandemie. Neue Zeitschrift für Verwaltungsrecht – Extra 9a:1–15

Häberle P, Kotzur M (2021) Die Covid-19-Pandemie aus der kulturwissenschaftlichen Perspektive einer europäischen und universalen Verfassungslehre. Neue Juristische Wochenschrift:132–137

Heinig HM (2020) Gottesdienstverbot auf Grundlage des Infektionsschutzgesetzes: Verfassungsrechtliche Rechtfertigung und Grenzen. Verfassungsblog. https://doi.org/10.17176/20200318-003209-0

Heinig HM (2021, August 21) Parlamente und Pandemie. Frankfurter Allgemeine Zeitung:6

Heinig HM et al. (2020) Why constitution matters. Verfassungsrechtswissenschaft in Zeiten der Corona-Krise. JuristenZeitung:861–872

Kersten J, Rixen S (2021) Der Verfassungsstaat in der Corona-Krise, 2nd edn. C.H. Beck, München

[121] The ongoing, rather short-sighted discourse regarding the pandemic also belongs in this context, cf. Münkler (2021), pp. 535–553.

Kingreen T (2021a) Der demokratische Rechtsstaat in der Corona-Pandemie. Neue Juristische Wochenschrift, 2766–2771

Kingreen T (2021b, February 21) Ein Sonderregime ohne Ende?. Frankfurter Allgemeine Zeitung, p 6

Klafki A (2020) Mehr Parlament wagen? – Die Entdeckung des Art. 80 IV GG in der Corona-Pandemie. Neue Zeitschrift für Verwaltungsrecht:1718–1722

Klafki A (2021) Kontingenz des Rechts in der Krise. Jahrbuch des Öffentlichen Rechts der Gegenwart 69:583–602

Klein E (1989) Grundrechtliche Schutzpflicht des Staates. Neue Juristische Wochenschrift:1633–1640

Kloepfer M (2021) Verfassungsschwächung durch Pandemiebekämpfung? Verwaltungsarchiv 112: 169–204

Kluckert S (2021) Die Generalklausel des § 28 Abs. 1 Satz 1 IfSG im Spannungsverhältnis zwischen epidemiologischer Fachlichkeit, rechtsstaatlicher Machtbegrenzung und demokratischer Verantwortlichkeit. Deutsches Verwaltungsblatt 136:96–102

Lehner R (2021) "Triage" und Grundrechte – Überlegungen aus der Perspektive von Schutzpflichtendogmatik und Diskriminierungsverboten. Die Öffentliche Verwaltung:252–262

Lepsius O (2020a, December 20) Lockdown ohne Kontrolle. Frankfurter Allgemeine Zeitung, p 11

Lepsius O (2020b) Vom Niedergang grundrechtlicher Denkkategorien in der Corona-Pandemie, Verfassungsblog. https://doi.org/10.17176/20200406-131152-0

Lepsius O (2021) Partizipationsprobleme und Abwägungsdefizite im Umgang mit der Corona-Pandemie. Jahrbuch des Öffentlichen Rechts der Gegenwart 69:705–761

Lieberknecht C, Gleicke I, Teuteberg L (2021, March 11) Corona-Diktatur?. Frankfurter Allgemeine Zeitung, p 6

Manssen G (2021) Staatsrecht II – Grundrechte, 18th edn. C.H. Beck, München

Martini M, Thiessen B, Ganter J (2020) Zwischen Vermummungsverbot und Maskengebot: Die Versammlungsfreiheit in Zeiten der Corona-Pandemie. Neue Juristische Online-Zeitschrift:929–935

Mayer F (2021, December 17) Die Freiheit aller. Süddeutsche Zeitung, p 6

Mehring R (2021) Überlegungen zur Aktualität Carl Schmitts. JuristenZeitung:745–751

Meinel F & Möllers C (2020, March 20). Das Recht des Ausnahmezustands ohne Krieg. Frankfurter Allgemeine Zeitung, p 9

Möllers C (2020) Parlamentarische Selbstermächtigung im Zeichen des Virus. Verfassungsblog. https://doi.org/10.17176/20200326-123121-0.

Muckel S (2021) Schutzpflichten des Staates bei der Bekämpfung der Corona-Pandemie. Juristische Arbeitsblätter:263–264

Müller R (2020, December 20) Weiter in Freiheit. Frankfurter Allgemeine Zeitung, p 10

Münkler L (2020) Expertokratie. Zwischen Herrschaft kraft Wissens und politischem Dezisionismus. Mohr Siebeck, Tübingen

Münkler L (2021) Nothing else matters. Jahrbuch des öffentlichen Rechts 69:535–553

Murswiek D (2021a) Die Corona-Waage – Kriterien für die Prüfung der Verhältnismäßigkeit von. Corona-Maßnahmen. Neue Zeitschrift für Verwaltungsrecht – Extra 5:1–15

Murswiek D (2021b) Schutz – Freiheit – COVID. Die Öffentliche Verwaltung:505–510

Richter C (2021) Die Schutzpflicht des Verfassungsstaates in der Pandemie. Deutsches Verwaltungsblatt:16–19

Scalia F (2020) The reasonable balancing of rights and interests at the time of pandemic. Rev Eur Adm Law 13:89–106

Schenk R (2020) Die Rechtsprechung der Verwaltungs- und Verfassungsgerichte in der Corona-Pandemie – ein erster Eindruck. Bayerische Verwaltungsblätter:793–803

Schmitz H, Neubert C-W (2020) Praktische Konkordanz in der Covid-Krise. Neue Zeitschrift für Verwaltungsrecht:666–671

Sinder R (2021) Versammlungsfreiheit unter Pandemiebedingungen. Neue Zeitschrift für Verwaltungsrecht:103–108

Viessman T (2021) "Corona-Entschädigung" für den Lockdown: der Vorbehalt des Gesetzes als Barriere. Bayerische Verwaltungsblätter:397–401

Volkmann U (2020) Heraus aus dem Verordnungsregime. Neue Juristische Wochenschrift:3153–3160

von Weschpfennig A (2020) Der Parlamentsvorbehalt in der Corona-Krise. Die Verwaltung 53: 469–500

The Impact of the Pandemic on the Greek Constitution

Ioannis A. Tassopoulos

Abstract This chapter discusses the main legal problems Greece faced during the various phases of the COVID-19 crisis. The impact of the pandemic on the protection of civil rights seems to be lasting and nefarious. Fundamental rights were subject to unprecedented restrictions for the sake of public health, without any effective judicial protection. Free movement, the right of assembly, religious liberty, freedom of speech, economic liberty, and ultimately personal autonomy limited by compulsory vaccination, were regulated exhaustively by detailed and intrusive administrative rules and prohibitions. Moreover, the pandemic put under great pressure the existing framework for the constitutional protection of fundamental rights where the principle of proportionality is the cornerstone of judicial review.

1 Introduction

The pandemic of COVID-19 had a catalytic effect on the Greek Constitution. It created a complex situation which has been constantly evolving. It began as an extraordinary emergency and continued as a continuous threat to public health. This chapter discusses how Greece managed the pandemic and the main problems it faced. The impact of the pandemic on the protection of civil rights seems to be lasting and nefarious. The challenge in Greece is to devise new flexible and effective methods, including judicial guarantees, to protect public health and constitutional rights, without sharpening the division within society between those who had been vaccinated and those who wish to avoid it.

I. A. Tassopoulos (✉)
Department of Political Science and Public Administration, National and Kapodistrian University of Athens, Athens, Greece
e-mail: itassop@pspa.uoa.gr

K. Chrysogonos, A. Tsiftsoglou (eds.), *Democracy after Covid*,
https://doi.org/10.1007/978-3-031-13901-7_9

2 The First Phase of the Pandemic and the Activation of the Law of Necessity

Initially, with the outbreak of the pandemic in February 2020, Greece, like other European countries, took measures at national level to limit the spread of the virus within its borders. The lack of sufficient scientific data on the virus and its uncontrolled spread led to the inability of national health systems to respond to the needs, particularly due to overcrowding in Intensive Care Units (ICU) and insufficient qualified nursing and medical staff.

The main constitutional problems raised at the initial stage of the pandemic were the classic law of necessity problems:[1] the excessive strengthening of the executive power manifested in the autonomous regulatory powers of the administration and the extreme restriction of fundamental rights. From February 2020 onwards, Acts of Legislative Content (hereinafter "A.L.C."[2]) began to be issued and restrictions and bans on the movement of citizens of unprecedented duration and severity were imposed.[3]

The 25 February 2020 A.L.C. included a series of delegations of power to the relevant ministers by which they could extensively restrict individual rights, and the 20 March 2020 A.L.C. imposed significant restrictions to prevent or control the spread of the disease.[4] It was thus envisaged to take measures such as compulsory submission to medical examination and hospitalization, restriction of contacts with countries where there was high spread of the disease, prohibition (closure) of schools and entertainment venues, religious worship, etc.

In an emergency, the main responsibility for dealing with the situation while protecting fundamental rights lies with the political institutions, particularly the Parliament. Of course, Greece did not declare the suspension of freedoms under the (formal) state of emergency of Article 48 of the Greek Constitution ("Gr.C."), because the latter does not provide for this in matters of public health. But a critical aspect of the problem is posed by the legal authorization of other administrative organs to impose restrictions on freedoms without the political safeguards provided by the Greek Constitution in Articles 44 para 1 (A.L.C.) and 48. Delegation cannot be extended validly over successive phases of the pandemic. As the restrictions on rights are prolonged the political safeguards of emergency legislation should be reaffirmed.

---

[1] See Tassopoulos (2020a), p. 81.

[2] According to the procedure enshrined in Art. 44 para 1 of the Greek Constitution.

[3] FRA (2020) - EU Agency for Fundamental Rights, Report on Greece.

[4] Law 4683/2020 (Government Gazette A 83/10.04.2020) Ratification of the 20.3.2020 A.L.C.

3 The Relationship Between Political Power and the Medical Scientific Community, and the Fading of Political Accountability

The first phase of the pandemic is particularly characterized by the emergence of the role of the Committee responsible for dealing with the coronavirus. Apart from the obvious provision that the restrictions on rights must respect the principle of proportionality, a particular feature of the pandemic legislation was the importance given to the National Advisory Committee for the Protection of Public Health against Coronavirus COVID-19, which is staffed by infectious diseases specialists and scientists from other related disciplines.

Although formally advisory and consultative in nature, in practice the COVID-19 Committee was quasi-decisional because the political authorities accepted its recommendations without being in a position to check what it recommended. Technically, nominally, the political and administrative bodies were responsible for decisions at the legal-political level, but in practice this was more likely to be true if they did not adopt the Committee's recommendations on the measures to be imposed, taking into account other considerations such as the resilience of the economy to the lockdown, with the result that public health was seriously affected.[5]

These circumstances created a regime of extreme restrictions on individual rights which, as the pandemic dragged on, also raised questions of democratic legitimacy. Political responsibility in conditions where the precautionary principle is applied marks the priorities of the welfare state in risk society[6] to prevent hazards to life, property, the environment, etc. without unduly burdening individual freedoms.

Prevention has gone hand in hand with scientific uncertainty, at least in the phase of testing measures against coronavirus, where there has been regression and vacillation, e.g., on the use of the mask (the necessity and suitability of the mask was initially questioned until its use became mandatory). In these circumstances, the *precautionary principle* justified the adoption of measures. However, the precautionary principle was developed in relation to environmental protection when there was no scientific certainty as to the risk of an activity.[7] But the environment sets a relatively stable standard, in the sense that it must not be degraded. Things change when the problem at hand is the conflict and balancing of rights in the context of a pandemic in flux based on many variables that make predictions about the spread of the disease difficult. What is the point, for example, of complying with preventive measures in public space when they are not observed on public transport?

With regard to the recommendations of the COVID-19 Committee, they did not mention dissenting opinions that could undermine public confidence in the measures

---

[5] Presumably, this happened in December 2021, when there was no lockdown notwithstanding a huge number of new cases of the Omicron variant of the disease in Greece.

[6] Contiades (2020), pp. 59, 103.

[7] Garnett and Parsons (2016), p. 502.

to deal with the pandemic. Overall, however, this policy had the opposite effect because the sense of representativeness of the Committee's decisions was undermined. At least in circumstances where the precautionary principle is applied, it would have been very important to record any dissenting opinion, so that the Committee's communications summarised the discussions that took place and reflected all views. This would not only help to better inform the public but would also greatly enhance the authority of the Committee's decisions when they are taken unanimously. The path of transparency is much safer than silencing the dispute. This is what the public use of reason in a liberal democracy requires.

After the previous decade of the Greek Crisis and of Memoranda (2010–2019) where the technocracy (economists) often dictated to the political power (government, parliament) the content of decisions to achieve the economic goals of austerity,[8] the pandemic has again led to a similar situation, but under completely different political circumstances. It had as an important constitutional implication the real upgrading of the political role of scientific medical bodies, indicating once again the cognitive and substantive limits of politics, which in modern technological society is circumscribed by scientific knowledge.

The government is politically responsible for the measures it adopts taking into account the opinion of experts. It decides what balance the public interest requires between public health and the fundamental rights being infringed. But what exactly remains to be attributed in terms of political responsibility for the recommendations of the Committee responsible for dealing with the coronavirus, at the moment of the pandemic outbreak is an important question that remains to be answered.

4 The Effects of the Pandemic on the Right of Assembly

The impact of the coronavirus legislation on the right of assembly has been drastic. The legal status of assemblies was amended by Law 4703/10.7.2020 which set the regulatory framework to harmonize the right with other rights with which it may conflict, particularly economic freedom and the freedom of movement. But the coronavirus regime in the March 2020 A.L.C. effectively put this normative framework in de facto suspension. The emergency legislation delegated to the head of the Police the power to restrict the right of assembly during the pandemic, in whole or in part (by imposing a restriction on the number of persons participating), in certain areas or even throughout the territory.[9] This power was exercised some months later.

The annual demonstration to commemorate the uprising of the students of the Polytechnic School of Athens on 17 November 1973 was banned in November 2020 when the Chief of Greek Police ordered a ban on assemblies throughout the country for four days. Both the interim order of the President of the Hellenic Council of State

[8]Tassopoulos (2020b), p. 203.

[9]Art. 68 § 2 of the March 2020 A.L.C.

and the plenary decision on the suspension of the operation of the ban on 19 November 2020 did not address the issue of the power of the Chief of Greek Police to ban assemblies throughout the country, at a time much later than the legislative ratification of the Legislative Act which had authorized him in the first place. The justices' decisions were limited to finding the existence of overriding reasons of public interest.[10] But the decision of the Chief of Greek Police was issued without fulfilling the essential formal condition of the previous opinion of the COVID-19 Committee.[11] This is a prime example of the effects of the pandemic on the exercise of rights in Greece.

On the contrary, in the logic of pragmatism, the authorities showed tolerance in relation to the gathering in front of the Court of Appeal of Athens when the verdict in the Golden Dawn trial, a highly political case concerning the defense of democracy, was about to be delivered.[12] In Greece, individual rights exercised collectively and linked to popular sovereignty enjoy special protection, not in legal theory (as is the case with freedom of speech in the U.S.A., preferred position) but in political practice.

5 The Issue of Compulsory Vaccination in the Second Phase of the Pandemic

The second phase of the pandemic, which coincides with the start of vaccinations in Greece in early 2021, raised a different set of issues regarding the mandatory or non-mandatory nature of vaccinations and the consequences for those who choose not to be vaccinated. The question raised in principle was whether the state, by making vaccination compulsory, violates the constitutionally enshrined limits of the autonomy of the person (Article 2 para 1 Gr.C., human dignity, Article 5 para 5 Gr. C., "All persons have the right to the protection of their health and of their genetic identity. Matters relating to the protection of every person against biomedical interventions shall be specified by law"). If the answer is in the negative with regard to the general population, a more specific question concerns the categories of persons (e.g., workers in areas such as education and health care) on whom compulsory vaccination may be imposed. A distinct issue is that of the sanctions for refusal to comply with vaccination and other coronavirus control measures, both in terms of their nature (e.g., fines) and their severity.

---

[10] Council of State (Suspension Committee, Plenary) 262/2020 held (para 7) that the temporary (from 15.11.2020 at 6.00 a.m. to 18.11.2020 at 9.00 p.m.) ban on public open-air gatherings of four persons or more throughout the territory was adopted because there were exceptionally urgent reasons of public interest relating to the protection of public health against the serious risk of spreading COVID-19. Moreover, the measure adopted by the contested decision is entirely provisional and, in the light of the circumstances, of reasonable duration.

[11] Kouroundis and Tsigaridas (2020).

[12] See, e.g., Guardian (2020).

The state may impose restrictions to prevent the spread of the virus. However, the direction of its action must be protective of the rights and interests of others, but not compulsory and binding on anyone regardless of the need to protect the legitimate interests and rights of others. There is no duty (legal obligation) to vaccinate outside of the obligation not to endanger the health of others. Therefore, where the right of some to remain healthy triggers the obligation of others to respect it, it is reasonable and legitimate to impose vaccination as an appropriate means of protection. But as long as one person does not put others at risk, e.g., because he has few social contacts, then the state cannot in principle deprive him of the right to choose not to vaccinate. This is particularly true insofar as there does not appear to be a procedure at present to predict who will be severely affected by the vaccine. We know that statistically the number is minimal. But the state cannot force someone to be exposed to this risk unless there is a reason relating to the rights of others, or a reason relating to an overriding public interest.

In this regard, in March 2020 Law 4675/20 "Prevention, protection and promotion of health, development of public health services and other provisions" was passed,[13] which provided (Article 4 para 3, A, iii, b) that: "In cases where there is a risk of spreading a communicable disease, which may have a serious impact on public health, vaccination may be made compulsory by decision of the Minister of Health, following an opinion of the [Covid-19] Committee, in order to prevent the spread of the disease."

Following a request by the Prime Minister, in June 2021 the National Commission for Bioethics and Technoethics issued a Recommendation on compulsory vaccination against COVID-19 of physicians, nurses and all staff in healthcare structures (public and private) or healthcare structures for vulnerable groups (elderly, patients with chronic diseases or the disabled).[14] However, the Commission did not extend its recommendation on compulsory vaccination of the general population, but only as a last resort. It would be contrary to the Constitution (Article 2 § 1, human dignity) to require vaccination by force.

In the prevailing view, compulsory vaccination can be imposed on certain categories of persons such as health workers and restrictions could be imposed on those who choose not to be vaccinated. The issue may not yet have been directly addressed by the ECtHR,[15] but the Strasbourg Court has had the opportunity to make its mark in relation to the issue of compulsory vaccination of children which, although falling within the scope of protection of Article 8, was ultimately held to

[13] Law 4675/2020 "Prevention, protection and promotion of health, development of public health services and other provisions" (Government Gazette A 54/11.03.2020).

[14] See National Commission for Bioethics and Technoethics (2021).

[15] Although this is a case concerning the compulsory COVID vaccination imposed on certain occupations, particularly the fire service, it is currently pending before the European Court of Human Rights, Thevenon v. France, Application no. 46061/21, filed October 7, 2021. See European Court of Human Rights Factsheet, COVID-19 Health Crisis (2022).

be compatible with the ECHR in Vavřička and Others v. the Czech Republic.[16] Moreover, the ECtHR has rejected requests for interim measures concerning compulsory vaccination of staff in the health sector.[17]

The Greek Council of State, particularly in the context of interim judicial protection, has held in favour of the possibility of imposing compulsory vaccination. In recent plenary decisions[18] it rejected applications for suspension of the obligation of the staff of health care facilities to vaccinate against COVID-19. The ground of irreparable harm due to the threatened suspension of duties, which would result in the loss of the applicants' earnings, social security, employment and social standing, was rejected on the ground (among others) that the harm did not justify the suspension of compulsory vaccination, weighed against the fact that vaccination is necessary to protect public health from the spread of coronavirus among hospital inpatients, who are a particularly vulnerable group, and the fact that the proper functioning of the hospitals would be disrupted if a member of the nursing staff were to contract coronavirus. Moreover, the Council of State has also held[19] that the vaccination of officials of the Special Units of the Fire Brigade (for emergency and particularly difficult disaster situations) is required by overriding reasons of public interest, which consists in the need to ensure their uninterrupted operation and the full availability of their staff.[20]

Law 4865/2021[21] provides in Article 24 the compulsory vaccination, for imperative reasons of public health protection against COVID-19, of all natural persons who have their residence within Greece and were born up to 31 December 1961. The deadline for the first or the single dose is on 16 January 2022. Exceptions were provided for health reasons only. In case of non-compliance with the vaccination obligation, an administrative fine of one hundred (100) euros per month is imposed.

In my opinion, in principle, the compulsory vaccination with the threat of a fine is constitutional in the context of an aggravated pandemic. But the provision can be challenged both substantively and procedurally. *Substantively* mainly because it does not provide for exceptions, for persons who have a serious, consistent and proven conscientious objection towards taking medication; for remote mountain villages of a few inhabitants; or for persons over 90 years old who are unable to move and stay permanently at home. Moreover, the sanction for ensuring

[16]European Court of Human Rights, Vavřička and Others v. the Czech Republic, Application no. 47621/13, April 8, 2021. See Vlachogiannis (2021).

[17]European Court of Human Rights, Refusal of requests for interim measures in respect of the Greek law on compulsory vaccination of health-sector staff against COVID-19, Press Release 266 (2021), September 9, 2021. https://eulawlive.com/app/uploads/request-for-interim-measures-against-greece-concerning-compulsory-vaccination-for-health-staff.pdf (last accessed 27 May 2022).

[18]Council of State (Suspension Committee, Plenary) 250 - 252/2021.

[19]Council of State (Suspension Committee) 133/2021.

[20]See also French Conseil d'État n. 440250 of 30.4.2020 (continuation of public services) as well as the pending case before the ECtHR, Thevenon v. France (application no. 46061/21).

[21]Law 4865/2021, Government Gazette A 238/4.12.2021.

compliance is mainly suitable for the poor, raising questions of equality and discrimination. Also, the provision could be challenged *procedurally* because it is of indefinite duration without an explicit obligation to review; it does not provide for an administrative procedure for objections in individual cases; and it does not contain the necessary justification to substantiate for the purposes of the principle of proportionality the public interest, particularly with official data on the relationship between vaccinated and unvaccinated persons, in hospitals and in the ICU.[22]

6 Balancing Rights Against Each Other and Against the Public Interest: The Principle of Proportionality and the Return of the Administrative State

Prohibitions on movement have affected a chain of other rights and freedoms, particularly those that require collective action (e.g., the right to assembly)[23] or are usually exercised collectively (e.g., religious worship). The pandemic has diluted, in the name of public health, both procedural and substantive guarantees against the risk of excessive restriction of rights. The peril of spread of COVID-19 is objective and undeniable and the disease can be fatal, especially for the elderly. Despite initial scientific uncertainty about the mode of contagion of the virus, it was known to be aggressive and asymptomatic. It was an insidious and invisible enemy.

In view of the above features, the protection of public health from the spread of coronavirus appeared to be beyond suspicion and justified additional precautionary measures in addition to measures to prevent the known and established risks from the virus. The situation was volatile and unpredictable and emergency conditions prevailed which required immediate state action.

Public health, due to the high contagiousness of coronavirus, ceased to be merely an abstract collective good and became individualized to each person who could contract the virus through interaction with asymptomatic carriers. The view that you are entitled to put those around you at serious risk and spread the virus because you do not want to, for example, wear a mask, is not seriously tenable on the basis of individual rights, primarily because one carrier may be asymptomatic and therefore the other cannot be protected. However the need to protect the right to life against COVID-19 does not have a uniform age distribution. There was a clear age differentiation of this threat, much more so for the elderly than for the young, resulting in an intergenerational gap. It was crucial that the measures taken should not discriminate between citizens based on unfair criteria such as age. The measures had to offer protection to every person on Greek territory,[24] including prisoners and those living in refugee structures. Eventually, however, age discriminations became inevitable,

---

[22] Tassopoulos (2021), p. 1201.

[23] See above Sect. 4.

[24] Per Art. 5 § 2 GrC.

as said, since compulsory vaccination was imposed on those over 60, in December 2021.

In the first phase of the pandemic, the scales were always tipped in favour of bans and restrictions on rights for the sake of public health. But the primacy of the public interest in public health was not matched by effective protection of freedoms and mechanisms to control and rationalize restrictions on rights. This situation has given rise to a sense of insecurity and skepticism about what it means to have constitutional rights under conditions of balancing conflicting rights. What is the meaning of the express constitutional provision (Article 5 para 3) that personal freedom is inviolable if it does not offer protection against such restrictive and prolonged measures as those against coronavirus?

The public interest has been immutable throughout the pandemic: the protection of public health. In contrast, during the pandemic the focus of restrictions on freedom for the sake of public health shifted to different individual rights, from freedom of movement to religious freedom, to freedom of enterprise, to the core of personal autonomy (compulsory vaccination). The longer the restrictions on a certain right were prolonged, the harder it was to be judged constitutional. For example, the prospect of businesses going bankrupt and their employees going unemployed became increasingly serious in the course of the pandemic. In compensation, however, it became necessary to combine the restart of the economy with appropriate personal protection measures, e.g., masks in the metro and public transport and in enclosed areas (shops, etc.). The logic of government action had to consider the number of cases in relation to the available ICU beds, initially in the N.H.S. and secondarily in private clinics.

Balancing public interest and rights, or fundamental rights against each other, and seeking the best equilibrium between them is the traditional method of resolving conflicts in constitutional law. But the difficulties of reconciling the various freedoms with the public health interest in fluctuating and rapidly changing circumstances made it reasonable to adopt uniform general regulation, peculiar to the Administrative state, through police provisions easily updated. Conversely, in pandemic conditions, judicial weighing of rights through the principle of proportionality seems to lose its sensitivity as a method for correcting excessive restrictions of rights, because judicial action is by nature fragmentary, case-by-case and inappropriate to follow, let alone anticipate, rapidly changing conditions. That inability was manifested both at the level of judicial protection, insofar as the Council of State refused to review administrative acts whose validity had expired, and at the level of substantive legal protection. Throughout the crisis, the Council of State has shown a consistent tendency in favour of the constitutionality of restrictions on rights, clearly demonstrating an attitude of judicial self-restraint.

At the *procedural level*, the Council of State 665/2021 (Plenary) held[25] that when the challenged act has ceased to be in force and no adverse effects of an administrative nature have been produced by it against the applicant, there is a case for

[25] Council of State 665/2021 (Plenary), para 8.

terminating the proceedings on a petition for the annulment of that act, according to which persons entering the country from any foreign state were subject to seven days of mandatory preventive detention at home or at their place of temporary residence. The Court held that: "The resolution of the legal questions raised *with a view to preventing the future adoption* of acts of a similar nature does not justify the continuation of the proceedings."[26]

On *religious worship*, the Council of State has rejected[27] an application for suspension of the legal effect of an act temporarily prohibiting the performance of all kinds of functions and ceremonies in religious places of worship for a certain period of time, in order to address the risk of spreading COVID-19, on the grounds that the granting of suspension is prevented due to the existence of imperative reasons of public interest, taking into account (a) the entirely temporary nature of the restrictive measures adopted by the contested act and their reasonable duration, and (b) the fact that, as is generally known, it does not appear at present that there were less restrictive means to ensure effective protection of public health. This position was followed by another interim measure decision[28] which stressed, however, that "substantiating the necessity of the measures taken to deal with the epidemic, in view of their particularly restrictive nature for the exercise of fundamental rights, such as freedom of religion and in particular freedom of worship, is an obligation incumbent on the administration in accordance with the principle of proportionality (Article 25 para 1 Gr.C.)," and that the time which has already elapsed since the first appearance of the emergency in order to take measures to prevent the spread of the epidemic is also considered in each case.

Moreover, the Court has recently held[29] that the maintenance by subsequent ministerial decisions of the restrictive measure prohibiting the presence of natural persons (with the exceptions provided for) during services and religious ceremonies of all kinds was adopted, following a reassessment of the epidemiological data, for the same exceptional reasons of protecting public health against the risk of further spread of the coronavirus disease.[30]

---

[26] Ibid, para 11.

[27] Council of State (Suspension Committee) 49/2020, para 6.

[28] Council of State (Suspension Committee) 60/2020, para 4.

[29] Council of State (Suspension Committee) 1/2021, para 3.

[30] Compare on injunctive relief for limits on attendance at religious services, this case-law of the US Supreme Court: South Bay United Pentecostal Church, et al. v. Gavin Newsom, Governor of California, et al. of 29 May 2020, 592 U. S. ____ (2021); Calvary Chapel Dayton Valley, Applicant v. Steve Sisolak, Governor of Nevada, et al. of 8.7.2020, 591 U. S. ____ (2020); Roman Catholic Diocese of Brooklyn v. Cuomo of 25.11.2020, 592 U. S. ____ (2020). For the relevant case-law analysis, see the contribution of Tsiftsoglou A. in the present volume.

7 The European Dimension

The problem of coordinating state action against the pandemic was raised not only at the national level but also at the European level for many reasons. The fundamental freedoms of the Common Market have at their very core the freedom of movement, which has been suspended in many EU Member States by the imposition of restrictions or even bans on cross-border movements. The specific nature of the European Union as a community of states was highlighted by the national responses to the problem and the lack of a common philosophy in dealing with the pandemic (e.g., Sweden's initial approach of limited restrictions was distinctively different from that of Greece), but also by the attempt to serve a common European public interest, both in pooling the negotiating power of the Member States vis-à-vis vaccine producers and in avoiding inter-state competition of the Member States over the commitment, supply and distribution of vaccines.

Lastly, the downturn in economic activity caused by the restrictive measures to prevent the pandemic led to a relaxation of the strict budgetary policy provided for in the Stability and Growth Pact[31] and to the adoption of measures that went beyond the taboo of a European public debt guaranteed by European institutions, even if for an exceptional, specific and limited purpose.[32]

8 The Regulatory and Coordinating Role of Law in Greek Society

The rapid mutations of the fundamental rights affected by the public interest and the unequal distribution of risk for different age groups have put the role of the state as a collective body that sets the legal rules for the regulation and coordination of social life to the test. In the first phase of the coronavirus, this difficulty was saved through the influence of soft law,[33] which imposed on citizens conditions for leaving their homes which they could and should observe themselves in an exercise of self-discipline and self-limitation, where the main object of control was the observance of certain formalities before moving and leaving home by sending an SMS to the civil protection service or by filling in a corresponding form. The accuracy of the formalities and information itself was less checked. This system worked satisfactorily and resulted in a reduction of COVID-19 cases and decongestion of the N.H.S.

However, the situation changed in the second phase of the pandemic because vaccination rates in Greece remained relatively low[34] and there was a strong

[31] Camous and Claeys (2020), pp. 331, 336.

[32] Ladi, Tsarouhas (2020), p. 1049.

[33] Tsourdi and Vavoula (2021), p. 59.

[34] See relevant data on https://emvolio.gov.gr/vaccinationtracker (last accessed 27 May 2022).

challenge to vaccination policy. The media undertook to play an educative role, instead of their traditional watchdog one. In addition, one of the most serious damages caused by the pandemic with long-term consequences is the imposition of further restrictions on freedom of expression by the amendment of Article 191 of the Penal Code for the dissemination of false news via the Internet to prevent fake news about vaccines, their side effects, and the pandemic itself.[35] The new version of the provision adds public health to the list of legal goods for which it is a criminal offense to disseminate or spread false news likely to cause concern or fear among citizens, or to undermine public confidence. If the act is repeatedly committed through the press or on the Internet, the offender is liable to a minimum of six months' imprisonment and a fine. The same penalty shall be imposed on the actual owner or publisher of the medium by means of which the acts were committed.

As emphasized by the Hellenic League for Human Rights, a statutory provision such as the above may freeze criticism and extend liability to those who reproduce information that: i. weighs legal goods (public health versus individual liberties); ii. addresses moral, political and legal issues about the mandatory or non-mandatory nature of vaccinations and its limits; iii. concerns controversial opinions and predictions of scientists; iv. discusses political considerations about the balancing of rights and the prevailing priorities, etc. But "the criminalisation of unorthodox opinions and views leads to 'dogmatic truths,' totally incompatible with a liberal and democratic Constitution."[36]

Finally, there was also serious concern about the recording of cases and the tracking of citizens' movements and contacts by electronic means to prevent the spread of the coronavirus. Emphasis was placed on the need to use software that does not personalize the user from the outset.[37]

9 In Lieu of an Epilogue

The pandemic is still unfolding in Greece and it is too early to say the last word. The question of the economy of the administrative measures that will have to be put in place in the exercise of rights to protect public health arises. Can a general obligation to vaccinate constitute a lesser evil than a complex system of detailed regulations and distinctions, which are hard and too cumbersome to observe? The social man's response is one thing and the lonely individual's is another. The pandemic poses this systemic dilemma in the most painful way.

---

[35] Law 4855/2021 (Government Gazette A 215/12.11.21), Art. 36.

[36] Hellenic League for Human Rights (2021).

[37] Contiades (2020), pp. 111, 120.

References

Camous A, Claeys G (2020) The evolution of European economic institutions during the COVID-19 crisis. Eur Policy Anal 6(2):328–341

Contiades X (2020) Pandemic, biopolitics & rights. Kastaniotis, Athens (in Greek)

European Court of Human Rights (2022) Factsheet, COVID-19 Health Crisis, January 2022, https://www.echr.coe.int/Documents/FS_Covid_ENG.pdf (last accessed 27 May 2022)

FRA (2020) EU Agency for Fundamental Rights, Coronavirus pandemic in the EU: Fundamental Rights Implications – Greece, Report, 4 May, 2020, https://fra.europa.eu/sites/default/files/fra_uploads/el_report_on_coronavirus_pandemic-_may_2020.pdf (last accessed 27 May 2022)

Garnett K, Parsons DJ (2016) Multi-case review of the application of the precautionary principle in European Union law and case law: application of the precautionary principle. Risk Anal 37: 502–516. https://doi.org/10.1111/risa.12633. (last accessed 27 May 2022)

Guardian (2020) Golden Dawn guilty verdicts celebrated across Greece. https://www.theguardian.com/world/2020/oct/07/golden-dawn-leader-and-ex-mps-found-guilty-in-landmark-trial (last accessed 27 May 2022)

Hellenic League for Human Rights (2021) Announcement of 1.10.2021. https://www.hlhr.gr (in Greek) (last accessed 27 May 2022)

Kouroundis H, Tsigaridas B (2020) The constitution, assemblies and the National Committee for the Protection of Public Health. Syntagma-Watch 20(11):2020. (in Greek) https://www.syntagmawatch.gr/trending-issues/to-syntagma-oi-synathroiseis-kai-i-ethniki-epitropi-prostasias-tis-dimosias-ygeias/ (last accessed 27 May 2022)

Ladi S, Tsarouhas D (2020) EU economic governance and Covid-19: policy learning and windows of opportunity. J Eur Integr 42(8):1041–1056

National Commission for Bioethics and Technoethics (2021) Recommendation for the compulsory vaccination of certain professional groups in the health sector, June 14, 2021 (in Greek), https://bioethics.gr/opinions-reports/2021-06-18-10-11-05-3021 (last accessed 27 May 2022)

Tassopoulos I (2020a) Political emergencies as challenges to the impartiality of public law. In: Albert R, Roznai Y (eds) Constitutionalism under extreme conditions: law, emergency, exception. Springer, Cham, pp 81–100

Tassopoulos I (2020b) EU strict conditionality from the perspective of the separation of powers. In: Baraggia A, Fasone C, Vanoni L (eds) New challenges to the separation of powers. Elgar, Cheltenham, pp 202–223

Tassopoulos I (2021) Compulsory vaccination and intermediate control of proportionality. ΘΠΔΔ 2021(12):1201–1203. (in Greek)

Tsourdi E, Vavoula N (2021) Killing me Softly? Scrutinising the role of soft law in Greece's response to COVID-19. Eur J Risk Regul 12:59–76

Vlachogiannis A (2021) The compatibility of compulsory vaccination with the ECHR. Syntagma-watch 8(4):2021. (in Greek) https://www.syntagmawatch.gr/trending-issues/h-symvatothta-tou-ypoxrewtikou-emvoliasmou-me-thn-esda-apofash-vavricka-and-others-v-the-czech-republic/ (last accessed 27 May 2022)

Protecting Political Rights During the COVID-19 Pandemic: The Emergence of Strict Scrutiny in Spain

Joan Solanes Mullor

Abstract The states of alarm declared in Spain to address the COVID-19 pandemic have restricted multiple fundamental rights. While such restrictive states of alarm are not new in our constitutional history since 1978, the scale of the restrictions and the nature of rights affected is unprecedented, as some of them, especially political rights, have never been the focus of the previous states of alarms declared in the country. This chapter explores how the state of alarm relates to the limitation of the right to political participation and to the Spanish judicial response in light of the challenge posed by the pandemic. It examines the legal basis for the restrictions on political rights under the state of alarm, the decisions taken by Spanish public authorities limiting those rights during the pandemic and the judicial response to the measures. Surprisingly, the customary deference of the courts during emergencies has vanished. The Spanish judiciary has actively protected political rights and deployed a model of judicial review that formally and substantially stresses the protection of political rights even in times of crisis.

1 Introduction

The role of the judiciary during crises has always been the subject of debate, especially in contexts of threats to national security[1] and economic stability.[2] Constitutional clauses for emergency powers do not only affect constitutional provisions and ordinary legislation by altering, limiting, even suspending their application, but also call into question the supervisory role of the judiciary itself.[3] Laws usually clarify the margin for exceptional measures at the normative level but remain

[1] Cole (2003), pp. 2568–2571; Fabbrini (2010), pp. 664–666.

[2] Fabbrini (2014), pp. 74–103; Mayoral and Torres Pérez (2018), pp. 732–733.

[3] Wiley (2020), pp. 179–183.

J. Solanes Mullor (✉)
Department of Law, Pompeu Fabra University, Barcelona, Spain
e-mail: joan.solanes@upf.edu

K. Chrysogonos, A. Tsiftsoglou (eds.), *Democracy after Covid*,
https://doi.org/10.1007/978-3-031-13901-7_10

silent about the role of judicial review in checking the activation of constitutional emergency clauses or the actual measures that invoke the constitutionally declared emergency. In other words, neither the constitution itself nor the emergency legislation specify the appropriate standard of judicial scrutiny over the action of public authorities under emergency declarations.

The proper level of judicial scrutiny during crises therefore remains open to discussion. The COVID-19 pandemic has brought new challenges for exceptionalism law, especially because of the extended duration of the constitutionally declared emergency and the intensity of the extraordinary measures taken. The activation of emergency constitutional clauses is not new,[4] but those constitutional emergency frameworks were not conceived with the idea of sustaining emergency measures with severe impact on fundamental rights for so long.[5] These unprecedented circumstances have led to limitations on political rights under the constitutional emergency clause for the first time in Spain. During the state of alarm, several demonstrations and four elections have been held.[6] For the first time under the activation of such an exceptional clause, Spanish courts have been asked to review public measures limiting the exercise of the political rights of voting and assembly. The COVID-19 pandemic has forced an assessment of the role of the judiciary during crises and brought with it an opportunity to conceptualize different tiers of judicial scrutiny.

I use the term "strict scrutiny" in a way that alludes to its use in the United States but is not its equivalent. To begin with, strict scrutiny in the United States legal doctrine is a specific test developed for the particular context of the United States, namely the protection of civil rights. It is the highest of three tiers of judicial review along with the rational basis review (the lowest level) and intermediate review. Arguably, the proportionality test that plays a similar role in European jurisprudence already represents as high a standard as strict scrutiny review in the United States,

[4]In the case of Spain, before the states of alarm declared during the COVID-19 pandemic, a state of alarm was declared on 4 December 2010 during an air traffic controller strike (See Royal Decree 1673/2010, of 4 December).

[5]The first state of alarm during the COVID-19 pandemic that affected the entire national territory was declared by the Government on 14 March 2020 and ended on 21 June 2020 (see Royal Decree 436/2020, of 14 March, which the Congress of Deputies or lower house of Parliament successively renewed six times). The second state of alarm, which only applied to certain municipalities in the Autonomous Community of Madrid, was declared by the Government on 9 October 2020 and ended on 24 October 2020 (see Royal Decree 900/2020, of 9 October). Finally, the third state of alarm, again with national scope, was declared by the Government on 25 October 2020 and ended the 9 May 2021 (see Royal Decree 926/2020, of 25 October, renewed once by the Congress of Deputies, Resolution 29 October 2020, an extension declared unconstitutional by the Judgment of the SCC n° 183/2021, of 27 October, para. 8).

[6]I will refer to some of the demonstrations held and the response of the Spanish judiciary in the pages that follow. Regarding the elections, parliamentary elections in the Autonomous Communities of the Basque Country and Galicia were held on 12 July 2020, on 14 February 2021 in the Autonomous Community of Catalonia, and on 4 May 2021 in the Autonomous Community of Madrid (this one will not be analyzed because it did not entail any legal challenge from the point of view of the pandemic).

although in truth both represent significantly different conceptions of rights themselves.[7] What my use of the term borrows from the United States legal doctrine is the notion that certain situations and areas of rights warrant special attention by the courts on actions taken by public authorities. In the United States, strict scrutiny requires judges to consider whether a state action that is restrictive of a right (1) serves a compelling purpose, (2) may be reasonably expected to attain that purpose and (3) cannot be replaced by a measure that is as effective and less rights-restrictive. For my purposes, strict scrutiny refers to the willingness of Spanish courts to incorporate scientific knowledge into their exercise of the proportionality test. This marks a notable departure, however slight, from the deference traditionally shown to the political bodies by the judiciary during times of crisis.

This chapter explores the role of the courts in times of crisis focusing on the two political rights that have been the focus of public debate in Spain during the COVID-19 crisis: the right to assemble in peaceful protest and the right to hold free elections.[8] First, I describe the Spanish constitutional emergency framework and its operation before the COVID-19 pandemic, showing that the role of the courts in this framework was left largely undefined before the current public health crisis. Second, I examine the emergency clause invoked during the pandemic and the specific restrictions placed on political rights. Third, I discuss the Spanish judiciary's review of those measures and the level of scrutiny deployed. I argue that the Spanish judiciary sought to clarify its role during crises in terms of an emerging doctrine of strict judicial review in the context of political rights.

2 Spanish Law of Exception Before the COVID-19 Crisis and the Judiciary's Undefined Role

The clause for exceptional measures in the 1978 Spanish Constitution is found in Article 116, which foresees three different tiers depending on the gravity of the crisis: alarm, emergency, or siege. This section defines the procedure and competent authorities for declaring these constitutional states of exception. Declaring states of alarm and emergency corresponds to the Government by royal decree of the Council of Ministers but, for a state of emergency, the Government requires previous authorization from the Congress of Deputies.[9] In both cases, the Congress of Deputies must approve any extensions.[10] Declaring a state of siege corresponds to

---

[7]Greene (2021), pp. 110–111.

[8]The right to peaceful unarmed assembly is recognized in Article 21 of the Spanish Constitution ("SC"), the right to hold free elections is recognized in Article 23 SC.

[9]Articles 116.2 and 3 SC.

[10]Ibid. In the case of the state of alarm, the initial declaration of the Government is only valid for 15 days and any subsequent extension requires the authorization of the Congress of Deputies. In the

the Congress of Deputies and requires an absolute majority.[11] The Constitution is clear in that the declaration of any of the three states does not alter the normal operation of the constitutional bodies, especially the legislative, which should remain in operation.[12] Moreover, the declaration of any state of exception does not modify the regime for the accountability of the Government or public servants.[13]

The details of the legal frameworks of the three states are left to the organic law that implements the constitutional clause.[14] The Constitution therefore only refers to the basic procedural norms regulating the declaration of the three states. A remarkable margin of discretion is left to the legislature to demarcate the circumstances and bounds that differentiate each state of exception.[15] With respect to fundamental rights, however, the Constitution does define the scope of the three exceptional states. Only in the cases of the states of emergency and siege can some fundamental rights be suspended, not in the case of the state of alarm.[16] The right to assembly is listed among the rights that may be suspended under the states of emergency and siege (Article 21 SC), but not the right to hold free elections (Article 23 SC).[17]

Such is the normative framework under which, before the COVID-19 pandemic, a state of alarm, the mildest of the three constitutional exceptional states, was only declared once. An air traffic controller strike during the peak tourist season affected so many travelers that the Government declared a state of alarm to allow air controllers to be marshalled and end the strike. This state of alarm was only in force for a limited period totalling 43 days.[18] Notwithstanding, constitutional scholars intensely debated the legality of the executive action and cast serious doubts over the justification for the state of alarm, the measures taken by the Government and the extension approved by Congress after the initial 15-day period.[19] The

---

case of the state of emergency, the declaration lasts no more than 30 days, and the Congress of Deputies may only extend it for one additional 30-day period.

[11] Article 116.4 SC. In the case of a state of siege, the duration is decided by the Congress of Deputies without any constitutional limitation.

[12] Article 116.5 SC.

[13] Article 116.6 SC.

[14] See Article 116.1 SC. Currently, this is Organic Law 4/1981, of 1 June, on the states of alarm, emergency, and siege.

[15] Under Organic Law 4/1981, a state of alarm may be declared in cases of catastrophe, health crisis, paralysis of essential public services or shortage of primary goods (Article 4); the state of emergency corresponds to cases of severe threat to the public order (when fundamental rights, the normal operation of the democratic institutions or essential public services are in grave jeopardy) (Article 13); and the state of siege may be declared in case of insurrection or when force is used to attack against the sovereignty, independence, territorial integrity or the constitutional order (Article 32).

[16] Article 55.1 SC.

[17] Ibid.

[18] The initial 15-day period of the state of alarm provided by Royal Decree 1673/2010, of 4 December by the Government was extended by the Congress of Deputies until 15 January 2011 (Resolution of 16 December 2010).

[19] Aba Catoira (2011), pp. 335–339; Vidal Prado and Delgado Ramos (2011), pp. 253–260.

discussions stirred by this first state of alarm presented an opportunity to delimit the exceptional clause of the Constitution and establish guidelines for the future. The indeterminacy of the constitutional and legislative provisions for the states of exception and the interpretative doubts that arose from them generated such intense scholarly and political debate that the Spanish Constitutional Court (hereinafter the SCC) was called to review their application in practice.

The response of the SCC, however, was inconclusive. In two separate decisions, the SCC only addressed formal challenges to the clauses on exceptional rules without delving into the substantive issues that were questioned.[20] The SCC only addressed, first, the royal decrees issued by the executive branch and, second, the resolutions issued by the Congress of Deputies extending the state of alarm in terms of their nature and rank in the system of sources of law. In both cases, the SCC recognized the value of both types of norms and, therefore, rejected the understanding that they comprised simple regulations—secondary legislation—below the rank of an act of Congress. This was important from the point of view of jurisdiction over the case, since the Constitutional Court, not ordinary courts, is the only body with the competence to exercise judicial review over legislative norms.

Thus, although the Constitutional Court clarified the normative weight of the declarations and extensions of the states of exception, many unresolved questions remained. It did not address the debate over the scope of each state of exception or the interpretation of the causes that the Government may legitimately invoke for declaring them. The SCC did not discuss the concrete measures taken by the executive during the state of alarm either. The royal decrees and congressional extensions were not challenged through the proper constitutional procedures—that is, through motions for constitutional challenge and the question of unconstitutionality—and for that reason the SCC refused to enter to the substance of the case.[21] The Court thus abstained from providing any substantive criteria for the proper level of scrutiny that should be applied, in this case at the constitutional level, to measures taken under the clauses for exceptional rule.

What the intervention of the SCC made clear is that royal decrees declaring the states of exception and congressional extensions have the rank of legislation and, therefore, their review pertains to the SCC. However, as the COVID-19 crisis reveals, exceptional measures are not only established by the royal decree declaring the state of exception. They are also articulated through regulations (decrees, orders, and other types of secondary legislation). Such exceptional measures established in secondary legislation are to be reviewed by ordinary courts, and the SCC failed to establish any interpretive guidelines for the proper level of judicial scrutiny they should deploy. In other words, in passing up the opportunity to establish constitutional guidelines for its own scrutiny of measures imposed through royal decrees of

[20] See SCC Judgment n° 83/2016, of 28 April and SCC Decision n° 7/2012, of 13 January.

[21] The case against the royal decrees declaring the state of alarm was brought before the SCC by individuals affected by the measures—air controllers—through an individual constitutional complaint (*recurso de amparo*).

states of exception, the SCC also missed a chance to help ordinary courts determine the adequate level of scrutiny for emergency measures established through secondary legislation. Before the COVID-19 crisis, therefore, the appropriate level of judicial scrutiny to be applied to exceptional measures was highly ambiguous and vague.

3 The State of Alarm During the COVID-19 Pandemic and Political Rights

During the COVID-19 pandemic in Spain, the state of alarm, the mildest state of exception established by Article 116 SC, has been declared three times. In all three cases, the exceptional clause was activated by royal decree issued by the executive, but they differed substantially in terms of duration, territorial scope and the measures implemented to address the health public crisis.[22] In a little over a year (from March 2020 to May 2021), Spain has thus experienced three different states of alarm whereas before the COVID-19 pandemic only once was the clause activated under the current constitutional framework. The indeterminacy of the constitutional clauses for exceptional rule that was not addressed by the SCC following the air traffic controller crisis in 2010–2011 together with the unprecedented duration of the pandemic-related states of alarm that imposed severe restrictions on personal and social freedoms placed the Spanish constitutional system under great strain.

In this context, the three states of alarm have generated intense debate in political and scholarly circles where they have been addressed from various angles. Inter alia, questions advanced include whether: (i) the state of exception would have been preferable to the state of alarm to address the COVID-19 crisis;[23] (ii) the ordinary legislation represented a sufficiently robust response to the crisis or whether exceptional law was needed;[24] (iii) the response to the crisis unduly centralized the territorial organization of the State;[25] (iv) the severe proliferation of restrictive norms of all kinds violated the principles of predictability and legal certainty;[26] or

[22]The first state of alarm (March-June 2020) had national scope and was in place for 98 days. It contained the most severe restrictions (particularly the stay-at-home order, Article 7.1 Royal Decree 463/2020). The second state of alarm (October 2020) was in place for 15 days and only applied to some of the municipalities in the Autonomous Community of Madrid (a municipal lockdown was established in the concerned cities by Article 5.1 Royal Decree 900/2020, of 9 October). The third state of alarm (October 2020-May 2020), again of national scope, was in place for 166 days and imposed restrictive measures such as prohibiting travel between Autonomous Communities and a curfew, but not a general stay-at-home order (see Articles 5 and 6 Royal Decree 926/2020, of 25 October).

[23]Álvarez García (2020), pp. 13–20; Garrido López (2020), pp. 383–388.

[24]Nogueira López (2020), p. 29; Villar Crespo (2020), p. 20.

[25]Velasco Caballero (2020), pp. 80–82.

[26]Perea González (2020), p. 1.

(v) the limitation of fundamental rights exceeded permissible levels under the declaration of the state of alarm.[27] In short, the unprecedented crisis has led to unprecedented debates.

Political rights have also been in the spotlight. The three states of alarm have provided a succinct normative framework for the exercise of political rights. The first formulation of the first state of alarm (March-June 2020) did not address political rights. Only in May 2020 did a modification of the royal decree declaring the state of alarm introduce two references to the right to hold elections.[28] These two references declared that the state of alarm would not represent an obstacle for the Autonomous Community elections and that the central Government would mobilize resources at its disposal to assist the electoral processes.[29] The Government clearly had in mind the impending elections in the Basque Country and Galicia. The second state of alarm (October 2020) did not refer to political rights at all. The third state of alarm (October 2020–May 2021) followed the path of the first by announcing that the state of alarm would not prevent Autonomous Community elections.[30] It introduced a fresh reference, however, to the right to peaceful assembly by declaring that demonstrations could be limited, conditioned, or prohibited when the conditions for adequate social distancing to prevent contagion could not be guaranteed.[31] The exceptional normative framework thus remained largely silent as regards the general criteria for limiting the rights to hold elections and demonstrations with only an incomplete reference to one criterion for the latter—the need to respect social distancing guidelines. In this regard, the judiciary lacked instructions for assessing the tension between political rights and the public health threat entailed by the COVID-19 pandemic.

Under this exceptional normative framework, Autonomous Communities have held four elections. In the case of the Basque Country and Galicia, the elections were scheduled for 5 April 2020 but the two regional Governments, considering the circumstances and in spite of the state of alarm's explicit approval of holding the elections, decided to postpone them until 12 July 2020 when the first state of alarm had been lifted.[32] No political party or private citizen challenged the postponement of the elections before a court so the judiciary was not called upon to review their decision. In the Catalan elections, however, the judiciary was asked to review the decision of the Catalan Government to postpone its elections. The elections were scheduled for 14 February 2021, in the middle of the third state of alarm. The

[27] Garrido López (2020), pp. 393–398; Siera Mucientes (2020), pp. 292–297.

[28] This modification was introduced by the Final Provision 1.1 of the Royal Decree 514/2020, of 8 May.

[29] See Article 7.1.bis and Additional Provision n° 7 of Royal Decree 463/2020, of 14 March.

[30] See Additional Provision n° 1 of Royal Decree 926/2020, of 25 October.

[31] See Article 7.3 of Royal Decree 926/2020, of 25 October.

[32] See Decree n° 45/2020, of 18 March, of the Galician Government and Decree n° 7/2020, of 17 March, of the Basque Country Government, both postponing the elections.

Catalan Government decided to tentatively postpone them until 30 May 2021.[33] Political parties and citizens filed complaints challenging the decision[34] and, as a result, the judiciary intervened, annulling the decision to postpone the elections, which took place on the originally scheduled day of 14 February 2021.

The right to peaceful assembly has also been affected during the three states of alarm. The specific decisions of the administrative authorities allowing, limiting, or prohibiting demonstrations across the territory have varied and lawsuits have been filed forcing the judiciary to review some of these decisions.[35] A common pattern in the behavior of public authorities in this matter is difficult to identify because the decisions ran in opposite directions depending on the territory and the circumstances. During the first state of alarm, when the most severe measures were in place, such as the stay-at-home order, different administrations authorized some demonstrations and others were prohibited.[36] During the second and third states of alarm, when the domicile lockdown was not in place, public authorities allowed demonstrations in most but not all cases.[37] When public authorities limited or rejected requests to hold demonstrations, the judiciary has been called to review those decisions. In these cases, the lack of proper normative guidance in the exceptional legislation has made establishing an adequate, common standard difficult.

4 The Judicial Response: Strict Scrutiny

The ongoing constitutional review of the first and third state of alarm Royal Decrees (March–June 2020 and October 2020–May 2021) represents another opportunity for the SCC to provide interpretive guidelines for the constitutional clauses on exceptional rule.[38] The constitutional challenge questions the adequacy of the state of alarm and calls upon the SSC to review the specific measures—inter alia, the

[33] See Decree n° 1/2021, of 15 January, of the Catalan Government.

[34] Lamelas (2021), p. 1.

[35] Ituren Oliver and Esteve Segarra (2020), pp. 6–11.

[36] Ibid.

[37] The demonstrations planned for Women's Day on 8 March 2021 provide an example of the confusion. Demonstrations were allowed everywhere in the country except in the Autonomous Community of Madrid, where the demonstrations were banned by the competent public authority because of the infection statistics in the region (Ugarte 2021).

[38] Up until now, the SCC has decided the constitutional challenge against the first state of alarm (Judgment of the SCC n° 148/2021, of 14 July) and the third state of alarm (Judgment n° 183/2021, of 27 October). In addition, still pending before the SCC is a question of unconstitutionality promoted by the High Court of Aragon regarding the power of ordinary courts of carrying out an ex-ante proportionality review of any public health restrictive measure decided by public authorities (see the decision of the SCC in case n° 6283-2020). This power was introduced by Law n° 3/2020, of 18 September, modifying the wording of Article 10.8 of Law n° 29/1998, of 13 July, of the Contentious-Administrative Jurisdiction.

restrictions on the right to peaceful assembly—that the exceptional normative framework was invoked to justify. So far, the SCC has declared unconstitutional (i) the mobility restrictions—especially the domicile lockdown—declared during the first state of alarm for being a suspension—not a mere limitation constitutionally allowed by the state of alarm—of freedom of movement (Article 19 SC);[39] (ii) the extension for six months of the third state of alarm for lacking a motivated justification;[40] and (iii) the delegation of powers to the so-called "delegated competent authorities" during the third state of alarm because of a blanket delegation of authority.[41] In relation to the right to peaceful assembly, the SCC only said that the declared first state of alarm was not per se a limitation of that political right (Article 21 SC), which preserved all its integrity.[42] Thus, individuals, despite the limitations of freedom of movement, were able to communicate the willingness of carrying out a demonstration to public authorities which could analyze case-by-case its compatibility with the public order or other public health considerations arising from the pandemic.[43]

In addition to this general challenge to the state of alarm, the SCC has only addressed limitations on the right to peaceful assembly justified by the COVID-19 pandemic twice.[44] These were the reactions of the SCC to two High Court decisions in Autonomous Communities where the authorities prohibited demonstrations because of the perceived risk of contagion.[45] The SCC added two new dimensions to the familiar proportionality test for addressing interferences with the right to peaceful assembly. First, it ruled that public authorities may legitimately weigh constitutional values and rights other than the classic preoccupation with public order against that right, values such as the values of life, public health, and the integrity of the public sanitary system.[46] Second, the SCC has not adopted a deferential stance or advanced a formalistic analysis in its proportional analysis. It reviews the measure prohibiting the demonstration in light of the scientific debate around COVID-19 and the preventive measures alleged by the petitioners and to be

[39] Judgment of the SCC n° 148/2021, of 14 July, para. 5. The SCC concludes in the same line regarding the third state of alarm and the measures provided for the limitation of permanent groups up to six persons in the public space (see Judgment of the SCC n° 183/2021, of 27 October, para. 6).

[40] Judgment of the SCC n° 183/2021, of 27 October, para. 8.

[41] Ibid. at para. 10.

[42] Judgment of the SCC n° 148/2021, of 14 July, para. 6.

[43] Ibid.

[44] See SCC Decision n° 40/2020 of 30 April, and the case before the SCC n° 1293-2021, which is still pending.

[45] In the case of Galicia, the High Court validated the decision of the public authorities to prohibit a demonstration on 1 May 2020 to mark International Workers' Day (see the Judgment of the High Court of Galicia n° 136/2020, of 28 April). In the case of Madrid, the High Court validated the prohibition of demonstrations on 8 March 2021 to celebrate International Women's Day (see the Judgment of the High Court of Madrid n° 184/2021, of 7 March).

[46] Decision of the SCC n° 40/2020, of 30 April, para. 4.

implemented during the demonstration.[47] The SCC concludes by validating the denial of a permit to hold the demonstration while affirming a place for substantive judicial review, that is, the prerogative of courts to engage the scientific debate and accordingly evaluate the measures taken by public authorities.

The SCC's restrained intervention may be due to the extremely varied lawsuits presented to the judiciary during the declared states of alarm and its similarly chaotic response. Indeed, ordinary courts have faced intense activity on all fronts. They have been called on to intervene in all the spheres of public and private life where restrictive measures taken by public authorities have impacted fundamental rights and constitutional values: the right to circulation or movement, the right to property and freedom of business, the principle of legality of the COVID-19 sanctions' regime and the mandatory enforcement of sanitary decisions.[48] The chaos stems not only from the diversity of the issues brought before the courts, but also from the variety of legal fora that have intervened in the debates.[49] In the end, this judicial cacophony should have been expected since the SSC only reserved for its jurisdiction the exceptional measures established by the royal decrees declaring the state of alarm, therefore leaving review of all the exceptional measures imposed through secondary legislation to the various ordinary courts and tribunals. Although the Spanish Supreme Court has as yet limited its intervention, it has a duty to unify and provide instruction for the ordinary courts' deliberations.[50]

Despite the variety of judicial results, a sort of robust judicial review seems to be emerging in the field of political rights. In this field, the courts appear prepared to engage the substantive issues of the cases. The SCC left space for such intense scrutiny and ordinary courts seem to have taken it as an invitation. In the case of the right to peaceful assembly, the courts have faced all manner of complaints and challenges, sometimes upholding the limitations on and prohibitions of demonstrations and other times invalidating them.[51] In their reasoning ordinary courts engage

[47] Ibid.

[48] Fernández de Gatta Sánchez (2020), p. 1.

[49] Indeed, ordinary courts of different jurisdictions have intervened, as have courts with different territorial scopes. Particularly, the High Courts of each Autonomous Communities have been called on to review the different restrictive measures adopted by the regional Governments in application of Article 10.8 of Law 29/1998.

[50] By the end of the third and the last state of alarm, Article 15 of Royal Decree Law n° 8/2021, of 4 May, introduced a new cassational appeal before the Supreme Court which may be used against the Autonomous Communities High Courts' judgments decided in application of Article 10.8 of Law 29/1998 (ex-ante proportionality review of public health restrictive measures implemented by public authorities). The utility and practicality of this new appeal for the post-state alarm era remain to be tested. Until July 2021, only three times the Supreme Court has decided under this new appeal (see SSC Judgement n° 719/2021, of 24 May, SSC Judgment n° 788/2021, of 3 June, and SSC Decision n° 6719/2021, of 20 May).

[51] See, inter alia, the following decisions in which the judiciary have validated the limitations and prohibitions on demonstrations: Judgment of the High Court of Navarra n° 70/2020, of 30 April; Judgment of the High Court of Castilla and Leon n° 90/2020, of 30 April; Judgment of the High Court of Madrid n° 195/2020, of 30 April. For examples of judgments annulling the prohibitions on

the scientific debate, much as the SCC did, evaluating the restrictive measures in light of the health risks posed and the nature of the demonstrations planned. For instance, the High Court of Navarra allowed one demonstration to go forward because it was "static" and therefore its potential impact on public health was limited.[52] Similarly, the High Court of Aragon permitted a demonstration on condition certain limitations be respected.[53] Especially noteworthy in the case of Aragon is not only the High Court's disposition to review the decision of the public administration to prohibit the demonstration, but also its decision to revise that decision by allowing the demonstration to take place under additional conditions.

This scrutiny deployed by the courts was even stricter in the decision to postpone the elections in the Autonomous Community of Catalonia.[54] The decision to postpone the elections was made with the approval of the main political parties participating in them and was thus clearly shared by the political establishment of that moment. The legal challenge by minor political parties and private citizens led to the annulment of the decision to postpone and, finally, the elections were held on the originally scheduled date. In reaching the decision to annul the postponement, the High Court of Catalonia exercised strict scrutiny combining formal and substantive analysis. From the formal standpoint, the Court analyzed the decision-making process that led to the postponement of the elections and found that the body who took the decision did not have that competence.[55] More importantly, however, was the substantive analysis. The Court affirmed that postponing of an election was only permissible, because of the importance of the right to vote in a democracy, when the public health risk was severe and in the Catalan case found the criterion was not satisfied. The High Court examined the epidemiological statistics—both at the moment the elections were scheduled and when the decision was made to postpone them—and the preventive measures to be adopted, such as mail-in ballots and health protocols for in-person voting.[56] This substantive analysis, quite unprecedented and surprising in the Catalan political sphere,[57] led the High Court of Catalonia to conclude that postponing the elections disproportionately restricted the right to vote. The public authorities decided not to appeal the decision before the Spanish Supreme Court and, therefore, the High Court's decision became final.

---

demonstrations, see: Judgment of the High Court of Navarra n° 69/2020, of 30 April; Judgment of the High Court of Aragon n° 151/2020, of 30 April; Judgment of the High Court of Castilla and Leon n° 462/2020, of 21 May; Judgment of the High Court of Madrid n° 214/2020, of 21 May; Judgment of the High Court of Catalonia n° 1391/2020, of 22 May.

[52] Judgment of the High Court of Navarra n° 69/2020, of 30 April, para. 6.

[53] Particularly, the demonstration was to respect the total limit of 60 participants, each in an enclosed vehicle with only one person per vehicle. See Judgment of the Superior Court of Aragon n° 151/2020, of 30 April, para. 6.

[54] See Judgment of the High Court of Catalonia n° 121/2021, of 1 February.

[55] Judgment of the High Court of Catalonia n° 121/2021, of 1 February, para. 6.

[56] Ibid. at para. 8.

[57] Bossacoma Busquets (2021), p. 1.

5 Conclusions

The COVID-19 crisis has forced the judiciary to rethink its position in the framework of government checks and balances during instances of exceptional rule. The role of judicial review in times of crisis was unclear before the pandemic, especially because the state of alarm had only been declared once in Spain, in 2010–2011, and its duration and measures were quite limited in scope. Neither the SCC nor ordinary courts had deeply contemplated their role or the proper intensity of judicial review of exceptional measures. When the pandemic broke out and exceptional measures became key tools in combating it, the undefined role of the judiciary meant it had to address a broad variety of scenarios. On the one hand, as in recent economic crises and national security threats, the judiciary could have chosen to show deference to the political bodies—executives and legislators—in this time of public health crisis. Put otherwise, political actors, who may or may not possess scientific expertise, would have been the key actors in charge of exceptional rule making. On the other hand, the judiciary could take the opportunity to vindicate its role as sentinel of political action by articulating a coherent, solid legal response.

In Spain, a pattern of strict scrutiny over public decisions that affect political rights is emerging, marking a shift in the judiciary's self-image. The judiciary seems to be moving in the direction of seeing itself as a relevant actor in times of crisis. During the pandemic, political bodies have declared the state of alarm and taken severe measures that limit political rights. Public authorities have decided to prohibit or limit demonstrations and postpone scheduled elections, in each case because of the COVID-19 public health threat. In reviewing those decisions, both the SCC and ordinary Spanish courts have deployed a substantive version of judicial review, that is, one that engages the political and scientific debates behind the decisions taken by public authorities. In exercising the proportionality test, both in the cases of the right to peaceful assembly and free elections, the judges incorporated the scientific data and arguments and considered alternative measures that could be less restrictive of political rights. The outcomes of that review have varied, with some upholding the public authorities' decisions and others annulling them but, in both cases, the message from the Spanish judiciary to the other constitutional bodies is clear. Even in times of crisis, it intends to perform its role as guardian of the constitution—and the clauses regulating exceptional rule—and is thus prepared to deploy a strict judicial scrutiny.

This pattern is emerging from the field of political rights. Whether this pattern is also emerging in other fundamental rights issues also warrants attention. These areas may include the right to circulation or movement or the right to property or freedom of business, rights which have also been deeply affected by measures imposed to contain the pandemic. In any event, the predisposition of the judiciary to engage actively in the public discussion when political rights are in question during crises could afford citizens a wider window of opportunity to exercise control over public power. This predisposition, which may also be due to the context of political rights in which courts are familiarized and feel comfortable, is also a first step towards normalizing the decisive role of judicial review during instances when a state of exception has been decreed.

References

Aba Catoira A (2011) El estado de alarma en España. Teoría y Realidad Constitucional 28:305–334

Álvarez García FJ (2020) Estado de alarma o de excepción. Estudios Penales y Criminológicos 40: 1–20

Bossacoma Busquets P (2021) Un poder perillós? Reflexions sobre l'activisme judicial contra l'ajornament electoral. Blog Revista catalana de dret públic, 10 February [online]. Available at: https://eapc-rcdp.blog.gencat.cat/2021/02/10/un-poder-perillos-reflexions-sobre-lactivisme-judicial-contra-lajornament-electoral-pau-bossacoma-busquets/ (Accessed 25 May 2022)

Cole D (2003) Judging the next emergency: judicial review and individual rights in times of crisis. Mich Law Rev 101:2565–2595

Fabbrini F (2010) The role of the judiciaries in times of emergency: Judicial review of counter-terrorism measures in the US Supreme Court and the European Court of Justice. Yearb Eur Law 28(1):664–697

Fabbrini F (2014) The Euro-Crisis and the courts: judicial review and the political process in comparative perspective. Berkeley J Int Law 32(1):64–123

Fernández de Gatta Sánchez D (2020) El Estado de Alarma y las medidas contra el coronavirus ante jueces y tribunales. Diario La Ley 9655, 3 June [online]. Available at: https://diariolaley.laleynext.es/dll/2020/06/17/el-estado-de-alarma-y-las-medidas-contra-el-coronavirus-ante-jueces-y-tribunales (Accessed 25 May 2022)

Garrido López C (2020) La naturaleza bifronte del estado de alarma y el dilema limitación-suspensión de derechos. Teoría y Realidad Constitucional 46:371–402

Greene J (2021) How rights went wrong: why our obsession with rights is tearing America apart. Houghton Mifflin Harcourt, Boston

Ituren Oliver A, Esteve Segarra A (2020) El ejercicio del derecho de manifestación (sindical o no) durante la pandemia por el Covid-19. Trabajo y Derecho 12:1–22

Lamelas M (2021) Inseguridad juridíca en Cataluña: aluvión de recursos contra la anulación del 14-F. El Confidencial, 19 January [online]. Available at: https://www.elconfidencial.com/espana/cataluna/2021-01-19/inseguridad-juridica-cataluna-aluvion-recursos_2912488/ (Accessed 25 May 2022)

Mayoral JA, Torres Pérez A (2018) On judicial mobilization: entrepreneuring for policy change at times of crisis. J Eur Integr 40(6):719–736

Nogueira López A (2020) Confinar el coronavirus. Entre el viejo Derecho sectorial y el Derecho de excepción. El Cronista del Estado Social y Democrático de Derecho 86–87:22–31

Perea González A (2020) Apología de la forma: Covid-19 y seguridad jurídica. Diario La Ley 9657, 9 June [online]. Available at: https://diariolaley.laleynext.es/Content/Documento.aspx?params=H4sIAAAAAAAEAMtMSbF1CTEAAmNDQxNDI7Wy1KLizPw827DM9NS8klQA9HwZeSAAAAA=WKE (Accessed 25 May 2022)

Siera Mucientes S (2020) Estado de alarma. Eunomía. Revista en Cultura de la Legalidad 19:275–305

Ugarte I (2021) La Delegación del Gobierno en Madrid prohíbe todas las manifestaciones del 8-M. El País, 4 March [online]. Available at: https://elpais.com/espana/madrid/2021-03-04/la-delegacion-del-gobierno-prohibe-todas-las-manifestaciones-del-8-m-que-le-han-sido-comunicadas.html (Accessed 25 May 2022)

Velasco Caballero F (2020) Estado de alarma y distribución territorial del poder. El Cronista del Estado Social y Democrático de Derecho 86–87:78–87
Vidal Prado C, Delgado Ramos D (2011) Algunas consideraciones sobre la declaración del estado de alarma y su prórroga. Revista Española de Derecho Constitucional 92:243–265
Villar Crespo G (2020) Repensando el derecho de excepción: la crisis del coronavirus y los tres aprendizajes sobre el derecho de necesidad en el ordenamiento jurídico español. Revista General de Derecho Administrativo 54:1–52
Wiley L (2020) Coronavirus, civil liberties, and the courts: the case against 'suspending' judicial review. Harv Law Rev Forum 133(9):179–198

Part IV
Conclusions: Liberal Democracy After COVID-19

Conclusions: Liberal Democracy After COVID-19: Challenges in Europe and Beyond

Kostas Chrysogonos and Anna Tsiftsoglou

Abstract The COVID-19 pandemic has been a stress test for liberal states and the rule of law worldwide. While not unprecedented, this global health emergency has challenged constitutionalism and the foundations of modern democracies, often pushing new boundaries in regulation, judicial review, and executive decision making. COVID was often treated as a state of emergency that called for exceptional crisis management, and strengthened the executive at the expense of parliamentarism. Even in EU countries with a long parliamentary tradition such as Germany and Italy, institutional innovations and the rise of "the administrative state" have raised rule of law questions. Courts, on the other hand, have addressed exceptional measures with an eye to their institutional limitations. While deferential in the spark of the crisis, they have progressively acquired a rather proactive role in the defense of human rights, particularly in Spain, Germany, and USA. Overall, the pandemic has highlighted the need for both flexible regulatory approaches and an active judiciary. Restoring and preserving the rule of law while preparing for the next emergency remains a constant challenge.

Over two years after the outbreak of the COVID-19 pandemic in Europe and the rest of the world, democracies still seem to struggle with this global health emergency. While not unprecedented,[1] the ongoing global pandemic seems to challenge the very foundations of modern liberal democracy, particularly parliamentarism, judicial scrutiny or even constitutionalism per se as we know it.

We attempted to study the COVID-19 pandemic as *another emergency*, another *crisis* that, like other exogenous to the state crises—be they financial or security/ terrorist crises—shakes our preconceptions of normality calling for immediate and effective action. This global health crisis, as it turns out, has been perceived differently among our case studies, which were all liberal democracies of the

[1] See the historical account of Honigsbaum (2020) on the pandemics of the past century.

K. Chrysogonos (✉) · A. Tsiftsoglou
Faculty of Law, Aristotle University of Thessaloniki, Thessaloniki, Greece
e-mail: atsif@law.auth.gr

K. Chrysogonos, A. Tsiftsoglou (eds.), *Democracy after Covid*,
https://doi.org/10.1007/978-3-031-13901-7_11

Western World. Several states have managed the crisis within their regular constitutional framework, respecting the rule of law, while others declared a state of emergency, or used exceptional legislation that, oftentimes, justified serious human rights erosions or significantly strengthened the executive power.

In **Part I** of this Volume, COVID-19 is conceptualized as an *exceptional* state of affairs, one that may jeopardize our constitutional acquis, or one that might be dealt with within the rule of law, safeguards attached. As Chrysogonos and Viopoulos argue, COVID resembles an "asymmetric threat for humankind" that could "have consequences comparable to a war." Seen through this lens, the pandemic may have served as an excuse for *even large-scale abuses.* Thus, the major challenge for liberal democracies, which in the 21st century must stand to face a plurality of risks-health, environmental or other, is how to achieve efficiency while respecting the rule of law. In other words, how to better apply the institutional knowledge acquired by modern crises to build more *sustainable* responses for tomorrow. Constitutionalism must stay *relevant* in the future, too.

The Portuguese case offers a fine example of "state of exception" management. As Violante explains, to tackle COVID-19, Portugal implemented a combination of *constitutional* and *statutory* emergency regimes. This choice in effect resulted in parliamentary abdication, governing through decrees, and "surrender to the executive." Nevertheless, the implemented measures enjoyed broad political consensus and judicial challenges against them in administrative courts were rather unsuccessful. According to Violante, institutional reasons, primarily the absence of a constitutional complaint, similar to the German *Verfassungsbeschwerde*, coupled by a systematic display of judicial deference to the political branches during the pandemic, contributed to the Portuguese Constitutional Court's passive role regarding the COVID measures. Portugal seems to have "learned" from the pandemic, since it has recently promoted new legislation specifically designed for pandemic emergency management in the future.

The difficulties of maintaining institutional balances during the pandemic is highlighted in **Part II** of this Volume, with insights from major parliamentary democracies such as Italy and Germany, as well as from Cyprus, a country that has been living in emergency practically since its foundation. As Merten explains, parliamentarism in Germany has been "stress-tested" during the pandemic, while trying to maintain its operations as well as conducting the 2021 Federal Elections. Acting within the regular constitutional framework, the German Parliament has gradually lost power at the outbreak of the pandemic, for efficiency reasons, with the executive, on both federal and state levels, disproportionately empowered. Nevertheless, no breach of the parliamentary assessment prerogative was found by the infamous German Federal Constitutional Court (BVerfG) in Karlsruhe. In the end, the COVID-19 pandemic turned out to be a good opportunity to make parliamentarism, as Merten remarks, "crisis-and future-proof," through the adoption of institutional innovations, for instance in electoral law (with postal voting) or parliamentary procedures (with digital meetings).

The German example is also studied through the lens of *federalism*. According to Hofmann, the federal structure of the German State has proved to be rather problematic for crisis management during the COVID-19 pandemic. IfSG

(Infektionsschutzgesetz), the German Federal Infectious Diseases Act, has been the principal legislative instrument used for COVID-19. However, its implementation was left to a diversity of German states (Länder) that, according to their needs, interpreted IfSG as deemed fit. This legislative complexity resulted also in a diverse body of IfSG case law, complicating matters even worse, undermining a national, well-coordinated, and democratic response to the pandemic. As Hofmann remarks, such a highly bureaucratic approach turned out to be inadequate and inefficient for COVID-19, since it was "a 19th century approach applied to a 21st century problem."

On the other side of the spectrum, executives during the pandemic, who were significantly empowered at the expense of national parliaments worldwide, have also proved to be very creative while experimenting. According to Delledonne, innovations such as the centralization of decision-making power in one executive member, such as the Italian Minister of Health, or the enhancement of internal collegiality in Germany, in addition to ad hoc legislative solutions, were all signs of pragmatic and flexible responses to the pandemic. Still, as Delledonne points out, such innovations should be reconciled with parliamentary oversight and, if formalized, should be more thoroughly examined in the long-term context. Unsurprisingly, the COVID-19 crisis seems to have only brought to surface issues of the preexisting crisis of representative democracy in many countries today.

The Cyprus case, which involved managing an "emergency within an emergency," brings another fresh perspective to questions of parliamentarism and the rule of law during the 2020–2022 global health crisis. As Stratilatis explains, historically Cyprus had to live in a quasi-permanent state of emergency since its independence in the 1960s, due to serious disputes between the Greek-Turkish communities on the island, but still managed to operate thanks to the *doctrine of necessity*. The latter, judicially created by the Supreme Court of Cyprus (through the infamous *Ibrahim* case), has allowed Cyprus and its democratic institutions to function under the rule of law up to present, despite all the political shortcomings. Ironically, as Stratilatis points out, the COVID-19 crisis in Cyprus has been dealt with on the verge of (il)legality. While Cyprus did not declare a state of emergency but was rather governed by decree like many other states, it recently introduced a bill that, if adopted, will replace an old British Colonial Quarantine law and grant vast authority to the executive, without any parliamentary oversight or other procedural guarantees. On top of that, courts in Cyprus have precluded any judicial control of COVID-19 measures by treating them as *actes de gouvernement*.

Judicial scrutiny of the COVID-19 measures and balancing during the pandemic is the focus of **Part III** of this Volume, with case studies from the US Supreme Court, the German Federal Constitutional Court, the Spanish Constitutional Court, and the Hellenic Council of State. Most of the studies involved the review of serious fundamental rights restrictions and, more recently, the issue of compulsory vaccinations in the workplace, with litigation still evolving in 2022.

In the United States of America, one of the hardest hit states by COVID-19 in the world, the pandemic has become the cause of multiple human rights restrictions, like First Amendment rights, primarily through State regulations. Applicants across the country challenged such measures both on States Courts and on the US Supreme Court, too, seeking interim relief. As pointed out by Tsiftsoglou, although "lurking in the shadows" and not on the merits of the cases, the US Supreme Court has produced an impressive body of COVID-19 case law, particularly on crucial issues such as freedom of religion and the compulsory vaccinations in public and private workplaces, where the Court literally split. Among the hotly debated topics were the role of the judiciary during crises, the scope of the free exercise clause and even the regulatory power of administrative agencies on mandatory vaccinations. While the internal balances of the Court recently changed after the appointment of more conservative justices during the Trump Era, controversial issues involving religion have been decided with rational balancing.

On the other side of the Atlantic, Germany addressed the pandemic challenges within the framework of the Rule of Law, since the Basic Law does not provide for any state of emergency. In fact, the traditional model of separation of powers has been, according to Kahl and Poulou, "sufficiently flexible" during this global health crisis. Judicial control in pandemic-hit Germany, from lower courts to the *Bundesverfassungsgericht*, has proved to be adequate in reviewing far-reaching encroachments on human rights. Primarily through applications for interim relief, the BVerfG has drawn notable limits to various rights violations, using the principle of proportionality. Still, the executive in Germany has been empowered to produce emergency legislation during the COVID-19 crisis, as in many other liberal states, without oversight, at the expense of German parliamentary democracy. As Kahl and Poulou correctly suggest, it is time to replace the current government-centered administrative state with a more liberal and parliamentary state during crises.

Rigorous judicial review has also been reported, inter alia, in crisis-hit Spain. As Solanes Mullor points out, political rights have been particularly curtailed when Spain declared a state of alarm and courts did not stay passive in this pandemic. From ordinary courts to the Spanish Supreme Constitutional Court, "a pattern of strict judicial scrutiny has emerged" in the field of political rights, particularly the right to peaceful assembly and the right to hold free elections. Moreover, courts have deployed a *substantive* version of judicial review, incorporating experts' data in the proportionality review. This pattern of strict scrutiny was certainly evident in the field of political rights, which might be indicative of a predisposition of the judiciary to be more actively involved in such questions affecting the public sphere. It only seems that here, too, the COVID-19 crisis has "forced the judiciary to rethink" about its role in the rule of law system, even more so in those stressful times.

Finally, the Greek case, presented by Tassopoulos, also stresses the importance of an active judiciary during crises, where fundamental rights can be constantly curtailed for a blanket public health reason. The impact of the pandemic on the protection of civil rights seems to be "lasting and nefarious." Tassopoulos highlights the absence of effective judicial protection during the pandemic in Greece, in addition to "the rise of an administrative state" that promoted complex and rapidly changing regulations that were difficult to interpret or to even be applied. Concerning compulsory vaccinations of all elderly people over the age of 60, a measure instituted in the end of 2021 in Greece following the positive impact of compulsory vaccination of healthcare workers, it is well argued that this measure would possibly not withstand strict judicial scrutiny.

As the COVID-19 pandemic still unfolds, and a large proportion of the global population still remains unvaccinated,[2] liberal democracies are viewed by many observers as facing a big dilemma: protect public health *or* respect the rule of law. In fact, *this dilemma is non-existent*. Liberal democracies in the 21st century must learn to live with global emergencies, be they COVID-19, climate change or security threats, and manage them *within the framework of the rule of law*. Unquestionably, this pandemic has overstretched the limits of the rule of law, the time has come to restore it. As Francis Bacon once said, "*Scientia potentia est.*"[3]

References

Bacon F (2010) Meditationes Sacrae and human philosophy. Modern Reprint. Whitefish, Kessinger Publishing

Honigsbaum M (2020) The pandemic century: a history of global contagion from the Spanish Flu to Covid-19. Virgin Books, London

[2] As of June 12, 2022, 60% of the global population has been fully vaccinated against COVID-19, while only 17.8% of people in low-income countries have received at least one dose. https://ourworldindata.org/covid-vaccinations?country=OWID_WRL Accessed June 12, 2022.

[3] "Knowledge is power." Bacon (2010).

The manufacturer's authorised representative in the EU is Springer Nature Customer Service Centre GmbH, Europaplatz 3, 69115 Heidelberg, Germany. If you have any concerns regarding our products, please contact ProductSafety@springernature.com

Printed and bound by CPI Group (UK) Ltd, Croydon, CR0 4YY
28/09/2026
02224070-0001